JANE B. SINGER, ALFRED HERMIDA,
DAVID DOMINGO, ARI HEINONEN,
STEVE PAULUSSEN, THORSTEN QUANDT,
ZVI REICH, AND MARINA VUJNOVIC

Participatory Journalism

Guarding Open Gates
at Online Newspapers

(W)WILEY-BLACKWELL

A John Wiley & Sons, Ltd., Publication

Blackwell Publishing was acquired by John Wiley & Sons in February 2007. Blackwell's publishing
program has been merged with Wiley's global Scientific, Technical, and Medical business to form
Wiley-Blackwell.

Registered Office
John Wiley & Sons Ltd, The Atrium, Southern Gate, Chichester, West Sussex, PO19 8SQ, United
Kingdom

Editorial Offices
350 Main Street, Malden, MA 02148-5020, USA
9600 Garsington Road, Oxford, OX4 2DQ, UK
The Atrium, Southern Gate, Chichester, West Sussex, PO19 8SQ, UK

For details of our global editorial offices, for customer services, and for information about how to
apply for permission to reuse the copyright material in this book please see our website at www.
wiley.com/wiley-blackwell.

Library of Congress Cataloging-in-Publication Data
Participatory journalism: guarding open gates at online newspapers / Jane B. Singer ... [et al.].
    p. cm.
  Includes bibliographical references and index.
  ISBN 978-1-4443-3226-1 (hardback) — ISBN 978-1-4443-3227-8 (paperback)
  1. Electronic newspapers. 2. Online journalism. 3. Citizen journalism. I. Singer, Jane B.,
1955– II. Title.
  PN4833.P37 2011
  070.4–dc22

                                                                            2011001829

A catalogue record for this book is available from the British Library.

This book is published in the following electronic formats: ePDFs 9781444340716; Wiley Online
Library 9781444340747; ePub 9781444340723

Set in 10 on 12.5 pt Century Book by Toppan Best-set Premedia Limited
Printed in Malaysia by Ho Printing (M) Sdn Bhd

1 2011

Contents

Notes on Authors

David Domingo is a senior lecturer in online journalism at the Department of Communication Studies of Universitat Rovira i Virgili in Tarragona, Spain. Domingo, who has a PhD in Journalism from the Universitat Autònoma de Barcelona, was a doctoral fellow at the University of Tampere (2004) and visiting assistant professor at the University of Iowa (2007–2008). His research interests include online journalists' professional ideology and work routines, as well as the dynamics of innovations such as participatory journalism and convergence. He is co-editor, with Chris Paterson, of *Making Online News: The Ethnography of New Media Production* (Peter Lang, 2008).

Ari Heinonen, PhD, is journalism teacher and researcher in the Department of Journalism and Mass Communication at the University of Tampere, Finland. A former newspaper journalist, he has focused his academic research on explorations of the changing nature of professionalism in journalism, concepts of journalism in the new media era and journalistic ethics. He has directed and participated in a number of national and international research and development projects in these areas.

Alfred Hermida is a digital media scholar, journalism educator and online news pioneer. Since 2006, he has been an assistant professor at the Graduate School of Journalism at the University of British Columbia, Canada. Hermida was a Knight–Wallace Fellow at the University of Michigan in 2005 and an IBM CAS Canada Research Faculty Fellow in 2010. An award-winning journalist who served for four years as a Middle East correspondent, Hermida is a 16-year-veteran of the BBC and was a founding news editor of the BBC News website in 1997. He has also written for *The Wall Street Journal*, *The Times of London*, the *Guardian* and NPR.

Steve Paulussen, PhD, is a part-time lecturer in journalism studies at both the University of Antwerp and the Vrije Universiteit Brussel, as well as a senior researcher at the IBBT research group for Media & ICT (MICT) at Ghent University, Belgium. In recent years, he has participated in a number of projects on different aspects of today's digital media culture. His main research interests lie in the field of journalism studies, where he has published on developments in online journalism, newsroom convergence and the sociological profile of professional journalists. Between 2006 and 2010, he also was involved in a multi-disciplinary strategic research project on digital news trends in Flanders, Belgium (FLEET).

Thorsten Quandt, Dr. phil. habil. is a professor in Communication Studies / Interactive Media and Online Communication at the University of Hohenheim, Germany. He has served as chair of the Journalism Studies Division in the German Communication Association (DGPuK) and as an officer in the Journalism Studies Division in the International Communication Association (ICA). His widely published research includes studies on online journalism, media evolution, network communication and computer games.

Zvi Reich, PhD, is a former journalist and a researcher in journalism studies at the Department of Communication, Ben Gurion University of the Negev, Israel. His book, *Sourcing the News*, was published by Hampton Press in 2009. Reich's research interests focus on online news, sociology of news, the relations between reporters and sources, authorship in journalism and the use of communication technologies in journalism. Two of his papers have won the top three papers prize of the Journalism Studies Division at ICA. Other research has appeared in *Journalism Studies*, *Journalism & Mass Communication Quarterly* and *Journalism*. He is a member of the editorial board of *Journalism Practice*.

Jane B. Singer is an associate professor in the School of Journalism and Mass Communication at the University of Iowa, USA, and a visiting professor in the School of Journalism, Media and Communication at the University of Central Lancashire, UK. From 2007 to 2010, she was the Johnston Press Chair in Digital Journalism at Central Lancashire. Her research explores digital journalism, including changing roles, perceptions, norms and practices. Before earning a PhD in Journalism from the University of Missouri, Singer was the first news manager of Prodigy Interactive Services. She also has worked as a newspaper reporter and editor.

Marina Vujnovic, PhD, is an assistant professor at Monmouth University, USA. Her primary fields of research are participatory journalism and new media studies, media history and gender, critical political economy, and cultural studies. Additional research interests include international communication and the global flow of information, as well as ethnicity and the media. She is the author of *Forging the Bubikopf Nation: Journalism, Gender and Modernity in Interwar Yugoslavia* (Peter Lang, 2009).

The authors have elected to donate all their proceeds from the sale of this book to Reporters Without Borders / Reporters Sans Frontières (http://www.rsf.org, http://en.rsf.org), a non-profit organization committed to press freedom around the world.

Acknowledgements

This book became a reality because dozens of journalists and news executives with precious little time to spare agreed to open their newsrooms to us and to carve out space to talk with us honestly, thoughtfully and at length. We are deeply grateful to them for their willingness to share their ideas and insights, as well as their reasons for both hope and concern as they contemplate an increasingly participatory future.

We also owe a large debt of gratitude to the Helsingin Sanomat Foundation in Finland for supporting the extensive fieldwork involved in this research. Without the foundation's generous support through multiple phases of the project, from its planning through its execution, this multi-national, multi-authored endeavor would have been impossible to coordinate or to carry out. The rest of the authors also send a big "kiitos paljon!" to co-author Ari Heinonen and the Tampere Journalism Research and Development Centre for negotiating this foundation support, as well as overseeing the conversion of that commitment into much-appreciated dollars, euros, pounds and shekels.

Our editors at Wiley-Blackwell, particularly Elizabeth Swayze, Margot Morse and Elina Helenius, have been unflaggingly enthusiastic and remarkably patient throughout our lengthy, long-distance laboring to turn a mountain of interview data into a manageable manuscript. They have been hugely helpful right from the start, not least in soliciting reviewers whose feedback has significantly strengthened the work you are about to read. These reviewers are outstanding thinkers and scholars in this field, and they and their colleagues – including those who have provided feedback at the academic conference venues in which some of our preliminary findings were initially presented – have been a resource and an inspiration for us.

Each of the authors also wishes to thank our respective academic institutions, which provided the time, space and resources that enabled us individually and collectively to do our thinking, researching, analyzing, writing and editing.

Several of us also would like to individually thank the following people for their invaluable aid:

David Domingo wishes to thank Erin Tiesman, for her assistance in transcribing the US interviews, and Sergio Martínez Mahugo, who conducted and transcribed the interviews with Spanish journalists.

Ari Heinonen wishes to thank Pauliina Lehtonen and Riina Hautala, both of the University of Tampere, for their assistance in this research.

Alfred Hermida wishes to thank Leslie Young, who conducted and transcribed the interviews with Canadian journalists, as well as Alison Loat of Samara for providing a space to think and write.

Thorsten Quandt wishes to thank Ansgar Koch, Laura Leithold, Agatha Pohl and Fabian Schwinger for their assistance in this research.

Zvi Reich wishes to thank Tal Waxman-Kushnir from Ben Gurion University for her thoughtful contribution in conducting the interviews and analyzing the data, as well as Dror Walter from the Hebrew University and Oded Jackman from Ben Gurion University for their assistance.

These authors, along with co-authors Steve Paulussen and Marina Vujnovic, also are grateful to Jane Singer for her precise and patient work in crafting a final manuscript that succeeds in giving one voice to this collective research project.

Jane Singer wishes to thank Jean-Yves Chainon, then of the World Editors Forum in Paris, for arranging, leading and transcribing the French interviews.

Finally, we must thank you, our readers and the readers of these and other online newspapers, for all that you bring to "participatory journalism." The future of this collective enterprise rests on you and your contributions, and we believe you will enrich it beyond measure.

Authors' Note

This book is the result of a research project carried out by eight researchers in eight languages and in ten different countries, over a period of several months in late 2007 and early 2008. Among us, we talked one-on-one with nearly 70 journalists, at more than two dozen leading national newspapers, about user contributions to the newspaper-affiliated website. The appendix, beginning on page 192, provides more details about what we did and how we did it.

Each chapter contains information gathered by all of us, asking similar questions of our interviewees and steering our newsroom conversations in the direction we collectively decided would be most interesting and illuminating.

To turn this mountain of quotes into a book, each of us took the lead in crafting one thematic chapter that explores a particular aspect of our topic in detail. Jane Singer, with the assistance of Alfred Hermida, then worked to integrate each of these chapters into what we hope is a cohesive whole that is easy and enjoyable to read as a unified package. We did not want our own individual voices to drown out the voices of the journalists whom you will "hear" throughout the pages that follow.

However, we have included the names of each lead author in the Table of Contents and at the start of each chapter to highlight the individual effort and perspective that went into each section of the book.

1

Introduction
Sharing the Road

The English words "journalism" and "journey" are cousins. Both stem from the Latin word *diurnalis*, which means "daily." Over time, one came to mean a daily record of transactions, while the other was used to describe a day's work or travel. Today, journalism is on a journey into uncharted territory – and the road is crowded with all manner of travellers.

Only very recently has the entrenched idea of a concrete daily record, prepared by people dedicated to its compilation, begun to lose its usefulness. A printed product may still appear just once a day, but as newspapers have moved online, they have evolved into something far more fluid and amorphous. The twenty-first-century newspaper is essentially never complete, neither finished nor finite.

Nor are journalists the only ones determining what gets recorded. A great many other people also contribute content, representing their own interests, ideas, observations and opinions. That content comes in a steadily expanding volume and variety of forms and formats – words, images and sounds, alone or in combination, turning the online newspaper into an open, ongoing social experiment.

This book is about the journey of the journalistic enterprise through an increasingly collaborative present and into a collective future that you will share, whether or not you ever set foot in a newsroom. It explores how newspaper journalists are handling the transition to a world in which vast numbers of strangers contribute directly to something that those journalists alone once controlled. The story is still being written, and you are the ones writing it.

Participatory Journalism: Guarding Open Gates at Online Newspapers, First Edition.
Jane B. Singer, Alfred Hermida, David Domingo, Ari Heinonen, Steve Paulussen, Thorsten Quandt, Zvi Reich, and Marina Vujnovic.
© 2011 Jane B. Singer, Alfred Hermida, David Domingo, Ari Heinonen, Steve Paulussen, Thorsten Quandt, Zvi Reich, and Marina Vujnovic. Published 2011 by Blackwell Publishing Ltd.

1.1 Participatory Journalism

Many terms have been coined to describe the contributions to online newspaper content from those whom media critic Jay Rosen (2006) describes as "the people formerly known as the audience." Some call it "**user-generated content**." Others prefer "**citizen journalism**." One scholar likes the term "produsage" to highlight the blending of producing and consuming information (Bruns 2008; 2005).

Our choice, though, is "**participatory journalism**" because we feel it captures the idea of collaborative and collective – not simply parallel – action. People inside and outside the newsroom are engaged in communicating not only *to*, but also *with*, one another. In doing so, they all are participating in the ongoing processes of creating a news website and building a multifaceted community.

Others like this term, too.[1] Back in 2003, online journalist and commentator J. D. Lasica defined "participatory journalism" as a "slippery creature" but offered a range of examples, some of them associated with mainstream media offerings and others not. Among the former, which are the focus of this book, he included **comments**, discussion **forums** and user **blogs**, along with reports (including visual ones), reviews and articles supplied by readers (Lasica 2003).

Those sorts of contributions remain very much part of today's participatory journalism, and they have been joined by newer forms of contributing, such as **reputation systems**, **micro-blogs**, **social networking sites** and more. Indeed, new participatory formats appear all the time; by the time you read this, there will be a dozen new examples that don't even exist as we write.

Since Lasica made his list, people outside the newsroom have contributed to a steady stream of material published on media websites (and, of course, elsewhere, as well) around the world. In a fundamental way, news has become socially engaging and socially driven, as millions of people not only create news but also share it (Pew Research 2010).

Ordinary people have captured and published, in words and images, stories of global impact, including the results of terrorist attacks on the commuters of Madrid and London, the abuse of prisoners at Iraq's Abu Ghraib prison, the lethal chaos surrounding elections in Iran, and the devastation caused by tsunamis, floods and earthquakes. They also have provided intimate looks within the smallest of communities, sharing local and even personal information and ideas in depth and detail. They have carried on millions of topical conversations through discussion forums, comment threads and blog posts. In all of these online activities and many more, they have taken on roles and carried out functions that sound quite a bit like, well … journalism.

In the same year that Lasica offered his definition of participatory journalism, Chris Willis and Shayne Bowman connected the rise of what they referred to as both "we media" and "participatory journalism" to the changes facing traditional newsrooms. "The venerable profession of journalism finds itself at a rare moment in history where, for the first time, its hegemony as gatekeeper of the news is threatened by not just new technology and competitors but, potentially, by the audience it serves," they wrote (Willis and Bowman 2003). The subtitle of our book, "Guarding Open Gates at Online Newspapers," suggests that this challenge remains a central one for journalists today.

Gatekeeping has been defined as "the process by which the vast array of potential news messages are winnowed, shaped, and prodded into those few that are actually transmitted by news media" (Shoemaker *et al.* 2001: 233). But when journalism becomes "participatory," the volume of transmitted information rapidly surges to flood levels, swamping traditional approaches to winnowing and the like. How newspaper journalists are thinking about and dealing with the change is a recurring theme in this book.

1.2 Why Look at Newspaper Websites?

Journalists produce content for all sorts of platforms and products, of course. They work for lots of different kinds of employers – including themselves – as the numbers engaged in increasingly entrepreneurial versions of the craft continue to grow (Shedden 2010). However, we have chosen to focus on journalists employed by companies that print (on sheets of paper), a traditional newspaper and maintain a website affiliated with that newspaper.

We made that choice for a number of reasons. First is the historical longevity of newspapers and their demonstrated ability to adapt successfully to other monumental changes in communications technology throughout the nineteenth and twentieth centuries. The newspaper industry has survived everything from the advent of the telegraph in the early 1800s to that of the **mobile** telephone a century and a half later – with landline telephones, film, radio, broadcast and cable television, and more in between. As a result, the culture of newspaper journalism is simultaneously – and somewhat paradoxically – the most deeply rooted and the most flexible of all **newsroom cultures**. This seemed to us an interesting backdrop for the current challenges posed to journalists by an open and interactive network.

The second reason is that despite the many and ongoing changes in the ways that people access information, leading newspapers generally retain an authoritative role as providers of "the news of record" – certainly in the eyes of their own employees, but also in the eyes of many other social and political leaders. Although print circulation has been declining steadily in many Western nations, particularly the United States (Pew Project for Excellence in Journalism 2010), the medium is likely to remain a staple for opinion leaders into the foreseeable future (Meyer 2008).

And the third reason for focusing on newspapers is that in the brief history of online media, newspapers have generally been the first to innovate, and with a few exceptions – the BBC in the UK and National Public Radio in the United States spring to mind – they have done so more extensively than their magazine or broadcast counterparts. Although their critics have pointed out, not incorrectly, that newspapers have missed a great many opportunities over the past two decades, those innovations have been quite significant indeed for the people whose jobs, roles and self-perceptions have been fundamentally shaken. Their reactions and responses form the heart of this book.

1.2.1 Online Newspapers

Changes never occur in a vacuum, and these are no exception. The news industry in the early twenty-first century faces a strikingly severe economic crisis, and the occupation of journalism has been buffeted by changes in newsroom structure, organization, tasks and working conditions (Deuze 2010; Fortunati *et al.* 2009; Ryfe 2009; Gade 2008).

"Even before the recession, the fundamental question facing journalism was whether the news industry could win a race against the clock for survival: Could it find new ways to underwrite the gathering of news online, while using the declining revenue of the old platforms to finance the transition?" the authors of a recent report about U.S. media said (Pew Project for Excellence in Journalism 2009). They were not especially optimistic about the answer, particularly for the newspaper industry, described in 2009 as being "in something perilously close to free fall" (Pew Project for Excellence in Journalism and Edmonds 2009).

While the revenue from online news is not booming, its usage is. Journalists who write for newspapers, in particular, have far more readers now than at any time in the past. Traffic to newspaper websites has grown enormously in the past few years, as their familiar and (at least to some extent) trusted brand names have successfully made the transition to the Internet.

The websites of some national papers, including many of the ones discussed in this book, routinely attract tens of millions of readers every month – far more than they have in print. They are not the same kinds of readers – the print kind tend to be more regular readers, and they are much more likely to see more than just the one or two items that the click-in-click-out crowd sees. But they are consumers of the newspaper product nonetheless.

There are not, however, far more journalists working for these newspapers than before. On the contrary, at a great many papers, considerably *fewer* people are in the newsroom than were there a decade ago. The journalists who remain typically generate content for both the print and online products, as well as other platforms such as mobile. And they are working – in various ways, with varying attitudes and with variable results – with some of those millions of readers and their contributions, from comments to photos to blog posts and more.

This cacophonous world of participatory journalism is an exciting place but one that is still largely unfamiliar to many of these journalists. This book, based on the insights and the early adventures of top-level professionals at some of the democratic world's biggest and best newspapers, will help you prepare for the adventure on which you are about to embark.

1.2.2 Participatory Journalism in Online Newspapers

This book is about participatory journalism in online newspapers. It draws on lengthy interviews with 67 print and online editors, and other journalists at about two dozen leading national newspapers in ten Western democracies. A full list and a brief description of each newspaper and its website, along with a list of interviewees (by job title in order to preserve the confidentiality that some requested), is provided in the appendix at the back of the book.

The fact that all are democracies is important because of the premise underlying this form of government: It rests on a public that is both informed about matters of civic importance and, importantly, able to talk about those matters with other citizens. Journalists have always seen themselves as fundamental to the democratic role of informing the public (Gans 2003), and that perception is a key aspect of a broadly shared journalistic culture. Today, the shift of journalism from a lecture to a conversation (Gillmor 2006) highlights the second requirement, too. Indeed, this connection between discourse and democracy (Habermas 1989; Dewey 1927) has been highlighted over many centuries and in many cultural contexts, and it surely is no less valid in our times.

This book is unusual in incorporating perspectives from journalists in so many different countries, even countries that broadly share a political ideology. It would have been logistically much easier, of course, to write a book based on interviews with journalists in a single nation, with a shared political, economic and legal culture informing their work. Journalists do think about their roles within the context of those aspects of their own society. And although website **users** can access a site from another country as easily as one from their own, the traffic to most (though not all) of the newspapers in our study comes mainly from within their national borders. These citizens also construct their identities and social roles within a particular national context.

That said, we are interested here less in the national culture than the professional one – the culture of journalism, at least as it is understood by practitioners in relatively free and open societies. All over the world, the nature of an unbounded, participatory network is challenging traditional journalistic practices, policies and self-perceptions. Our interviews did suggest some national idiosyncrasies (as well as some personal ones), and you'll read about them as you go along. But we also found a great deal of similarity among journalists in the various countries in the ways they thought about themselves, their products and their audiences. Those similarities suggest to us that the fundamental change currently under way transcends national boundaries, and it is the nature of that change that we will explore together in the pages of this book.

1.3 Chapter Preview

After this introduction, we begin the exploration by offering a fuller overview of the audience participation options offered by online newspapers, describing how they fit into the multifaceted process of producing news. In Chapter 2, Alfred Hermida provides a summary of journalists' views of the newly active audience in connection with a series of **news-production stages**, proposing ideas that are then explored in more detail throughout the book.

In Chapter 3, Ari Heinonen explores changes in the relationship between journalists and readers who once were undifferentiated members of a relatively passive "**audience**" but who, in increasing numbers, are emerging as active individual "users" and even co-producers of website content. Heinonen provides an overview of our journalists' attitudes toward these users, examining the ways in which traditional journalistic roles are being shaped by new relationships and exploring the various roles that practitioners see website users filling – or not filling.

The second section of the book, beginning with Chapter 4, offers a closer look at how journalists are managing user contributions. Steve Paulussen leads off by focusing on the reasons why online newspaper editors have decided to develop audience participation platforms, as well as the effects of their decision within today's newsrooms. What are their motivations and their rationales, and how are those influencing their organizations' structural changes?

In Chapter 5, David Domingo takes us inside these newsrooms to investigate changes in workflows and news production routines that journalists have made to accommodate and integrate contributions from users. Domingo discusses various approaches and investigates the reasoning behind them, then highlights the best strategies identified by our interviewees.

With Chapter 6, we focus still more tightly, as Zvi Reich turns user comments into a framework for exploring a host of issues raised by participatory journalism in all its forms. Comments are enormously popular on newspaper websites, but their popularity causes management problems, particularly when user contributions are seen as superficial or offensive.

The third and final section of the book broadens the perspective to consider wider issues and implications of participatory journalism. In Chapter 7, Jane Singer looks at the ethical and legal issues that editors see as important in handling user contributions, as well as their strategies for dealing with those issues. She considers challenges to long-standing professional norms, along with the difficulty of heading off potential legal problems created by this ongoing global discourse.

It is painfully evident that economic pressures play a significant role in all manner of journalism, and that certainly is no less true for the participatory kind. In Chapter 8, Marina Vujnovic explores the impact of user contributions on commercial models for media organizations, as well as journalists' responses to both existing and potential economic pressures. In Chapter 9, Thorsten Quandt begins the process of tying the pieces together by considering the broader impact of participatory journalism on traditional media and on journalists, both historically and in today's environment. Quandt examines how journalists think about themselves and users, delving into the ideological and professional essence of journalism.

In the last chapter, Alfred Hermida returns to offer lessons learned and a look ahead. In addition to providing a summary, he outlines recommendations for better practices, considering the future in light of journalists' experiences, practices, perceptions and aspirations.

There is a lot of ground to cover, and much of it may be unfamiliar to you at first. Because we include newspapers in so many different countries, published in eight different languages, you probably won't have read them all yourself! So we have incorporated some things that we hope will be helpful, such as:

- A unique model for breaking the process of "making news" into five readily understandable stages. The model, which is explained in Chapter 2 and referred to throughout the book, will help you understand how newspaper editors are thinking about audience participation at each stage.
- Profiles or descriptions of the various newspapers in an appendix, which you can use as a refresher when you encounter references to them in the chapters. They are listed in alphabetical order by country, starting with Belgium and ending with the United States. We identify each newspaper by the URL of its affiliated website. Participatory journalism is a rapidly changing subject, so we strongly recommend that you visit these sites to track new and ongoing developments.
- Questions at the end of each chapter, inviting you to think more deeply about the issues raised and to probe further to understand the current paths that newspapers are navigating.
- A glossary of terms related to participatory journalism. Within each chapter, the first significant reference to a glossary term is highlighted in this **bold typeface**. You may already have noticed some of these terms in this introductory chapter.

The journey on which journalism embarked in the twenty-first century is not an easy one; it requires journalists not only to change their everyday work routines and practices but also to take up the much harder task of changing their occupational culture and even their self-perceptions.

Journalists, who long have cultivated a professional distance from their readers and sources, find themselves integrated into a network in which the distances have collapsed. Physical distances have been erased by a global network that instantaneously delivers information everywhere and anywhere, while social ones have been erased by the inherently open and wholly participatory nature of that network. The journalists whom you will meet in the pages that follow, are figuring out where they fit into this world and how to help make it an even better one.

Which is where you come in …

Note

1   The work of Mark Deuze, who has been conducting research and doing a lot of serious thinking about participatory journalism for more than a decade, has been especially valuable to us. Examples of his work include the book *Media Work*, published by Polity Press in 2007, and a series of journal articles that include "Participation, remediation, bricolage: Considering principal components of a digital culture" (*The Information Society* 22, 2006: 63–75); "Towards professional participatory storytelling in journalism and advertising" (*First Monday* 10/7, 2005: http://firstmonday.org/htbin/cgiwrap/bin/ojs/index.php/fm/article/view/1257/1177); and "The Web and its journalisms: Considering consequences of different types of media online" (*New Media & Society* 5/2, 2003: 203–230).

References

Bowman, Shayne, and Chris Willis (2003) Introduction to participatory journalism. In: *We media: How audiences are shaping the future of news and information*, The Media Center at the American Press Institute. Accessed 23 December 2010: http://www.hypergene.net/wemedia/weblog.php?id=P36

Bruns, Axel (2005) *Gatewatching: Collaborative online news production*, New York: Peter Lang.

Bruns, Axel (2008) *Blogs, Wikipedia, Second Life and beyond: From production to produsage*, New York: Peter Lang.

Deuze, Mark (2010) *Managing media work*, Thousand Oaks, CA: Sage.

Dewey, John (1927) *The public and its problems*, New York: H. Holt and Company.

Fortunati, Leopoldina, Mauro Sarrica, John O'Sullivan, Aukse Balcytiene, Halliki Harro-Loit, Phil Macgregor, Nayla Roussou, Ramón Salaverria and Federico De Luca (2009) The influence of the Internet on European journalism, *Journal of Computer-Mediated Communication* 14 (4): 928–963.

Gade, Peter J. (2008) Journalism guardians in a time of great change: Newspaper editors' perceived influence in integrated news organizations, *Journalism & Mass Communication Quarterly* 85 (2): 331–352.

Gans, Herbert J. (2003) *Democracy and the news*, New York: Oxford University Press.

Gillmor, Dan (2006) *We the media: Grassroots journalism by the people, for the people*, Sebastopol, California: O'Reilly Media.

Habermas, Jürgen (1989) *The structural transformation of the public sphere* (Thomas Burger, trans.), Cambridge, Massachusetts: MIT Press.

Lasica, J.D. (2003, 7 August) What is participatory journalism? *Online Journalism Review*. Accessed 21 March 2010: http://www.ojr.org/ojr/workplace/1060217106.php

Meyer, Philip (2008, October/November) The elite newspaper of the future, *American Journalism Review*. Accessed 11 September 2010: http://www.ajr.org/article.asp?id=4605

Pew Project for Excellence in Journalism (2010) Newspapers: Audience. The state of the news media: An annual report on American journalism. Accessed 11 September 2010: http://www.stateofthemedia.org/2010/newspapers_audience.php

Pew Project for Excellence in Journalism (2009) Overview: Introduction, The state of the news media: An annual report on American journalism. Accessed 21 March 2010: http://www.stateofthemedia.org/2009/narrative_overview_intro.php?cat=0&media=1

Pew Project for Excellence in Journalism and Rick Edmonds (2009) Newspapers: Introduction, The state of the news media: An annual report on American journalism. Accessed from: 21 March 2010: http://www.stateofthemedia.org/2009/narrative_newspapers_intro.php?media=4

Pew Research Center's Project for Excellence in Journalism (2010) Understanding the participatory news consumer: How Internet and cell phone users have turned news into a social experience. Accessed 21 March 2010: http://www.journalism.org/analysis_report/understanding_participatory_news_consumer

Rosen, Jay (2006, 27 June) The people formerly known as the audience, PressThink. Accessed 21 March 2010: http://journalism.nyu.edu/pubzone/weblogs/pressthink/2006/06/27/ppl_frmr.html

Ryfe, David M. (2009) Broader and deeper: A study of newsroom culture in a time of change, *Journalism* 10 (2): 197–216.

Shedden, David (2010, 18 August) Entrepreneurial journalism, PoynterOnline. Accessed 7 September 2010: http://www.poynter.org/column.asp?id=132&aid=176024

Shoemaker, Pamela J., Martin Eichholz, Eunyi Kim and Brenda Wrigley (2001) Individual and routine forces in gatekeeping, *Journalism & Mass Communication Quarterly* 78 (2): 233–246.

Part I

The Impact of Participatory Journalism

2

Mechanisms of Participation

How audience options shape the conversation

Alfred Hermida

Reader participation in journalism has a long history. It dates at least to eighteenth-century England, when newspapers regularly left space at the end of the third page for reader comments, with a blank fourth page so that the paper might be folded and addressed like an ordinary letter (Wiles 1965). Readers of newspapers such as *The Evening General-Post* were able to add their own observations – complete with spelling and grammatical mistakes, erroneous facts and inane comments – before sending the paper on to friends or relatives; indeed, a copy of the *General-Post* kept at Oxford University includes a long hand-written letter in unprinted space on page 3.

The first newspaper in the American colonies adopted a similar approach. Benjamin Harris' *Publick Occurrences* was printed on three pages, with the fourth page blank so readers could add their own news before passing it on to someone else (Martin and Hansen 1998). The *Publick Occurrences*' experiment in reader participation was short-lived, however, as was the paper itself: After the first issue appeared on September 25, 1690, British authorities shut the publication down because Harris lacked the required license.

These early forays into enabling readers to contribute to the newspaper after it was published came to an end with the professionalization of journalism.

Participatory Journalism: Guarding Open Gates at Online Newspapers, First Edition.
Jane B. Singer, Alfred Hermida, David Domingo, Ari Heinonen, Steve Paulussen, Thorsten Quandt, Zvi Reich, and Marina Vujnovic.
© 2011 Jane B. Singer, Alfred Hermida, David Domingo, Ari Heinonen, Steve Paulussen, Thorsten Quandt, Zvi Reich, and Marina Vujnovic. Published 2011 by Blackwell Publishing Ltd.

Newspapers became finished products with no blank spaces and with virtually all their editorial content authored by individuals – the professional journalists – according to laws of spelling and grammar (Stephens 2008). There was no longer room for the personal observation of the reader, at least within the newspaper itself. The main exception was the formal channel of the letter to the editor, which was vetted by a journalist and, if the journalist decided it was acceptable, printed along with the other contents of that edition.

With online media, newspapers are once more metaphorically leaving blank space on their pages, offering a myriad of opportunities for readers to participate and interact with the news or the publication. The ability of readers to contribute to professional journalism thus has more in common with the newspapers of the eighteenth century than with newspapers published during the centuries of institutionalized production that followed.

This chapter examines the opportunities for **users** to participate in journalistic processes and discusses the extent to which available participation technologies and formats give formerly passive **audience** members greater agency or authority to influence news making. Through the multi-national interviews described in Chapter 1, as well as a consideration of the websites themselves (see the appendix for a list plus a description of our research methods), we explore how those tools of interaction are defining the relationship between journalists and users in today's online media.

The tools and formats themselves are developing continually and rapidly, so many will have changed – in some cases quite dramatically – since we collected our information back in 2007 and 2008. But what journalists were doing and saying then remains important for understanding how and why **participatory journalism** is evolving, as well as what its development means both inside and outside the newsroom.

This chapter provides an overview of the participation options offered on these major newspaper websites, provides a framework for analyzing what we learned and identifies broad perspectives about **user-generated content**. The findings suggest that most of the available options for participation frame the user primarily as a consumer of journalism – similar to the audience role in a more traditional print or broadcasting environment – rather than as a co-collaborator in the gathering, selection, production and dissemination of news.

2.1 The Emergence of Participatory Journalism

As highlighted in Chapter 1, journalists in modern Western societies see themselves as central to the proper functioning of democracy: News practitioners believe their job as gatekeeper is to ensure that citizens have the credible information necessary to govern themselves wisely (Kovach and Rosenstiel 2007; Gans 2003).

The journalist as a gatekeeper has become a core premise not only for practitioners but also for the people who study them; the concept has been integral to communications research since its first application to news more than six decades ago (White 1950). **Gatekeeping** is the "overall process through which the social reality transmitted by the news media is constructed" (Shoemaker *et al.* 2001: 233). Within the newsroom, it involves "selecting, writing, editing, positioning, scheduling, repeating and otherwise massaging information to become news" (Shoemaker, Vos and Reese 2008: 73).

The role of the journalist as gatekeeper rested largely on professionals' privileged access to the means of producing and disseminating information. However, that role has been undermined by digital media technologies, which enable users, as individuals or as groups, to create and distribute information based on their own observations or opinions. These technological advances, coupled with contemporary problems in journalism as an institution and an industry, present new challenges to the media.

Journalists now are a part of a network in which the long-standing hierarchy among contributors to the public discourse has been significantly flattened. A participatory media culture, scholar Henry Jenkins writes, "contrasts with older notions of passive media spectatorship. Rather than talking about media producers and consumers occupying separate roles, we might now see them as participants who interact with each other according to a new set of rules that none of us fully understands" (Jenkins 2006: 3).

In our own earlier work, we suggested that this change "might lead to a new model of journalism, labelled 'participatory journalism'" (Domingo *et al.* 2008: 331), where individual citizens and community organizations perform some of the communication functions previously controlled by media institutions.

Terms such as "participatory journalism," "**citizen journalism**" and "user-generated content" have been used interchangeably to refer to "the act of a citizen, or group of citizens, playing an active role in the process of collecting, reporting, analyzing and disseminating news and information" (Bowman and Willis 2003). As you know from Chapter 1, Axel Bruns (2005) coined the term "produsage" to refer to the blurring of the line between media producers and consumers, while Dan Gillmor (2006: 136) spoke of the "former audience" to stress that the public should no longer be regarded as a passive group of media consumers.

We use the various terms throughout this book, but as we said at the very start, the one we like best is "participatory journalism." We feel it comes closest to capturing both the processes and effects of ordinary citizens' contributions to gathering, selecting, publishing, distributing, commenting on and publicly discussing the news that is contained within an institutional media product such as the newspaper websites in our study.

2.2 Analyzing Audience Participation

For several years now, established media – and newspapers in particular – have been exploring participatory forms of content production, hoping to "connect more effectively with changing usage patterns and the 'real' needs and preferences of their public" (Paulussen *et al.* 2007: 132). The Internet's participatory potential may be instigating a fundamental shift in established modes of journalism by bringing new voices into the media.

Proponents of participatory models argue that in a changing society, the democratic role of journalism needs to be redefined so that it is more inclusive than the notion of an institutional "gatekeeper" allows. These critiques address the top-down approach of the past and re-imagine journalism as a conversation with citizens, which encourages them to take an active role in news processes (Gillmor 2006; Jarvis 2006). But just what might such an active role look like? In this section, we break the news-production process into five stages to address that question.

2.2.1 Tools of Participation and Analysis

News organizations have integrated a range of technical processes and capabilities into their websites to facilitate reader participation. The newspaper websites we describe throughout this book all offered similar kinds of participatory journalism formats at the time of our study though, again, they have since continued to expand and in some cases diverge. The options we encountered were similar to the kinds of user-generated content identified by other researchers, as well (Hermida and Thurman 2008). Table 2.1, below, shows the main ones.

We are interested in more than simply the different ways that users can contribute content, however. We want to explore all the opportunities that active audience members have to influence the processes of producing and distributing news, ranging from ranking stories to using **social networking** platforms, so that we can understand their impact on the norms and practices of journalism. The generic formats are common across a number of online newspapers, and the culture of journalism is broadly shared across national borders. But the similarities can mask the diverse attitudes of journalists working with this material as well as the diverse ways in which those journalists are implementing and managing participation options, as we explore in detail in Chapters 4, 5 and 6.

This chapter draws on our previous work in developing a model that analyzes participatory journalism practices in the context of the historical evolution of public communication (Domingo *et al.* 2008). Table 2.2 suggests five **news-production stages**, providing us with a strategy for systematically analyzing users' opportunities to participate in this process of making news.

The grid illustrates the common components of the communication process, which include access to and observation of something that can be

Table 2.1 Examples of formats for user participation (Developed from Hermida and Thurman 2008)

Format	Description
Citizen blogs	Blogs created by users hosted on the news organization's website.
Citizen media	Photographs, video and other media submitted by users, usually vetted by journalists.
Citizen stories	Written submissions from readers on topical issues, including suggestions for news stories, selected and edited by journalists for publication on the website.
Collective interviews	Chats or interviews with journalists or invited guests, with questions submitted by readers and typically moderated by a news professional. These usually are webcast in audio or video formats, or transcribed live, offering a sense of interactivity and immediacy.
Comments	Views on a story or other online item, which users typically submit by filling in a form on the bottom of the item.
Content hierarchy	News stories ranked according to audience ratings, often based on the most read or emailed content.
Forums	1) Discussions led by journalists, with topical questions posed by the newsroom and submissions either fully or reactively moderated. These often are open for a limited number of days. 2) Places where readers can engage in threaded online conversations or debates, with discussions staying open for weeks or months. The readers usually initiate these forum topics.
Journalist blogs	Authored by one or more journalists, with short articles in reverse chronological order. Journalist blogs (also called "j-blogs") often are associated with a specific topic or perspective, with the facility for readers to comment on entries.
Polls	Topical questions posed by journalists, with users asked to make a multiple choice or binary response. These polls provide instant and quantifiable feedback to users.
Social networking	Distribution of links to stories through social media platforms, such as Twitter and Facebook.

communicated, selection and filtering of that information, and then processing or editing, distributing and interpreting it. Traditionally, professional journalists have been employed full time to handle the first four of these stages. They also interpret information themselves – for instance through news analysis articles or opinion columns – and control the distribution of others' interpretations, for instance through the letters to the editor mentioned above. This role came about

Table 2.2   Stages of the news production process (Developed from Domingo *et al.* 2008)

Stage	Description
1) Access/observation	The initial information-gathering stage at which source material for a story is generated, such as eyewitness accounts and audio-visual contributions.
2) Selection/filtering	The "gatekeeping" stage when decisions are made about what should be reported or published.
3) Processing/editing	The stage at which a story is created, including the writing and editing of an item for publication.
4) Distribution	The stage at which a story is disseminated or made available for reading and, potentially, discussion.
5) Interpretation	The stage at which a story that has been produced and published is opened up to comment and discussion.

as large and complex societies made it increasingly difficult for individual community members to perform the communication functions necessary for the whole process to work effectively, as described in Chapter 9.

But digital technologies enable the audience to assume some of these communication functions, within institutional media as well as outside the structures and strictures of professional journalism. The widespread adoption of participatory tools suggests that journalists are seeking to accommodate input from the audience within the spaces that media institutions once tightly controlled.

We now take a look at the ways online newspapers are incorporating participation formats into each stage of creating a news story.

2.2.2 Access / Observation

The newspaper websites studied provided various ways for users to participate in the **access and observation stage of news production**, often within operational procedures based on established news practices. At the time of our study, these primarily involved tools that allowed users to send text or audio-visual material to the newsroom. Our interviewees also described opportunities for readers to post questions, which typically were filtered by a professional journalist. Editors saw these options as successful for engaging users in a debate on issues; for example, one interviewee described online discussions as an "extraordinarily high-end interactive" feature.

Most of these newspapers offered users some way to contact the newsroom or specific journalists (or both), though relatively few explicitly encouraged audience members to submit story ideas or otherwise guided their coverage. The main channel offered for suggesting a story was email, either via a form on the website, through a generic newsroom email address or by direct contact using a journalist's individual address. Regardless of the actual recipient, email enabled users to submit news tips or story suggestions; however, it was then up to the professional journalist to decide if the idea was newsworthy and merited further attention.

In Israel, for example, online users of different websites had various ways to contact the newsroom. At the Ynet and *Haaretz* sites, they could send an email message to either the reporter or the newsroom. At NRG, only emails to the newsroom were allowed, via a "Scoop Mail" feature. The Ynet website had a similar feature for reader alerts called the "Red Mail" button. Journalists said this tool proved popular with readers, particularly during major news events, when the newsroom could be bombarded with hundreds of emails. These messages went directly to editors who decided whether to follow up any story leads and, if so, assigned them to the appropriate reporter.

Some newspapers, such as the two Finnish dailies in our study, *Helsingin Sanomat* and *Kaleva*, actively asked for news tips and provided email addresses for individual reporters, as well as the overall newsroom. At *Het Nieuwsblad* in Belgium, editors could create a separate email address for each local news page on the website, which they said had proved to be a valuable way of receiving tips, photos or videos about specific towns. However, they also said that the newsroom struggled to handle the unsolicited emails, with a lot of the material getting "lost amidst all the information we receive." A few years earlier, Belgian online newspapers had experimented with an SMS service for people to send their tips or photos, but the service was abandoned. Editors said the response was poor and they rarely receive a useful text message.

The most widespread method of involving users at this stage of the news-production process was through enabling them to submit photos and video, which journalists divided conceptually into news-related events and lifestyle-related topics. At the time of the interviews, newspapers received far more photos than video, though several interviewees said they had to explicitly solicit the material. "You really have to invite people actively to send in pictures. You have to put a message on the site that says 'please send us your photos,' because people will not do it automatically," said the online editor at *De Standaard* (Belgium).

Other editors said calls for particular kinds of lifestyle-related material could result in a deluge of submissions. "We asked people to send in their own jokes, and nobody did – whereas if we ask people to send in a picture of their dog, we get 1,200 a day," recalled the managing editor at *The Globe and Mail* (Canada). The online news editor at the *National Post* (Canada) also described dog pictures as "wildly popular." At *USA Today*, many of the photos uploaded were related to weather and travel.

Overall, the way in which user participation tools were implemented at this stage of the news-production process indicated that newspapers were reluctant to allow audience members to set the news agenda, a sentiment that also came through in our interviews, as we'll see throughout this book and especially in Chapter 3. Instead, journalists were extending established newsgathering practices to the web, seeking to limit the user role at this stage to serving simply as a source of information or raw audio-visual content – particularly for material that journalists wanted to have but for whatever reason were unable to get. As one French editor put it: "What's interesting for journalists is to have contributions that really relate to news, of the witness type."

Many of our interviewees expressed a similar attitude. Editors at *De Standaard* (Belgium), for example, placed far greater value on journalists approaching audience members as sources for a specific story or issue than they did on users providing unsolicited story ideas or news tips. Similarly, journalists at *Le Figaro* (France) described appealing for eyewitness accounts on breaking news events, while an editor at *The Globe and Mail* (Canada) expressed frustration that reporters did not ask for information from users "as often as I would have liked." Even newspapers that did not offer much user-generated content, such as the *Washington Post* (USA), saw value in the reader as a source, particularly at the community level. An editor there admitted that it made more sense to have "a thousand people" telling the newspaper what is going on at a local level than to rely on one reporter trying to cover everything.

This approach can be considered a form of **crowdsourcing**, a practice through which journalists try to loosely steer the priorities of contributors by requesting data, analysis or other assistance with specific stories or with topics of investigation. An editor at the *Guardian* (UK) described how readers had helped the newspaper in its coverage of Burma by providing details of events on the ground, while a *Globe and Mail* editor highlighted audience contributions in response to a series on mental health. At the other Canadian newspaper in our study, the *National Post*, editors experimented with crowdsourcing to cover a huge propane gas explosion that happened overnight in Toronto, setting up a **blog** and appealing for eyewitness accounts.

Another example of crowdsourcing was a project on cycle paths by *Het Nieuwsblad* (Belgium), which asked readers to submit complaints, tips and photos. The newspaper's editor in chief said the project proved that "citizens can help set the agenda," but in all these cases, the reality was that the journalist shaped the users' involvement, assessed the content that resulted and made the final decisions about its editorial value.

The way these tools have been implemented, then, suggests that journalists tightly limit the **agenda-setting** capability of citizens. There were exceptions, however, such as the user-dominated spaces of LePost.fr in France (part of the *Le Monde* newspaper group) or My.Telegraph.co.uk in Britain, as discussed later in this chapter. Another exception was the online edition of the Spanish free daily, *20 Minutos*. The site was launched in 2005 with an innovative approach that involved publishing users' original content under a Creative Commons license and allowing free republishing with credit to the author. This online edition of *20 Minutos* provided channels for both solicited and unsolicited user material; it received 150 items a day – by "snail mail," fax, email and online forms – at the time of our study in 2008. The content ranged from hard news to complaints about local issues to poems.

While the newspaper used similar tools to the other newspapers in our study, comments by editors at *20 Minutos* reflected a difference in attitude. "We also get proposals about very diverse topics, such as education, transport, health care, street safety, infrastructure, traffic," said an editor. "That is, very specific things that may be improved, immediate and bonded to everyday life and the closest environment of the reader."

Such comments suggest that papers such as *20 Minutos*, which are relatively new and have begun building their reputation as news providers in an online era, may be more open to the idea of users as a co-collaborators in the access/observation stage of news production than some of more traditional publications we studied. We return to this theme in subsequent chapters.

2.2.3 Selection / Filtering

The **selection/filtering stage** was by far the most closed of the five news-production processes to users at the time of our study, and we believe that has continued to be the case since. The notion of enabling readers to decide what is news was generally taboo for the journalists we interviewed. None of the newspapers discussed in this book allowed readers any meaningful agency over what went into the main news product at this stage of the journalistic process. Other researchers also have found that participation tools have not empowered citizens in any meaningful way to change or challenge established news selection criteria (Harrison 2010).

A very few of the papers in our study did allow readers a semblance of control over the selection and filtering of news at the time of our interviews – but in areas separated from the main website of the parent organization. The best example was LePost.fr, the spinoff website of French newspaper *Le Monde*, which enabled contributors to perform a news monitoring function. Launched in September 2007, the website is an innovative online-only entity based almost entirely on user contributions. Users are encouraged to filter news from other sources and, in the words of the editor in chief, "give them an angle." Contributors thus have some leeway in deciding what is news – albeit on a site that is viewed by the parent organization as an experimental laboratory and distinct from the more traditional newspaper brand.

2.2.4 Processing / Editing

The newspapers in our sample also tended to shy away from allowing citizens to write their own news stories. Indeed, some comments from our interviewees suggested a decided resistance to opening up this **processing/editing stage** of the news process. "Somebody can send a story in and say you should publish this story. But they're probably going to get nowhere with it," said an editor at the *National Post* (Canada).

When newspapers did offer an option for citizen stories, the process was subject to strict editorial controls. At *El País* (Spain), users had to register with the website and provide a telephone number and an email address, with story submissions filtered and fact-checked by journalists. The stories would then be published in a separate section of the website, rarely making it to the homepage. For a while, the newspaper offered a monetary prize for citizen stories, but this practice was discontinued. Participation subsequently declined, in part because citizens who contributed did not feel their efforts were recognized by the online newsroom.

Similarly, the other Spanish newspaper in our study, *20 Minutos*, offered a space in its local pages for short news items from citizens, titled "the reader informs." However, journalists viewed these contributions more as news tips than as news stories in their own right. Journalists selected what they saw as the best ones and developed them into larger stories that only generically acknowledged the source by adding the tagline "with a tip-off from a reader."

At other newspapers, notably the Belgian ones, some editors saw value in citizen coverage of **hyperlocal** news. "We should publish as much as we can on our local news pages," said an editor at *Het Nieuwsblad* (Belgium), though he emphasized that content from users must be "double-checked." Rather than relying on users to take the lead, another Belgian newspaper, *Het Belang van Limburg*, provided journalistic training to users who volunteered to become local correspondents for the newspaper's website, creating a network of around 80 amateur journalists to contribute citizen news. Material from these citizen journalists was labeled to distinguish it from the content produced by professionals.

More broadly, hard news tended to remain the preserve of professional journalists at the newspapers we visited. When the papers did enable citizen participation in producing content, this option typically was limited to lifestyle topics, such as travel and culture. The Been There section of the *Guardian* (UK) website, for instance, allowed users to contribute travel reviews and advice, with some of the content selected and published in print. In Germany, *Der Spiegel* offered *Einestages*, a site about twentieth-century history that invited users to submit contemporary eyewitness accounts. Amateur and professional content was published side by side but was labelled with different icons to indicate the source.

The decision to explicitly distinguish between professional and amateur content was also evident among websites that adopted user blogs as a participation option, which one editor described as "quite a radical step" for newspapers. Citizen blogs enabled news organizations to offer a hosted space for users to create their own content that was self-contained – and, more importantly, at an arm's length editorially – from the professional publication. These blogs, where available, also tended to be the most open form of participation among the various formats on offer, as there typically was no content moderation prior to publication.

24 Hours and *Vecernji List* (Croatia), *Le Monde* (France, through its LePost. fr spinoff), *El País* (Spain), the *Telegraph* (UK) and *USA Today* all hosted collections of thousands of citizen blogs at the time of our study. Most required user **registration** but were otherwise open to all comers and all content. A *Telegraph* executive described the My Telegraph community section of the website as an opportunity to give users "a place on the web to go to meet like-minded people to talk about things that they were interested in."

Other newspapers, such as *De Standaard* (Belgium), *Helsingin Sanomat* and *Kaleva* (Finland), and the *Guardian* (UK) only offered citizen blogs to approved guest writers at the time of our study. For example, *De Standaard* hosted a number of blogs written by Belgians living abroad, selected by editors who expressed scepticism about offering blogs to everyone. "All people who want a weblog already have one, I think, so also economically, it is not interesting any more," said one editor. An editor at *FAZ* (Germany) went further: "It is out of the question for us to broadly install a user blog and to offer all users the option to inscribe their name for eternity."

2.2.5 Distribution

Users' ability to exercise a degree of decision-making over the **distribution stage of the news-production** process also was very limited at the time of our study. Most of the newspaper websites we explored created user-driven story rankings, based on automatic counts of most-read or most-emailed stories and often featured on the homepage. *Le Monde* (France) also tested a format called "hottest topics," which linked to five interesting posts and five associated **comments**, ranking them on the basis of the discussion they provoked.

But again, there appeared to be a reticence about handing over too much decision-making about content hierarchy – that is, the prominence with which an item is displayed, an indication of its perceived value or importance. Making such judgments is another role journalists seemed to feel they could and should exercise themselves. "You have to give your users the opportunity to personalize content to their own preferences and needs," said an online editor at *Het Nieuwsblad* (Belgium). "But at the same time, I think it is still important to provide a 'package' of news chosen by the professional newsroom, a package that says 'this is what happened today.'"

Most of the newspapers in our study also enabled users to share articles by email and through **social bookmarking** services, such as del.icio.us or digg. com, a capability that has continued to expand in recent years. In addition, some papers allowed users to distribute links to stories through **social media** platforms, such as Facebook and Twitter – another increasingly popular option. "Everybody is engaged in Twitter," said the managing editor for online news at *The Globe and Mail* (Canada). "You don't expect people to come to your content; you want to send it out to people. And so everybody is scrambling to figure out, how do you do that?"

Some interviewees highlighted the fast pace of technological change, along with frustration at the need to keep up with the latest web innovations. Belgian editors, for example, explained that their newspaper websites had few social networking features because of technological limitations. They were optimistic about offering these features when new online news production systems were introduced.

Journalists expressed mixed attitudes about opportunities for users to personalize content. There was a general recognition of a need to offer additional options to create a more personal and social news experience, however, and several newspapers had taken steps in that direction.

For example, Ynet (Israel) began setting up its own social network, and editors talked about developing functionality to provide users with their own space to aggregate their comments, as well as website content such as cooking recipes and favorite articles. At *USA Today*, registered users could set up a profile and add other users as friends. In practice, most users did not develop their profile page, but the managing editor defended the value of this feature, saying it is an option that users appreciate having and helps build a community.

In France, *Le Figaro* went a step further by enabling registered users to set up a personalized page with customized feeds of news and topics. The Mon Figaro section of the site used the web aggregation platform Netvibes to pull together content from all over the web, which an editor said "helps to create a link with the online audience."

What emerged from our interviews and review of these websites, then, is a picture of editors trying to balance a shift toward a more social experience of the news while, at the same time, retaining a degree of control over the hierarchy and distribution of information. The online executive editor of *The Globe and Mail* (Canada) summed up the general attitude when he stressed the importance of journalism to the newspaper's website. "It's not a social networking site," he said. "It offers social networking functionalities along with its journalism."

2.2.6 Interpretation

By far, the greatest number of options for users to participate in online newspapers came at the **interpretation stage**, where users are encouraged to have their say on the day's news. The simplest and most immediate tools were **polls** on issues and stories of the day. These tended to attract the highest volume of participation, as anonymous voting demands the least amount of effort from a user.

Beyond polls, there were two main participatory journalism strategies at this stage of the news process. Most websites at the time of our study allowed comments through a form available below each story, while others separated news sections from areas for debate, such as **forums**. Comments, which we discuss in more detail throughout this book and especially in Chapter 6, were the most widely offered user-participation options at these newspapers.

Although our interviewees expressed mixed feelings about their value, most seemed to see **comments** as a significant tool to enable users to discuss the news content produced by professional journalists. The executive editor of *The Globe and Mail* (Canada), for instance, described the ability to comment on the news as a way for "readers to come online and express their views on any article that's written on our site."

Editors generally viewed comments as one of the most successful forms of interaction with audiences, often equating success with the number of comments left on a story. Editors at the website of *Le Monde* (France) highlighted the fact that they received a thousand comments every day, while journalists at *Süddeutsche Zeitung* (Germany) described how, in just one year, the volume had risen from fewer than 400 comments a day to as many as 2,000. These figures, however, paled in comparison to the 12,000 daily comments at *20 Minutos*, the first Spanish newspaper to allow comments on every news story.

Although comments on stories were the most successful participatory feature in terms of quantity, journalists recognized that successful participation was more than just a numbers game. At *20 Minutos* (Spain), editors declined to estimate how many of the thousands of daily comments were relevant – and they said that from 25 to 30 percent typically were deleted as inappropriate. An editor at *USA Today* said that "a lot of the comments are just opinions, and they don't necessarily lead individually to an understanding of the situation."

In general, our interviewees tended to see comments less as journalistic input and more as conversations among users that can inform the newsroom about the interests and concerns of their audience. "We don't really see them as contributions unless we actually ask for contributions," said the executive editor of the *National Post* (Canada), where journalists select the "rational elements of the debate" and package them for the letters page of the printed newspaper. "I think we see it as [*users having a*] conversation with each other." The editor in chief of LePost.fr (France) put it more bluntly: "For us, that's not really participation. It's just debate."

Journalist blogs also featured user input alongside professionally produced content. Journalists viewed this participation option as an important way for them to communicate and engage with readers by writing in a more personal and opinionated style about a particular topic or issue. At the *National Post* (Canada), in fact, this was the only avenue for user comments due to technological limitations at the time of the interviews. At other newspapers, such as the two British papers in our study, blogs were one of the main forms of interaction with users. And *Haaretz* (Israel) specifically encouraged its journalists to converse with their audience through blogs. However, website editors said they also had to dampen demands from reporters for blogs, making them aware of the burden and the benefits of constant correspondence with readers.

The type and tone of user participation on journalists' blogs differed from comments on stories, interviewees said – and the participation of the journalists themselves also tended to be much greater. "It feels like a slightly different space for people to comment," said an editor at the *Telegraph* (UK). "The best of our blogs tend to work with the bloggers coming back on the thread quite a lot more than they would do if they'd written a column."

There were some indications that narrow topics targeting specific audiences worked best as vehicles for audience interaction. Editors at *USA Today*, for example, cited their success in developing lively online communities around blogs on pop culture and ocean cruises. "When they start talking, it may go on forever," one editor said. Journalists said the loyalty of members of these specialized *USA Today* communities was valuable. They highlighted benefits stemming from the quality of the contributions rather than simply the size of the audience.

The other main approach adopted by online newspapers was to keep participation separate from professional content through the use of forums, which were either journalist-led or audience-led. Editors at *Der Spiegel* (Germany) boasted about having the largest online discussion platform in German-speaking countries, with nearly 100,000 registered users and at least 800 posts daily. Forums were the main Spiegel.de participation channel, with the newsroom initiating discussion on topics that "promise controversial debate."

Journalists at the *Helsingin Sanomat* (Finland), who said their discussion forum was "absolutely the most popular," also would kick off discussions by posting a link to a news article on the forum. While the main discussion took place in its own space, the opening comment would appear below the story. Journalists took an even more active role at *De Standaard* (Belgium), not just initiating the debate but also **pre-moderating** user submissions before they were published.

Most often, though, newsrooms ceded a significant level of independence to audience-led forums. An editor at *Focus* (Germany) explained that the newspaper did not apply the same strict criteria to forums that it did to comments, such as demanding a clear focus and proper spelling. "In the forums, the space is much bigger," he said. "You can link to other websites and communicate with other users if you want. You can argue. All that isn't permitted in the comments."

This hands-off approach to audience-led forums was common. Editors at *Het Nieuwsblad* (Belgium), for example, did little to enhance the discussions or suggest new forum topics. Where contributions were **post-moderated**, or reviewed only after publication, newsrooms relied heavily on selected users to oversee the debate. A forums on Britons living abroad hosted by the *Telegraph* (UK), for instance, used expatriates as community "mentors."

However, journalists held divided views over the value of forums as a tool for audience participation. Some saw them as making a worthwhile contribution. A senior editor at the *Washington Post* (USA) viewed forums as a way to attract an engaged and loyal group of contributors. He described the level of discourse at the newspaper's discussion group on international politics as "extremely interesting and high-level," with contributors who could offer expert perspectives. Editors at *FAZ* (Germany) also capitalized on this potential by creating a special-interest forum on contemporary literature, divided into two levels. On one level, the debate was restricted to invited experts, while a second level was open to all users.

Other editors were dismissive of forums. The *Gazet van Antwerpen* and *Het Belang van Limburg* (Belgium) closed down their forums, citing the poor quality of user input. At the time of our interviews, NRG (Israel) was in the process of closing its forums, which were perceived as a declining, old-fashioned platform. In contrast, the *Guardian* (UK) had kept the forums, or "talkboards," that it first set up in 1999; they remained popular with users even though other forms of participation had since become available. That said, *Guardian* journalists clearly saw the forums as separate, distant provinces and barely mentioned them in the interviews.

What, then, do these diverse approaches suggest about how journalists view the wide-ranging options for user input? In addressing that question, we will briefly set the stage for the more detailed explorations of participatory journalism in the chapters that follow.

2.3 Perceptions of Participatory Journalism

As we have just seen, the different types of participatory journalism available on these newspaper websites at the time of our study in the late 2000s gave users only limited options to engage in most stages of news production. At least at that point, online newspapers were generally reluctant to open up the news-making process to input from outside the newsroom.

Most opportunities for users to contribute came at the end of the process, with the ability to comment on or otherwise discuss content that the professional journalists had already produced and published. Journalists retained control over nearly everything that came first, including the tasks of identifying, gathering, filtering, producing and distributing news. Only after those processes were essentially completed were audiences invited to offer their interpretation of the result, primarily through comments.

2.3.1 The View from the Newsroom

The journalists we interviewed held three broad views of their website audiences: as active recipients of the news; as sources of information, including both breaking news and hyperlocal content; and as members of an online community. Let's briefly examine each of these perceived user roles before taking a closer look in the next chapter. We'll also come back to this idea at the end of the book.

First, these journalists generally cast audience members as active recipients of the news, rather than as active participants in the process of constructing it. As active recipients, audience members are expected to react to the news, with a variety of avenues provided to facilitate this process. As other studies (Domingo *et al.* 2008; Hermida and Thurman 2008) have suggested, the notion that participatory journalism is more than a right to reply had yet to be widely accepted in the profession at the time of our study. The choice and implementation of participation options provided few opportunities for users to take on the role of news producers rather than to remain in their long-standing role as news consumers.

However, journalists did clearly recognize users' potential as valuable sources of information. While there were a variety of mechanisms for users to contact the newsroom, there was consistency in the type of material most valued by journalists: eyewitness accounts or audio-visual material, especially related to breaking news events. As Harrison (2010) found in her study of the BBC's use of audience contributions, journalists at online newspapers considered user-generated content as a form of source material and story enhancement, rather than as a way to elicit new stories or substantively alter the journalists' narrative.

In effect, then, newsrooms were simply extending established newsgathering practices to the Internet, albeit using rapid and cost-effective digital technologies to gather input from a much more far-flung net. The user as a primary source is nothing new; journalists have always recognized the value of eyewitness accounts. Although the tools of participation are new, our study suggests they have been designed and implemented in a way that steers user submissions toward conformity with pre-determined news selection processes. The journalist still retained agency and authority in determining what constitutes news in the first place. As one Croatian editor put it: "We publish everything that we believe is newsworthy."

That said, online newspapers by the late 2000s also were exploring more collective, collaborative approaches around the edges of their news operations. In particular, our study identified experiments in tapping into citizens' knowledge to broaden hyperlocal coverage.

There were many examples. The *National Post* (Canada) created a Google map for users to add information following a major Toronto fire. An online editor described the map as "an experiment on the fly, and out of the first few hours, we were able to actually build a lot more than you can from one person." In Belgium, editors at *Het Nieuwsblad* described the cycle paths project, which solicited user complaints, tips and photos, as a "very good example of the fundamentally new ways in which users and user-generated content can now contribute to our news-making."

For the 2008 French municipal elections, *Le Figaro* created 38,000 pages for each of the nation's local communes. As well as providing hyperlocal information about the commune, users could participate by ranking their mayor or submitting ideas for municipal projects, among other options. "We were very innovative on that one, the only ones in France to do so," said the paper's director of new media. "It was a mix between a polling platform, based on common questions on a local level, and specific pages for each town where users could contribute content."

Beyond these one-off initiatives, there were indications that newspapers were adopting a more systemic approach for collaborating with audiences through dedicated hyperlocal sites. *Het Nieuwsblad* was investing in a significant hyperlocal news project, aimed at creating a network of professional and local volunteer correspondents. "We want them to create a local community of people who are willing to contribute to the local news pages of Nieuwsblad.be," said the website's news manager. In Finland, *Helsingin Sanomat* published a section called "Oma kaupunki" (My Town), where users could post reviews and comments about places and services in Helsinki. The other Finnish paper in our study, *Kaleva*, was reviving neighborhood community sites it had previously discontinued, after an initial trial in the late 1990s, through a project with the University of Tampere.

These initiatives suggested newspaper editors believed the potential of citizen journalism was in large part at the hyperlocal level, where journalists seemed more willing to accept users as collaborators in gathering, reporting and producing news. The extent to which this openness represents a shift in attitudes – as opposed, for instance, to an economically driven necessity as newsroom budgets and staffs continue to shrink – is an area for further research.

2.3.2 Arm's Length

In the meantime, though, our findings suggest that such citizen journalism initiatives tended to be kept at arm's length from professional news operations. For example, the Concentra media group, owners of two of the Belgian newspapers in our sample, set up a **citizen journalism** website in 2006 called *HasseltLokaal*. The website offered a platform for about 20 citizens who volunteered to cover local news from the city of Hasselt, with two online editors employed to coordinate, train and motivate them. While the website was closely related to the website of *Het Belang van Limburg* newspaper, the print newsroom was not involved in the project. Instead, *HasseltLokaal* was set up by the group's research and development department, and managed by the digital media business unit.

Similarly, *Süddeutsche Zeitung* (Germany) had a youth community website called Jetzt.de that published content from users. Again, though, Jetzt.de was organizationally separate from the newspaper operations and even was housed in a different building. The editor of *Süddeutsche* described Jetzt.de as an experimental lab for the publisher, where new ideas could be tested outside the constraints of the news website.

Indeed, a number of the newspapers we studied had adopted a strategy of creating dedicated spaces for user participation that were distinct and separate from professional content. These spaces suggest a third broad role that our interviewees identified for their website users: as members of a distinct online community clearly distanced from the newsroom.

It would be overly simplistic to assume that motivation for such separate spaces stemmed solely from journalists' unease about placing professional and amateur content side by side – though this certainly was one factor. "If you want to give people a space to chime in, that's fine. Give them a space to chime in," said an online editor at the *National Post* (Canada). "But give them a controlled space."

However, before examining each of these types of user roles more closely in Chapter 3, it is important to consider the spirit in which these spaces were set up in the first place.

In some cases, interviewees said, these spaces were viewed less as places for news content and more as areas for the community of readers to gather and connect with each other. Newspapers such as *Haaretz* and *Yedioth Aharonoth* (publisher of Ynet) in Israel, as well as *Der Spiegel* and *Süddeutsche Zeitung* in Germany, offered sites with a degree of social networking functionality, for example. At the *Telegraph* (UK), the My Telegraph section of the website was set up with the explicit aim of creating a user-generated blogging community that, in the words of a **community manager**, "belongs to the readers. It's their part of the site."

As we discuss in greater detail in Chapter 8, journalists viewed the sense of user belonging generated from online communities as a benefit not only to audiences but also to their own news organizations, for whom such communities serve as a way to both attract and retain users. Interviewees at the Belgian newspapers, for example, talked about the growing importance of social media platforms, enabling newspapers to eventually "create a true social network, in which all people can share information with other people. That way, we hope that there will emerge different communities of interest," as the online editor of *Het Nieuwsblad* said.

The adoption of social networking tools as part of the range of participation options, which has picked up additional momentum in recent years, suggests that news websites may be evolving into hybrid sites that focus on both content and community.

2.4 Conclusion

This chapter has provided an introductory overview of audience participation options at the leading online newspapers in our study. It suggests that while digitalization and **convergence** have blurred the distinctions between producers and audiences, established news institutions have tended to rely on existing norms and practices as they have expanded into digital media.

In theory, notions of participatory journalism signal the ability of users to become active collaborators in the journalistic process, with a degree of agency and authority over media content. In reality, our findings suggest that despite a diversity of strategies, many major newspapers remained generally averse to opening up significant stages of the news-production process to the audience.

Three centuries after early newspapers left a blank space for reader comments, online newspapers continue to frame participation primarily as the public's ability to engage in a debate on current events – as already identified and framed within the newsroom.

The way participatory tools are implemented and managed in newsrooms is not determined just by the availability of the technology; it also is shaped by the newsroom ethos, and that ethos varied somewhat from place to place. The two U.S. newspapers in our sample provide an example. The *Washington Post* has a longer tradition of engaging users than *USA Today*, but it has distanced the brand from outsiders by strictly separating user-generated content from journalistic content. The only direct interaction with users at the time of our study was through collective interviews or **chats**, discussion boards and journalist blogs. In contrast, *USA Today* relied on comments on news stories as a primary participatory mechanism but did so in a more collaborative spirit, integrating the discussion far more fully into its news pages. "We have tried to make [*user participation*] visible at all levels," a *USA Today* editor said, "beyond what other sites have done."

A similar picture emerged in the participation strategies of the two Spanish newspapers in the sample, *20 Minutos* and *El País*. The less traditional publication, *20 Minutos*, was very open to content at the access stage and to comments at the interpretation stage. The user content section was featured on the website's homepage, and two to three pages of the print newspaper carried user material. "User participation at *20minutos.es* is acknowledged and celebrated in the print newspaper," the online editor said.

El País had adopted almost every participation feature available. Yet judging the extent to which it was embracing participatory journalism based on the number of options would be misleading. In practice, the online newsroom paid virtually no attention to user input; in fact, members of the **participation team** expressed frustrating that user contributions were not promoted on the site's homepage and thus were essentially invisible. *El País* had effectively separated participation from the news production routines and, as discussed further in Chapter 5, set up segregated "playgrounds" for users.

In short, participatory journalism is not simply a technology-driven process. Rather, it results from complex interactions involving the professional culture of journalism, as well as both journalists' and users' understanding of the Internet and expectations about the potential of the technology. Professional, market and social factors all play an important part (Domingo *et al.* 2008). The online tools are mechanisms whose application is shaped by professional and organizational protocols, as well as by the way people outside the newsroom use them and think about them.

The rest of this book focuses on various ways in which the ethos of the newspaper organizations and their journalists – in other words, their **newsroom culture** and fundamental set of values – forms a prism to shape the opportunities for audience participation.

Participate!

1. What are the audience participation options available in your favorite online newspaper? How does it present or highlight content from users? At which stages of the news production process described in this chapter do users seem to have the most input? The least?
2. What is the value to journalists of offering a range of options for participation? What is the value to users?

References

Bowman, Shayne and Chris Willis (2003) *We media: How audiences are shaping the future of news and information*, The Media Center. Accessed 23 January 2010: http://www.hypergene.net/wemedia/weblog.php.

Bruns, Axel (2005) *Gatewatching: Collaborative online news production*, New York: Peter Lang.

Domingo, David, Thorsten Quandt, Ari Heinonen, Steve Paulussen, Jane B. Singer and Marina Vujnovic (2008) Participatory journalism practices in the media and beyond: An international comparative study of initiatives in online newspapers, *Journalism Practice* 2 (3): 326–342.

Gans, Herbert J. (2003) *Democracy and the news*, Oxford: Oxford University Press.

Gillmor, Dan (2006) *We the media: grassroots journalism by the people, for the people*, Sebastopol, California: O'Reilly.

Harrison, Jackie (2010) User-generated content and gatekeeping at the BBC hub, *Journalism Studies* 11 (2): 243–256.

Hermida, Alfred, and Neil Thurman (2008) A clash of cultures: The integration of user-generated content within professional journalistic frameworks at British newspaper websites, *Journalism Practice* 2 (3): 342–356.

Jarvis, Jeff (2006) Networked journalism, BuzzMachine, July 5. Accessed 18 September 2008: http://www.buzzmachine.com/2006/07/05/networked-journalism/

Jenkins, Henry (2006) *Convergence culture: Where old and new media collide*, New York: New York University Press.

Kovach, Bill, and Tom Rosenstiel (2007) *The elements of journalism: What newspeople should know and the public should expect*, New York: Three Rivers Press.

Martin, Shannon E., and Kathleen A. Hansen, (1998) *Newspapers of record in a digital age: From hot type to hot link*, Westport, Connecticut: Praeger Publishers.

Paulussen, Steve, Ari Heinonen, David Domingo and Thorsten Quandt (2007) Doing it together: Citizen participation in the professional news making process, *Observatorio Journal* 1 (3): 131–154.

Shoemaker, Pamela J., Martin Eichholz, Eunyi Kim and Brenda Wrigley (2001) Individual and routine forces in gatekeeping, *Journalism & Mass Communication Quarterly* 78 (2): 233–246.

Shoemaker, Pamela J., Tim P. Vos and Stephen D. Reese (2008) Journalists as gatekeepers. In: Karin Wahl-Jorgensen and Thomas Hanitzsch (eds.), *Handbook of journalism studies*, New York: Routledge, 73–87.

Stephens, Mitchell (2008) New media, new ideas: Escape from the holy of holies, *Journalism Studies* 9 (4): 595–599.

Thurman, Neil and Alfred Hermida (2010) Gotcha: How newsroom norms are shaping participatory journalism online. In: Monaghan, Garrett, and Sean Tunney (eds.) *Web journalism: A new form of citizenship*, Eastbourne: Sussex Academic Press, 46–62.

White, David M. (1950) The gatekeeper: A case study in the selection of news, *Journalism Quarterly* 27: 383–96.

Wiles, Roy M. (1965) *Freshest advices: Early provincial newspapers in England*, Columbus, Ohio: Ohio State University Press.

3

The Journalist's Relationship with Users
New dimensions to conventional roles
Ari Heinonen

See, you just can't make a newspaper without a living audience. I mean, the audience is the basis, not some sidetrack.

This Finnish journalist's remark encapsulates the crucial role that journalism professionals acknowledge members of their audience play. At a general level, there is no journalism without **audience**; journalism exists because – and if – it is capable of attracting and maintaining public attention. On a more concrete level, professional news workers justify their special role and privileges in society by referring to their public service function, which requires not only a mass audience ("the public") but also customers, who buy media products and who can be sold as "eyeballs" to advertisers.

James W. Carey (2007) aptly described this intimate relationship by stating that the "public" is "the god term of journalism." According to Carey, journalists refer to themselves as representatives of the public when they justify their actions and defend their civic role. But in the midst of daily journalistic work, "audiences" and "public" have tended to be abstractions rather than an active presence in the newsroom – until the era of interactive communication.

In this chapter, we look into how the online newspaper editors in our study described the relationship between journalists and audience members, many of whom have taken on a new, more active role as "**users**" of media websites.

Participatory Journalism: Guarding Open Gates at Online Newspapers, First Edition.
Jane B. Singer, Alfred Hermida, David Domingo, Ari Heinonen, Steve Paulussen, Thorsten Quandt, Zvi Reich, and Marina Vujnovic.
© 2011 Jane B. Singer, Alfred Hermida, David Domingo, Ari Heinonen, Steve Paulussen, Thorsten Quandt, Zvi Reich, and Marina Vujnovic. Published 2011 by Blackwell Publishing Ltd.

3.1 Rewritten Roles

The social role or function of journalism in the democratic process, which we outlined in Chapter 1, typically provides the context for defining the nature of the relationship between audience members and journalists. From the Commission on the Freedom of the Press in the United States and the Royal Commission on the Press in the United Kingdom in the 1940s to the ethics codes of present-day practitioners (Mäntylä and Karilainen 2008), journalists in democracies have been expected to act in the **public interest** and to be accountable to the public.

3.1.1 The Journalists' Tasks

The basic tasks of journalism can be grouped into three categories (Christians *et al.* 2009). First, it is the task of journalism to observe and inform. Second, journalism participates as an actor in public life when media practitioners comment on the news or advocate particular positions. And third, journalism has the task of providing a platform for voices from outside the media.

In the context of this book, the first and the third tasks are particularly important. In thinking of the journalist in a democratic society as an information provider, we traditionally assign the role of receiver to the audience. In this view, the public is made up of people who receive information and interpretations of events provided by journalists (McNair 2000). Although audience members are kept informed, they remain outside the journalistic process, as our exploration of the various **news-production stages** in the previous chapter indicated.

As we saw there and will explore further in this chapter, this perception of the audience as being at some distance from the process of producing news remains prevalent among many professional journalists today, including many of our interviewees. Scholar John Hartley (2008: 43–44) calls this idea "representative journalism," in which a dedicated profession exercises freedom of speech on behalf of the audience, supposedly in the public interest.

On the other hand, the journalistic task of providing a platform for other voices clearly requires at least a somewhat more active audience than one whose primary role is to get information from media professionals. In this context, the audience ceases to be merely a mass somewhere out there. The individuals who form this more involved "public" – the people we refer to as "users," rather than simply as audience members – not only receive information, but also search out their own information, produce additional information themselves, and consult and interact with other participants in the process. This major shift in their role enables individuals to become more active participants in journalism (McNair 2000; McQuail 2000).

3.1.2 Changes in the Audience

Traditional organizational patterns and forms of mass media have tended to hinder the emergence of this more active audience, both by limiting access and by discouraging participation and dialogue (McQuail 2000). The concept of an audience made up only of passive information receivers was questioned and indeed largely dismissed by many media observers well before the advent of the Internet era. But the communication network has made the issue topical in novel ways.

While traditional media, such as newspapers, radio and television are inherently linear – one-way carriers of messages – communication networks are two-way streets. The Internet enables many-to-many communication, allowing conversations and other reciprocal contributions by and among the people whom journalists once thought of as their passive audience. This non-linear, interactive structure of digital news media forms has been crucial in redefining the relationship between journalists and audience members, as well as the way in which journalists interpret their own professional role (Heinonen 1999).

At the same time that the Internet has become a vital information medium, both general education levels and communication competencies have risen in democratic societies overall, including those in our study. The combination means that in today's media environment, the "people formerly known as the audience" (Rosen 2006) have found an outlet for "interactive communication between widely separated individuals" (McQuail 2000: 131). More important, the new setting is characterized by joint or collaborative communication among individuals, and those individuals' engagement with network technologies is often characterized by cooperation (Deuze 2007).

3.1.3 Power Shift

For traditional journalists and media organizations, the new setting implies a shift in the balance of power from the sender to the (former) receiver of a communication message (McQuail 2000). The roles of both audiences and journalists have changed notably, as this chapter will describe.

For starters, the mere behavior of receiving "journalism" is different in a digital network than in analogue media. Clicking to play an online news video and taking time to rank a set of online news stories are conscious acts. They require more determination and engagement than simply watching the flow of a television show or seeing a static newspaper headline. Again, readers, listeners and viewers all become "users"; they have many more options in deciding when, where and how they consume journalists' products.

Moreover, these users are competent to talk back to journalists – and they can use tools that did not previously exist to do so. During the past 15 years, journalists have had to become accustomed to a much greater audience presence in newsrooms than ever before.

The third dimension in the recent power shift between the sending journalist and the receiving audience relates to the journalist's role in the communication process. If the audience is inspired to move away from traditional information providers toward emerging alternative channels, the foundations on which journalism rests are challenged. As described above, journalism exists for, and by, its audience. If audiences leave, the status of journalism professionals in determining the extent and nature of social communication is significantly diminished. Their essential power as the **gatekeepers** is at risk, undermining a key pillar in journalists' professional identity (Christians *et al.* 2009; Deuze 2008; White 1950).

Given this multi-dimensional power shift and the premise that journalists' once-distinctive news production practices now can be adopted, in principle at least, by anyone, professionals have been engaged in a considerable amount of recent soul-searching. They are revisiting not only the practice of daily tasks but also the values and conceptions underlying those tasks (Hayes, Singer and Ceppos 2007).

A crucial aspect of these renewed considerations of journalism – by journalists – is their relationship with audience members who, again, are now constituted as more active "users," and are taking on a variety of new or newly reconfigured roles. Our interviewees provided insights into whether they see a need to redefine that relationship with users and if so, how they might approach such a task.

Their responses suggest that while journalistic culture is broadly identifiable everywhere, specific attitudes vary across organizations and **newsroom cultures**. And other factors influence practitioners' role perceptions, as well (Metykova 2009; Deuze 2007). The historic national tradition of the profession, the institutional cultures of particular media organizations and the business pressures of commercial media all come into play as part of journalists' ongoing reassessment.

This chapter focuses on journalists' views of their audiences as users and producers of **participatory journalism**, illustrating various dimensions of the new and emerging relationships between the people inside and outside the newsroom. We look first at the crucial user roles that our interviewees identified at the first and last **stages of the news-production** process. We'll then consider new inclinations in the way journalists see themselves and their own professional role as it relates to those users, part of the process of self-reflection instigated by the changes in today's newsrooms described above.

3.2 How Journalists See Users: Before the story is written

3.2.1 Users as Sensors and Scouts

The ability of users to expand the reach of journalism at the **access/observation stage of news production** came up repeatedly in our interviews. There are always only so many journalists, and they can never be aware of everything that is going on. However, there is the "mass" of users in close contact with an enormous range of possible news topics. As a Croatian editor said, users are where events are happening. The online editor at *Le Monde* (France) pointed out that users also have a good sense of which issues other people are interested in – which ones are likely to "engage the audience in the most vivid debates." In addition to the inherent news value of what such users provide, this kind of information about audience interests is essential to journalists.

This user role of a "public sensor" has grown in importance for at least two reasons. One is the availability of enabling communications technologies, such as increasingly "smart" **mobile** phones, which greatly facilitate the flow of information from users to newsrooms. The other reason is bleaker: Now that newsroom staffs everywhere are becoming leaner, there simply are fewer professionals available to sniff for news and take the pulse of the community. Journalists are pressured by a heavy workload that demands, among other things, continual updates across multiple media platforms. Under these circumstances, user contributions become increasingly valuable if not vital for newsrooms, particularly in the initial stages of the journalistic work process that we described in Chapter 2.

One of the ways in which users act as newsroom scouts, our interviewees said, is by serving as idea generators. "Our journalists say they increasingly get tips from readers, especially for local news," said an editor at *Het Nieuwsblad* (Belgium). An editor at *Kaleva* (Finland) praised users' contributions as an endless stream of story ideas pointing to problems that newsrooms then can tackle. However, these ideas will go to waste if journalists are not attentive to the stream of information from users, monitoring it for worthy news leads. An editor at *USA Today* provided the example of a follow-up to a published story:

> The reporter went back to the original story as it appeared online and read through the comments. And so she saw [*a particularly interesting*] comment. She got in touch with the individual, they then took that conversation offline on the phone, and [*the commentator*] ended up being the focus of the story she followed up with.

3.2.2 Users as Exemplars and Eyewitnesses

In this instance, the user not only provided the idea for a story but also served as an exemplar or expert witness, another role that came up repeatedly in our interviews. For example, an editor at *Focus* (Germany) noted that keeping on eye on what users are talking about in discussion **forums** is useful. Journalists can get in touch with people who are discussing their experiences and generate stories from those exchanges.

A community editor at the *Telegraph* (UK) gave the example of a citizen blogger in the county of Suffolk whose daughters had been killed by a drunk driver on their way home from a concert. The resulting court case would have gotten little or no play in the national newspaper without the personal information the user provided. "We were able to use some of his **blog** posts in the story. We were able to do a half-page feature about something that would have just been a news-in-brief probably, if it had made the paper at all," the editor said. "What we normally lack is the detail that turns those things into a story."

In this example, a user served journalists by shedding light on the topic from a personal perspective, making the sterile news piece into a human story. More often, though, users act as eyewitnesses who report about events they either participated in or just happened to bump into.

Calls for these eyewitness reports are increasingly common in online newspapers. As users learn that journalists genuinely welcome their contributions, they may take the initiative to offer such first-hand accounts themselves. For example, an editor at *Süddeutsche Zeitung* (Germany) described how a user reported the 2007 Virginia Tech University campus shooting in her comments. As she was on the spot, many thousands of miles away from the German newsroom, the journalists asked her to submit an account of events, which was published online.

3.2.3 Users as Experts

Journalists also acknowledge that users have an important role as experts in various areas. Observers such as Dan Gillmor (2006) have been saying for years that journalists need to accept the fact that their readers may well know more than they do themselves. But seeing users as possible experts alongside regular sources is not easy for all journalists, and doing so is far from commonplace in many newsrooms. An editor at *USA Today* pointed out that there is a tendency to think of user-generated **comments** as strictly amateur content or "drive-by" remarks.

However, editorial routines are changing. A manager of **user-generated content** at NRG (Israel) said it is now possible to find many journalists collecting facts from users, wandering around the discussion forums, asking for help and just generally treating users as information sources.

This new "assignment" for the audience means journalists must cultivate active users, providing support and guidance to enable them to become expert sources and contributors of content that can add significant value to news reporting. At the online-only LePost.fr in France, journalists are serving as "coaches," mentoring users and helping develop the skills of those who show the most promise. A *Washington Post* (USA) editor offered an example from a more traditional news organization: "By setting up a discussion platform on world affairs, we were able to have relatively well-informed people, leading journalists – and in most cases leading journalists that are natives or citizens of the country they're filing from – in place to comment on what's going on in their part of the world in four dozen countries."

But our interviewees also pointed out that relying on users to generate ideas or serve as either witnesses or experts may create new problems. User information may not be totally reliable, as journalists frequently pointed out. Although the same can be said of any information source and it is a basic journalistic routine to verify facts, some interviewees felt it necessary to underline their view that users are *particularly* unreliable, a topic to which we'll return in Chapter 7.

The trustworthiness of information was only one problem. Adding to the difficulties were journalists' views about its haphazard delivery and overall quality, as an interviewee from the *National Post* (Canada) explained. This skepticism about relying on user input also suggests difficulties in working out the best practices for managing and cultivating that input, as described in more detail in Chapter 5.

3.3 How Journalists See Users: After the story is written

3.3.1 Users as Reflectors

The roles we have just described involve user input at the early stages of the news production process described in Chapter 2. At the other end of the process, in what we labeled the **interpretation stage**, users provide feedback about what journalists have already produced. Our interviewees seemed to value this user role as a "reflector." In fact, journalists have always claimed to want audience feedback, and the online environment provides a wide variety of tools to offer it – if newsrooms wish to make those tools available.

Many of our interviewees said reflections by users are inherently important, almost regardless of their nature. Getting any kind of user reaction implies that the journalists' message has reached at least some members of the audience. "The performers on the stage are after the applause," said an editor at the *National Post* (Canada). "That's what we want. We want the applause." Newsrooms can then decide to adapt their activities based on those responses.

As a Croatian editor explained, users who contribute feedback thus fulfill an essential role for newsrooms, informing journalists whether and how their products resonate with audiences and helping journalists see what needs to be done in future stories.

3.3.2 Users as Commentators

The most commonly mentioned interpretive role, as well as the most valued – albeit with reservations – was that of a *commentator*. By definition, this role positions users outside the actual journalistic production process as newsroom professionals see it: Media practitioners gather material about an issue and, by publishing it, set the agenda for public debate. Only then is it users' turn to express their opinions on the topics chosen and presented by the professionals. "So far, the impulse remains in the hands of journalists, who launch the debate. Users react to these," explained an online executive at *Le Figaro* (France).

Journalists have a certain ambiguity toward the comments that users provide, as we will see in more detail in Chapter 6. On the one hand, journalists do appreciate the feedback provided through the comments; interviewees pointed out that user contributions include important information as well as the feedback on the story itself. But they also keenly want to keep a clear line between user comments and editorial material that the journalists produce.

In other words, professionals want to keep audience members in their place in order to preserve a sort of journalistic purity. "We try to keep that line between opinion and editorial and actual reporting, like everybody else," said an editor at the *National Post* (Canada). "You don't want that bleeding into your reporting."

The underlying assumption is that what users say are merely opinions and therefore of lesser value than other journalistic content. That said, some interviewees pointed out that that the opinions have value, too. An online editor at *Le Monde* (France), for example, commended the site's users for their concerns about social issues, explaining that the newsroom can solicit their views and build content based on these contributions. An editor at the *Guardian* (UK) remarked that even if the comments were opinionated, they can benefit attentive journalists anyway because user interpretations help define the edges of an issue.

With this insight, of course, we connect the roles of "sensor," described in the previous section, and that of the "reflector." By reflecting on the stories and expressing their opinions about them, users also are acting as sensors, feeding into newsrooms new perspectives on existing topics as well as new ideas for fresh stories. Opening stories up to comments, for example, thus may launch a virtuous circle in which users play important roles in multiple ways.

3.3.3 Users as Audience Pulse-takers

Another example of this dual role is the journalists' perception of their users as important in taking the broader audience pulse. Interviewees highlighted the value of comments and discussion forums as indicators of what hits home with audiences. An editor at Ynet (Israel), for example, said that if an article gets hundreds of responses, it is a sign that the topic has not been exhausted. It is a cue to the professionals – if they care to take heed of it – to continue discussing that topic on a variety of levels. Active users thus serve as an important complement to other monitoring mechanisms, such as readership surveys and market analyses.

Journalists in a number of newsrooms described plans to cultivate these various reflector roles among their users. For instance, they said that one way to encourage comments was to demonstrate that those comments really are appreciated within the newsroom. Another online executive at *Le Figaro* (France) described plans to give more prominence to "quality commentators" in order to boost the importance of user-generated content. "The main project is to organize all comments on the site in a centralized location," he said. "It's a first step of a longer-term project that will enable us to flag commentators who have the most relevant contributions, who are considered as 'favorites' by the most other users."

3.4 A Collaborative Role: Users as co-workers

In our description so far of the different roles that journalists see users playing in the stages of news production that we outlined in the previous chapter, we have leaped from the beginning of the journalistic work process to its end. The reason is that these are the two phases in which our interviewees most readily expressed the value they saw in an active audience.

In contrast, the journalists in our study were clearly more ambivalent about the role users might play in the core journalistic task of producing actual editorial content. They expressed various doubts about the appropriateness of letting users pitch in and become, in essence, *co-workers* in journalism, in what some have labeled a "**pro-am**" relationship.

Many journalists freely admitted that the types of user-generated content they were inviting at the time of our study had more to do with people sharing their personal experiences and photos, for instance of their pets or other things that few would consider newsworthy. Such contributions do not extend to what one *Washington Post* (USA) interviewee described as "true reporting."

Some interviewees remarked that, actually, users may not be willing to submit journalistic content, as an online editor at *Le Monde* (France) mused:

> In terms of production of news, there should a multiplication of calls to the audience, but this doesn't mean getting readers to write articles or forcing them to enter classic journalistic formats. Maybe finding other ways to interact with the audience and offer them possibilities to contribute, but that maybe won't be to directly contribute articles. One must acknowledge that few people have the time and resources to do so, and it's not their goal, either.

3.4.1 Users as Guardians of Quality

But if users are not considered willing or suitable as co-workers in hard news, their input as guardians of quality on the newspaper website is more widely valued. In this role, users are helping shape content – but not as authors. Rather, they act as proofreaders – for instance, by flagging misspellings – and as quality filters, recommending some comments and alerting journalists about problems with others. Users, therefore, feel involved in policing the content and in pushing particular items forward, journalists said.

Users' contributions to comment moderation offer one example of how online newspapers have engaged audiences in the content formation process as quality monitors. For instance, some online newspapers give users a role in managing discussion forums, a topic to which we return in Chapter 5. Users may act as forum administrators, with the ability to delete problematic messages and manage the community, as at *Haaretz* (Israel).

Not all the journalists we interviewed supported this particular policy, but even the sceptics acknowledged that at least some users are willing to participate in quality control. A **community manager** at the *Telegraph* (UK), for instance, said some users – annoyed at delays in dealing with what they perceived to be problems, for instance with removing spam – had asked for all moderation control to be handed over to them so that they could maintain the level of quality they wanted. The *Telegraph* did not agree to this request, citing concerns about potential bias and the lack of legal expertise among users, as discussed further in Chapter 7. Indeed, across the newspapers in our study, users were generally allowed only to point out dubious comments or discussion posts to official **moderators**, who then decided whether to act on their alerts.

3.4.2 Users as Ancillary Reporters

Another co-worker role for users is that of an ancillary reporter, who provides material for professionals. In the typical arrangement, professionals provide the framework, for instance, by publishing a story and soliciting user contributions to add to the available information or by requesting user input beforehand. "We can't know every topic as well as we know some," explained an editor at the *Washington Post* (USA). "But if we can facilitate people who do know those things that we don't know, if we can facilitate them to produce information and we can get that to our audience, then we're doing our audience a favor."

A community manager at *Het Belang van Limburg* and *Gazet van Antwerpen* (Belgium) explained that user-generated content may not be a sufficient information source by itself, but "a marriage" between material from users and journalists can result in something strong. In this view, professional and non-professional content producers are complementary.

However, not all newsroom experiments in this direction are considered worthwhile. At *FAZ* (Germany), for example, journalists felt that organizing a joint effort with users to cover certain topics would be too expensive.

That said, a common (though not unanimous) attitude among our interviewees was that in the near future, users would be seen in the role of co-worker more frequently. One reason was the perception that users' media competency was increasing. Users understand the logic of journalistic work much better in the digital environment than they did before, journalists suggested. For instance, an editor at *El País* (Spain) said that a user who submits a photo is effectively saying: "I know you are not here right now, but I know that if you were here you would be reporting on this. I send it to you because I understand you can't have someone here getting this picture right now."

In addition, interviewees believed professionals are beginning to more fully realize the potential benefits of user contributions. Hundreds or even thousands of people who think they can send a photo or a news tip to the newsroom if they see something interesting can add up to quite a valuable journalistic resource. The necessary condition, explained an editor at *Kaleva* (Finland), is that the newspaper must be seen as a co-produced effort more commonly than is now the case.

Journalists in some newsrooms were already keeping on eye on particular users whom they identified as likely to provide contributions that might deserve wider attention than they would get if they appeared only in separate sections devoted to user-generated content. This is a form of talent-spotting and indicates professionals' increasing appreciation of users' ability to offer journalistically meaningful content.

An editor at Ynet (Israel), for example, said journalists sometimes find interesting items on user blogs; the newsroom then asks the author to send the piece to the newspaper's news section. He said most users accept the offer, and the newsroom credits the user and links to his or her blog when it publishes the piece.

3.5 Community Members

So far, we have concentrated on the relationship between journalists and audiences in the context of the journalistic work process, but members of the media audience have roles that go beyond those related to producing journalism. Audience members are also citizens forming a public, and as we already have seen, in democratic societies such as those in our study, journalism has certain commitments related to the functioning of democracy (Christians *et al.* 2009). In particular, journalism has a social role to play in the formation of a diverse community.

The journalists we interviewed also talked about this aspect of participatory journalism. They pointed out that the widening user participation in online news redefines the roles of audience members in different but overlapping media-based communities. In this section, we consider professionals' assessments of users as members of customer, peer and civic communities.

3.5.1 Communities of Customers

Media organizations that produce journalism typically are businesses seeking economic profit. In the context of this aspiration, audience members are seen as part of a revenue source whose loyalty is crucial for the success of the media enterprise. From this perspective, users belong to a customer community, an essential collective that deserves to be acknowledged by professionals.

Several interviewees pointed out that user participation is one of the most important tools for engaging audiences with online newspapers. "We look at community tools as a way to build validity, to get people coming back and also keeping them on the site for a longer period," explained an editor at the *National Post* (Canada).

The underlying assumption is that even in today's fragmented and rapidly changing media environment, newspapers can serve as collective community nodes, as they have in the past. Of course, there are business calculations behind these strategies, as we discuss further in Chapter 8, but journalists also seem to feel that audiences are seeking a sense of belonging that can be lacking in a media landscape marked by overabundance and incoherence.

For example, a community editor at the *Telegraph* (UK) pointed out that in the print era, readers identified themselves with "their" paper, but that sense of personal ownership is harder to come by in an online environment marked by many choices and more sporadic selection of news sources. From this viewpoint, sections of the website devoted to user contributions can provide a place for audience members to connect and identify with other like-minded individuals.

3.5.2 Communities of Peers

This perception relates to users' roles as members of a peer community. In peer communities, users take on a collective role as people who engage with a particular media product, and participatory journalism provides a mechanism for enacting that role.

The online newspaper provides both the tools and the framework to help people inform and communicate with one another, as an interviewee from *USA Today* explained. Peer community members are, significantly, also "customers": "We launched blogs and [*a section devoted to user contributions*] a couple of years ago," said a *Telegraph* (UK) editor. "That was all about giving our customers a place on the web to go meet like-minded people to talk about things that they were interested in."

Providing a space for horizontal communication among users, rather than merely the conventional top-down communication from journalists to readers, offers both social and economic benefits for newspapers. That is, it builds both communities and markets. The journalists in our study saw facilitating "them-to-them conversation," for instance by rewarding registered users or by allowing personal screen names, as helping newspapers maintain a foothold in the journalism industry and in the online world in general.

However, seeing users as collections of "like-minded people" who can converse with one another restructures the audience-journalist relationship and affects journalists' own roles, as well. For instance, accentuating peer community features within the space provided by a news medium detracts correspondingly from the traditional journalistic role of communal aggregator.

It is noteworthy that not all our interviewees were happy about these developments. For example, an interviewee at the *Washington Post* (USA) said emphatically that it is not in a newspaper's interest or capacity to be a **social networking site**. Although this attitude can be interpreted as indicating a disregard for the benefits of peer communication within an online newspaper, it may be a realistic assessment of the core role and capabilities of news media.

3.5.3 Civic Communities

Closely related to the perception of users as members of a peer community is the view that they are members of a civic community. In this configuration, the news organization provides a "community center" whose members are its users.

Seeing their users as civic community members requires that journalists accept the idea of socially involved journalistic enterprises. Again, the image of media users expands from passive audience members to active citizens – people entitled to expect support from the media for justified social actions. "I'm hoping that we'll be able to help people use our site as a base for local campaigns," said a community editor at the *Telegraph* (UK). "We've done a little bit with, you know, save your post office, that kind of stuff. But if they want to do things that are focused on their community, I'm hoping that we can lend them those tools."

However, while media-led campaigns are common in Britain, the activist attitude was far from widespread among our interviewees. Most held the more conventional perspective of users as conscious citizens. To return to the user roles with which we began, they saw users as members of civic communities to whom they might turn when making their own decisions as journalists.

For instance, users can be approached when journalists need to get background or first-hand information about socially significant issues that the professionals consider worth putting on the media agenda. When *Helsingin Sanomat* (Finland) made a neighborhood tour after launching a user-driven neighborhood website, the newspaper sought input from readers in different boroughs about topical local issues and problems. Journalists then organized panels and other activities with community decision makers, resulting in a series of articles for both the print and online products.

Similarly at *Het Nieuwsblad* (Belgium), readers were invited to share their experiences and opinions about the security of cycle paths. Journalists said they learned that if the newsroom offers a platform, readers will use it and see it as a way to communicate their complaints to policy makers. Citizens thus hold an **agenda-setting** function, but it is exercised through the media website.

It is noteworthy in terms of the democratic function of journalism that some of our interviewees believed users who take on the role of civic participants can complement or even counterbalance regular sources. A citizen who lives in a particular neighborhood may not be known to the journalist but can become – at some point and for some period of time – a very valuable and relevant source. This role helps offset the usual journalistic dependence on politicians, celebrities and other high-profile sources, people with whom journalists often have a symbiotic relationship: Journalists get information, and sources get visibility, as a journalist at *20 Minutos* (Spain) explained.

Our interviewees clearly recognized the potential for new forms of audience engagement in an online media environment. That recognition was evidenced in the many diverse roles that journalists assigned to users. Although our interviewees tended to see users' roles as primarily connected with the creation of journalism by journalists, they did outline wider and more civic-oriented roles.

We now turn to a juxtaposition of these views about user roles with the journalists' views about their own roles as media professionals, a consideration that is important because journalists' self-perceptions help guide their approach to active audiences.

3.6 How Journalists See Themselves

Our interviews suggested three categories of self-perceptions among journalists. First, the people we talked with emphasized the need to preserve a clear demarcation line between the journalism produced by professionals and user-generated content. This perspective reflects what we call a "conventional journalist" role.

A second view was more inclusive, with journalism more likely to be seen as a joint or collaborative project of professionals and users. We call this a "dialogical journalist" role.

And third, as suggested above, many journalists described a period of soul-searching about the relationship between what they did and what users did, an intermediate attitude that reflects an "ambivalent journalist" role.

These three perceived roles are abstract conceptual definitions, based on analyses of all our interviews across the ten countries in our study. No one individual journalist wholly represented a single role definition. Rather, the three categories illustrate different discourses about professional roles that together comprise an ongoing debate about who is and is not a journalist. In fact, even in the limited time we spent talking with them, many interviewees articulated more than one perspective about the role of the journalist in a network.

3.6.1 Defending Demarcation: Conventional role

An extreme version of the conventional journalist role perception is the view that professionals would do better journalism without audience members putting their paws in it. This attitude was rare – or at least, few of our interviewees expressed it to us – and most of the related comments referred to the extra work that user participation creates for newsrooms.

Moderating discussion forums, checking the credibility of users' contributions, removing improper content from user sections, responding to users' queries and other similar tasks were seen by some as stealing time from "proper" journalistic work. For example, a journalist at *Helsingin Sanomat* (Finland) pointed out that by and large, journalists tend to think that they live by the stories they produce: "One wants to focus on doing as well as possible the thing where one's byline stands. Our wages and self-respect are based on what is below our own name in the paper."

A central argument defending the conventional role was that although user participation may be a positive trend, professional journalists couldn't be replaced. Expressions of professional pride were common. For example, the online executive editor of *The Globe and Mail* (Canada) insisted that "journalism remains journalism, and it's not going to change its fundamentals." These interviewees underscored their belief that citizens can be a good source of material, but journalists still do the job. Regardless of the criticism they receive, a Croatian editor said, journalists are professionals and know best how to inform people in a way that is timely, correct and proper.

Such statements suggest some journalists take a rather defensive posture toward user participation. It is important to clearly distinguish between what professional journalists write and what readers think, said an editor at *De Standaard* and *Het Nieuwsblad* (Belgium). Journalists, he added, now fear that their work will be drowned in the flood of reader opinions.

Related to this wish to preserve the status of professionals in the process of making journalism was the desire to maintain the (assumed) reputation of the news media. A conviction that the established brand itself conveys such qualities as credibility and trustworthiness underlies this view. Its adherents believe that journalists therefore must continue to play a decisive role in the production of journalistic content. "What we have to offer as our brand is a newspaper and a site that can be trusted to uphold the standards we've built our business on," explained an editor at the *Washington Post* (USA). "Turning the place over to every Joe or Sally on the street isn't going to be at the core of that mission."

Journalists who articulated this conventional view of their role emphasized that although readers are allowed to participate and collaborate, it must be made clear that in the end, there is professional work behind journalism, as an interviewee from *20 Minutos* (Spain) put it. Interestingly, some journalists claimed to be speaking on behalf of their audiences in holding this view, arguing that users still demand "good old-fashioned journalism, and investigative and enterprise journalism" – and it is established brands that provide it, as a *Washington Post* editor said. An editor at NRG (Israel) similarly said that users don't want to see what other users thought happened but rather what *really* happened – and to serve these users, news should continue to be written by professionals.

3.6.2 Making It Together: Dialogical role

Along with views that emphasized a wish to maintain the traditional journalistic role, our interviewees described a need to open up journalism to direction from users. Even those who saw the traditional journalistic role as vital also valued the audience as a defining element for journalism, but those who expressed views about a more *dialogical role* believed professionals should have the courage to embrace users as genuine co-workers.

"If we allow more user-generated content on our website, to what extent should we make a distinction between what is created by our own professionals and the rest?" wondered an editor at *De Standaard* and *Het Nieuwsblad* (Belgium). "Now we are still shouting that the distinction must be very clear, but I am convinced that after a while, it will become more blurred." An editor at *USA Today* also highlighted the evolving nature of this relationship, saying users are becoming an active part of a group that is presenting the news and soon will be elbow to elbow with trained journalists.

Comments such as these, referring to practices that traditionally have defined journalism as a distinct profession, indicate that at least some journalists are admitting those practices can be mastered by people who are not media professionals. An editor at *El País* (Spain) suggested that practicing journalism involves following certain rules, for instance related to impartiality and fact-checking – but, he added, anyone who adheres to those rules is doing journalism.

Obviously, this is not the same as claiming that everything users happen to send in constitutes journalism. Nevertheless, this kind of attitude is far less protective about "proper" journalism than the views of interviewees who emphasized the more conventional role. It is also more realistic, considering the abundance of high-quality news blogs and other online media formats.

This openness to a dialogical role should not be interpreted as journalists surrendering journalism to users. Rather, they are advocating, or at least entertaining the notion of, a fruitful co-existence that can result in better journalistic performance.

For example, a journalist at *Het Belang van Limburg* (Belgium) stressed that the professional journalist will continue to play an important role in society – which is how it should be, in her view. Professional news media, she added, should view participatory journalism as a new form of communication that simultaneously enriches journalists' stories and produces original news reports. In other words, she saw users not just as sensors at the service of journalistic gatekeepers but, at least to some extent, as co-workers. A news website still has to provide professional stories that are relevant, correct and cogent, but she felt that content can be supplemented by user contributions foregrounding social and personal aspects of a story.

If the comments reflecting the more conventional journalistic role positioned users as professionals' competitors, those leaning toward the dialogical role saw users more as companions. The need to make journalism more relevant in the everyday lives of media audiences commonly went along with this view. As the editor of the user-dominated LePost.fr (France) website put it:

> We really try to be something different, to accompany users editorially in the news process. The idea is that we are useful as journalists, instead of being competitors to users. We have a profession and we know what it is … and we're putting it at your service to help you have news that's closest to your daily lives, so there isn't that disconnection between users' lives and news.

As we highlighted at the start of this chapter, the idea that journalists are public servants is not alien to those who hold a more conventional role perception; indeed, the notion of public service underlies most articulations of journalism ethics. But most traditional interpretations of the audience-journalist relationship raise professionals on a podium somewhat distant from – and above – the audience. The dialogical role suggests a more equal standing. In fact, although it may be a blow to their pride, journalists need to accept that published material often carries a user's byline instead of a journalist's, as an interviewee at *El País* (Spain) pointed out.

Does that material require an editor's hand? A journalist at *Kaleva* (Finland) said journalistic professionalism is still needed; users may have something newsworthy to say, though they typically do not possess the skills necessary to say it well. In this view, journalists are needed to transform users' messages into understandable formats, and some interviewees were convinced of the need for journalists to edit what users provide. Again, though, even from this perspective, journalism results from the joint efforts of users and professionals.

The shift demands a novel approach to thinking about what professional journalistic work is. Conventional print professionals may be interested only in their own piece for the next edition, but the online journalist must pay more attention to the audience, including the social context in which people consume the news, as well as user communities and networks. As a community manager at *Het Belang van Limburg* and *Gazet van Antwerpen* (Belgium) argued: "This implies a very different approach to journalism."

That said, some interviewees reminded us that the wall between audience members and professionals is not, and has not been in the past, as impenetrable as it is sometimes portrayed. "It's always been a conversation. It's just that [*journalists*] never heard the other side of it," said a community editor at the *Telegraph* (UK). "People just shouted at their newspaper over the breakfast table or in pubs. So we were just never in the conversation. And now, we really have to be." An editor at *Helsingin Sanomat* (Finland) remarked that today's phenomenon of having users as contributors has its roots in the tradition of using amateurs as rural correspondents, in the days before journalism became fully professionalized.

Journalists often referred to the dialogical role in the context of a need to regain audience trust in the news media – something they pointed out might not be an easy task. A *USA Today* editor explained:

> We know the press has a damaged relationship with the public; they don't trust [*us*] like they used to. ... And with that lack of trust, when you throw open the doors and say "Talk to us!" there really isn't a friendship underlying the relationship from the beginning. So we have a lot of work to do there, to repair the relationship, to regain people's trust.

3.6.3 Role Ambivalence

It is worth keeping in mind that our interviewees did not express either of these two role perceptions –conventional or dialogical – in a pure form. Some individuals were inclined to speak more about the need to safeguard the journalist's professional status and the media brand, while others more readily promoted the idea that users are integral to the process of creating journalism. But most often, journalists expressed ideas that contained elements of both views.

Hence, the most common newsroom attitude we discovered might best be labeled an ambivalent role perception. An illustrative musing comes from a Spanish journalist at *El País*:

> Once [*participating users*] are here, they are not going to fade away. This does not mean that they are going to replace professional production of content. In order to have relevant and critical information, professional media are and will be necessary, even if there are thousands or hundreds of thousands of readers eager to send in texts, comments, participate in **polls**, make photos. ... Both will live side by side.

This journalist expresses reservations about users as participants in the process of making journalism but at the same time recognizes the journalistic value of a more active audience. Similar attempts to strike a balance between the problems and advantages of user participation were common across the interviews, as we saw in the previous section. An editor from *Helsingin Sanomat* (Finland), for example, warned that professionals should not run with every wind; although they should encourage user participation, journalists should also maintain their professional integrity and use it to inform their editorial judgments. User activity alone should not be sufficient information on which to base decisions in the newsroom.

In other words, professionals are simultaneously encouraging users to engage in as many ways as possible with their news sites *and* holding the hard core of news production as a sanctuary of professionalism – and both activities are carried out, allegedly, in the **public interest**. The basic idea underlying this ambivalent role perception seems to be that professional journalism is a necessary but not sufficient prerequisite for a news site: The work of professionals is needed but that work alone is not enough.

3.7 Conclusion

In this chapter, we have described how professional journalists assess the nature of their relationship with audience members-turned-users, considering both participatory features and journalistic practices.

We have shown that newspaper journalists assign users important roles, particularly in the initial phases of the journalistic work process, as idea generators and observers of newsworthy events. Our interviewees also valued users' interpretive role as commentators who reflect upon the material that has been produced through the journalistic work process.

However, these journalists were more hesitant to assign users proactive roles as co-workers or otherwise integral participants in the actual process of creating journalistic news content. Although many were open to dialogue with users, the journalists still saw themselves as the defining actors in the process of creating news.

These findings give little support to the visions of changing journalistic role descriptions introduced in the literature and discussed at the start of this chapter and elsewhere in this book. From the perspective of most journalism professionals, the public continues to be distinctively an audience for the media product – even if the relationship has more interactive features than before, enabling formerly passive audience members to be more directly present in the everyday work of journalists.

Our interviews suggest that a prevailing tendency among professionals thus tends to be toward inertia or at least conservatism.

Of course, as we mentioned at the start, the views that journalists hold about themselves and their audiences are formed by several factors, not solely by the immediate nature of the audience-journalist relationship. Journalists are salaried employees whose jobs are framed by corporate interests, available technologies, legal limitations and more. None of these constraints is constant – on the contrary, as we already have described, today's news media are evolving rapidly and continually – and each varies somewhat within particular national contexts. Journalists therefore must construct their professional identity in the context of this fluid, even precarious, work environment.

Self-perceptions also are a compromise between seemingly contradictory aspirations: Noble societal values of the profession sometimes collide with more mundane individual interests of the professionals.

Despite these confounding factors, however, it is possible to speak about a dominant occupational ideology or culture among journalists, at least in Western democracies such as those included in this study. One characteristic of such cultures is that outside forces are kept largely at bay by the self-referential nature of news work, which draws primarily on arguments based on values shared among journalistic insiders to justify the role and status of professionals (Hermida and Thurman 2008; Deuze 2007).

Our study also suggests that the origins of practitioners' ideas about audiences lie in the complex process through which journalists form such self-perceptions. In a way, then, we can say that how journalists see themselves shapes how they see users, as well as how they see the relationships between those inside and outside the newsroom.

When journalists have a relatively inclusive view of their own role, they are open to the idea of sharing that role with users. On the other hand, when journalists see themselves as kings or queens of the journalism castle, users are inherently viewed as people best kept on the far side of the moat. Active users may be a valuable resource for the professional journalist, but making use of that resource involves work that the journalists see as their special province.

So our findings reveal ruptures in this conventional way of envisioning the relationship between professionals and users as participants in the journalistic work process. There is a growing awareness – and, one might say, concern – about the effects that overall changes in social communication patterns have on journalism.

It is obvious that networked communication, particularly **social media**, enables people to be more than simply members of an audience. In enhancing the public's capacity to communicate, networks also craft journalism as a competence found outside conventional media realms. Moreover, the culture of participation extends well beyond journalism; it is a broad social phenomenon. From public governance to product design, "users" are increasingly recognized as partners and, at a minimum, invited to have their say in the process (Heinonen and Luostarinen 2008; Deuze 2007).

Trends inside and outside journalism thus are molding journalists' self-perceptions, so that more and more newsroom professionals are coming to see themselves as less self-sufficient and more reliant on the contributions of others. In the next three chapters, we take a closer look at how journalists are managing this transition and, more specifically, how and why they are attempting to manage the users whose many roles have become so instrumental.

Participate!

1. Which user roles does your favorite online newspaper seem to offer you?
2. What do you see as the advantages and disadvantages of the traditional or conventional journalistic self-perception described in this chapter? The dialogical self-perception?
3. What are the potential benefits of enabling audience members to become co-workers in journalism? What are the potential problems?

References

Carey, James W. (2007) A short history of journalism for journalists: A proposal and essay, *The Harvard International Journal of Press/Politics* 12 (1): 3–16.

Christians, Clifford G., Theodore L. Glasser, Denis McQuail, Kaarle Nordenstreng and Robert A. White (2009) *Normative theories of the media: Journalism in democratic societies*, Urbana: University of Illinois Press.

Deuze, Mark (2008) Professional identity in a participatory media culture. In: Quandt, T. and Schweiger, W. (eds.) *Journalismus online – Partizipation oder Profession?* Wiesbaden: VS Verlag für Sozialwissenschaften: 251–261.

Deuze, Mark (2007) *Media work*, Cambridge, UK: Polity.

Gillmor, Dan (2006) *We the media: Grassroots journalism by the people, for the people*, Sebastopol, California: O'Reilly.

Hartley, John (2008) "Journalism as human right: The cultural approach to journalism." In: Löffelholz, Martin and David Weaver (eds.) *Global journalism research: Theories, methods, findings, future*, Malden, Massachusetts: Blackwell: 39–51.

Hayes, Alfred S., Jane B. Singer and Jerry Ceppos (2007) The credible journalist in a digital age, *Journal of Mass Media Ethics* 22 (4): 262–279.

Heinonen, Ari (1999) *Journalism in the age of the Net: Changing society, changing profession*, Tampere: Acta Universitatis Tamperensis, 685.

Heinonen, Ari, and Heikki Luostarinen (2008) "Reconsidering 'journalism' for journalism research." In: Löffelholz, Martin and David Weaver (eds.) *Global journalism research: Theories, methods, findings, future*, Malden, Massachusetts: Blackwell: 227–239.

Hermida, Alfred, and Neil Thurman (2008) A clash of cultures: The integration of user-generated content within professional journalistic frameworks at British newspaper websites, *Journalism Practice* 2 (3): 342–356.

McNair, Brian (2000) *Journalism and democracy. An evaluation of the political public sphere*, London: Routledge.

McQuail, Denis (2000) *McQuail's mass communication theory*, London: Sage.

Mäntylä, Jorma, and Juha Karilainen (2008) Journalistietiikan kehitys Suomessa ja Euroopassa 1995–2007 (Development of journalism ethics in Finland and Europe 1995–2007), University of Tampere, Department of Journalism Mass Communication. Publications B 49/2008. Accessed 11 February 2010: http://tampub.uta.fi/tiedotusoppi/978-951-44-7262-6.pdf

Metykova, Monika (2009) "A key relation: Journalists and their publics." In: Preston, Paschal, *Making the news: Journalism and news cultures in Europe*, London: Routledge: 129–143.

Rosen Jay (2006) The people formerly known as the audience, PressThink. Accessed 11 February 2010: http://journalism.nyu.edu/pubzone/weblogs/pressthink/2006/06/27/ppl_frmr.html

White, David M. (1950) The gatekeeper: A case study in the selection of news, *Journalism Quarterly* 27: 383–96.

Part II

Managing Change

4

Inside the Newsroom
Journalists' motivations and organizational structures
Steve Paulussen

Newspapers' recent experiments with **audience** participation in online news production should be considered in the broader context of media **convergence** and innovation.

At the end of the twentieth century, newspaper companies began to undergo a transition to multimedia organizations. This shift was driven by the emergence of the Internet, which opened up new opportunities for publishing both in print and online. Faced with a general decline of readership and ever-increasing competition from new players in the information market, print media companies hoped to find salvation by embracing innovation and integrating digital media.

4.1 Incentives for Innovation

4.1.1 Economic Incentives

The attractiveness of the business model of "convergence," as this shift to a multi-platform environment was called, basically lay in its implicit promise "to produce more news for the same or little more money, which means that media organizations should be able to cut costs through increased productivity" (Quinn 2005: 29). So although often associated with the "new" Internet economy, media

Participatory Journalism: Guarding Open Gates at Online Newspapers, First Edition.
Jane B. Singer, Alfred Hermida, David Domingo, Ari Heinonen, Steve Paulussen, Thorsten Quandt, Zvi Reich, and Marina Vujnovic.
© 2011 Jane B. Singer, Alfred Hermida, David Domingo, Ari Heinonen, Steve Paulussen, Thorsten Quandt, Zvi Reich, and Marina Vujnovic. Published 2011 by Blackwell Publishing Ltd.

convergence strategies have been guided principally by "old" economic motives of cost efficiency, productivity and profit consolidation.

These motives also go a long way toward explaining the high interest of newspaper editors and managers in **user-generated content**. Organizations such as the World Editors Forum (WEF), which is part of the World Association of Newspapers (WAN), have done their utmost to convince newspaper editors all over the world of the great potential of audience participation in news making.

In the 2008 edition of its influential annual *Trends in Newsrooms* report, the WEF said the biggest change in news production since the 1980s "is that the overwhelming majority of universally accessible content is produced by everyone, everywhere, all the time. Since professional media organizations no longer have a monopoly on easy content production and distribution, they need to learn how best to include amateur material, most commonly known as User-Generated Content (UGC) or **citizen journalism**, into their everyday functions" (World Editors Forum 2008: 91).

Journalists offer various rationales to support the inclusion of user-generated content in the online news product. Broadly, however, they incorporate **participatory journalism** in an overall strategy for innovation. "There's a point around innovating," said a news executive at the *Telegraph* (UK). Innovation, he added, "is a very over-used term these days, but you have to continually create the products and the services – and also the content – that fit well with [*the newspaper's*] model."

However, "innovation" has many meanings, and different people can, and do, interpret it very differently. Quinn (2005) distinguishes between economic and journalistic interpretations, and other researchers have found support for his idea. Journalists seem to be most likely to favor innovation if they believe it can improve the quality of journalism (Gade and Perry 2003: 329). Newspaper managers, on the other hand, tend to follow the economic logic of producing the most possible content at the least possible cost.

These two visions – journalistic and economic – are evident in the interview material we have gathered for this book, and we look at them more closely in Chapter 8. However, the opinions of journalists and editors are less polarized than the previous paragraph might suggest. Most journalists also seem to be well aware of the economic reality in which news is being produced and consumed.

A **community manager** at *El País* (Spain), for instance, admitted that, aside from journalistic motives, one of the main reasons for adopting audience participation is that "it clearly adds value, increases visits and helps foster user loyalty. … That's mainly the point, because readers will see their own contributions published in the website, and that encourages them to come back again and again."

Journalists in other countries also said that tools for audience participation have to make commercial sense first and foremost. According to a Canadian editor, for example, this is "part of the game in the web publishing business: It's not just getting the eyes on your site, it's getting them to stay on your site. And if contributing to the **forums** gets them lingering, well, that's great."

A journalist at *Der Spiegel* (Germany) said print media are looking for ways of "using the possibilities of the Internet for attracting the adolescents to the brand," while a Finnish journalist pointed to the newspaper's efforts to figure out "how to make readers more engaged" with the paper, "and then one can sell this engagement to advertisers."

4.1.2 Journalistic Incentives

Newsroom managers are well aware that economic motivations are not enough, however, to convince their journalistic staff to adopt audience participation. Journalistic motivations are equally, if not more, important. Organizational studies of newsroom restructuring have suggested that journalists are more open-minded about change if they see how it can contribute to better journalism (Singer 2004; Gade and Perry 2003).

In other words, newspaper managers need to develop a clear vision about the future role of professional journalism, since having that vision may be the first step in convincing the newsroom's rank-and-file of the necessity and value of change (Ryfe 2009; McLellan and Porter 2007; Gade 2004).

When asked about the journalistic vision behind participatory practices in the newsroom, many interviewees referred to the need for journalists and the public to reconnect. "We would alienate ourselves from our readers and remain high in our ivory tower if we would not understand this issue," said a journalist at *Kaleva* (Finland). Online journalists seemed to believe strongly that to remain relevant, news media need to develop a closer and more interactive relationship with their audience.

Nonetheless, as shown in the previous chapter, some of the editors we interviewed added that not all journalists in their newsrooms were convinced. A print editor at the *Telegraph* (UK), who was not especially supportive of participatory journalism in general, described the reaction as "a mixed bag, in that some columnists, for example, welcome the mailbag … and like getting into a debate, and others don't." The newsroom response to user input, he added, "completely mirrors what goes on in print. Some columnists would, in the old days, if they received a letter, be keen to respond personally, and others would give it to their secretary, basically."

4.2 Changing the Newsroom Culture

The idea that digitization and convergence require a change of **newsroom culture** existed long before user-generated content or participatory journalism became hotly debated topics. In fact, since the 1990s, cultural change has been a crucial goal – and a major challenge – of efforts to turn traditional newsrooms into multimedia workplaces (Gade 2004; Singer 2004).

Newsroom culture consists of the unwritten rules, tacit norms and shared professional values that define the way journalistic work is done. These rules, norms and values are embedded in the habits, hearts and minds of journalists; cultural changes happen slowly and are rarely radical or revolutionary, at least in the short term (Boczkowski 2004a).

In our study, for example, a Finnish editor called the adoption of interactivity in journalism "a quite natural evolution." Others also found it "natural" or "inevitable" that newsroom culture adapt to the changing media environment. The best way to integrate audience participation in the news production process "would be to succeed in a cultural change," an editor at the *Guardian* (UK) said, describing that change process in his newsroom as one that "rolls on" and was only slowly taking place.

His remark suggests a rather relaxed attitude about the speed and pace at which newsrooms were adapting to participatory journalism practices, at least at the time of our study. Indeed, the interviewees seemed to understand that changing a newsroom culture just goes more slowly than proponents might expect or hope. A French editor, for instance, said the impact of audience participation "on the cultural level" should not be underestimated: "It's a real cultural change for a brand like *Le Figaro*, where the only space for interaction were letters to the editor, once a week on a quarter of a page for the last 180 years."

The managing editor at *Het Nieuwsblad* (Belgium) acknowledged that online newsrooms "actually expect nothing less than a mind shift." Journalists who have always been able "to work in a specific way and control their own agenda," he said, suddenly are supposed to dedicate more time and attention to interacting with the public and managing different types of user contributions.

To meet the challenge, he advocated a gradual approach. Instead of trying to force a radical shift, he said, newsroom leaders should try to let the more skeptical (mostly print) journalists on their staffs experience the benefits of user-generated content themselves. The creation of a new newsroom culture that favors audience participation "goes slowly, and you cannot force it," he argued. "But you can facilitate it by providing [*journalists*] with the technological infrastructure and by showing them the benefits for their own journalistic work."

This realistic approach of encouraging rather than forcing the adoption of audience participation was also seen as the best by an interviewee at the *Telegraph* (UK). "Obviously, over time, it's going to become the custom and practice that people will be expected to get into a dialogue. But we're not forcing the issue," he said. Journalists are "not under any compulsion" to interact with **users**. "We're still at the stage where we are reliant on individuals who kind of get the project to make it happen," he added. "I can't see that changing for a long time."

4.2.1 Individual Factors

Individual enthusiasm and commitment seem to be important factors for the incorporation of participatory journalism in newspaper culture.

In many newsrooms, individual journalists still make most of the decisions about how audience contributions are used. This ad hoc approach suggests a high degree of reluctance, pragmatism and aversion to change, all of which are in line not only with the attitudes we highlighted in the previous chapter but also with what earlier research tells us about how innovations are implemented in media organizations. Boczkowski (2004a), for instance, has described newsroom change as a step-by-step process that initially involves a limited number of employees and then gradually spreads over the entire news organization.

This slow diffusion allows the people involved to pick up new practices, such as moderating **comments** or editing user-generated content, as soon as they have learned and experienced the benefits of those practices.

In our study, for example, an editor at *Le Monde* (France) explained how only a handful of the newspaper's employees initially were engaged in the development of participation channels. This role, he said, was given "to journalists who were more oriented towards the audience." He called such journalists "role pioneers: Once the channels are well established and can be standardized, they become part of the job for all journalists."

Newsroom leaders seem to count on the initiative and creativity of engaged members of their staffs, but their own role in promoting audience participation in news production is also considerable. The managing editor at *The Globe and Mail* (Canada), for instance, told us that the newspaper is "only doing it because … I just came back from a conference of the Online News Association, and I felt like we might as well be chiseling on rocks like the Flintstones compared to what some people are doing."

At the *Süddeutsche Zeitung* (Germany), the chief editor played an important role in "pushing" the development of options for audience participation. At *USA Today*, the online editor-in-chief, an enthusiast about the potential of participatory journalism, subsequently became executive editor in the merged newsroom.

Likewise, journalists at *De Standaard* and *Het Nieuwsblad* in Belgium acknowledged the crucial role of the general editor-in-chief. "Since our chief editor says user interaction is important, more and more editors are making a mentality shift," said one Belgian interviewee. A colleague added that "change is made possible by the new editorial management. [*They*] truly believe in this [*citizen journalism*] project, and that opens a lot of chances." In particular, interviewees said, having newsroom managers who believe in the added value of user-generated content helps newsrooms obtain the resources needed for participatory journalism.

4.3 Time, Space and Staff

Back in the 1970s, media sociologist Herbert Gans observed that efficiency considerations heavily defined the daily work of news decision-making in print and broadcast newsrooms. "Journalistic efficiency exists to allocate three scarce resources: staff, air time or print space, and, above all, production time," Gans wrote (1979: 283).

Recent studies show that these three resources – staff, space and time – are still crucial in shaping newsroom practices, both offline and online (Lewis, Williams and Franklin 2008; Paulussen 2004). Moreover, these resources have become even more important in a contemporary digital media environment characterized by ongoing staff reductions, multimedia publishing and constant deadlines (Pew Research 2008; Preston 2009).

4.3.1 Resource Constraints

Indeed, our interviewees repeatedly confirmed that available resources profoundly shaped the development of participatory journalism. An editor at *Helsingin Sanomat* (Finland) argued that journalists' reluctance to adopt participatory practices had less to do with individual attitudes than with the "economics of work. The journalist is supposed to write stories in a given deadline, and because our working time is so limited, there just is no energy." An editor at the *Telegraph* (UK) agreed that given the volume of user input, "there's no way we could ever read everything."

Faced with the fact that they had to make choices, many journalists felt they should give priority to what they saw as the core of journalism – centered around the **selection/filtering** and **processing/editing** stages of the news production process, as described in Chapter 2 – rather than spending too much time with user contributions in the **access/observation** and **interpretation** stages.

"Obviously, a journalist shouldn't be spending half of his time reading comments on his stories, or we would never get through it," said an editor at *Le Figaro* (France). A Canadian journalist at the *National Post* said he hoped that newsroom managers will keep the value of the journalists firmly in mind when making budget decisions. "The person out there generating content by finding stories and getting quotes and writing it is more important than the person who is sifting through comments," he added. "So I hope it doesn't have to come to making that either-or choice."

4.3.2 Need for Investment

Among journalists in all ten countries in our study, there seemed to be a broad consensus that the development of participatory journalism required investment. And slowly but surely, most said, these investments were being made. The interviewees suggested that fostering interactivity, community and audience participation have moved high on their newspapers' agenda following the integration of the Internet in their media strategy.

For example, an editor at *Helsingin Sanomat* (Finland) said interactive features initially were treated as "a sort of orphan child, set up at a time when all [*online newspapers*] set up these options but then left without real resources." However, he said, this mentality had shifted in recent years. To illustrate this change in mind set, the community manager referred to his own position: Faced with the challenges of integrating user participation in its daily operations, the newspaper recognized the need to devote extra resources to manage user contributions.

In fact, almost all the newspapers in our study appeared willing to invest resources in community management, our interviews suggested. One rare exception was at *De Standaard* (Belgium), where two of the journalists we interviewed voiced skepticism about the need for a community manager. They said moderating user participation was a manageable task for existing staff because there was so little input to deal with. "It only takes half of my working day," said the online editor responsible for moderation at *De Standaard*.

4.4 New Job Profiles

The experiences of this Belgian journalist, however, were in sharp contrast to the views of a journalist at *Kaleva* in Finland, a country with a media market similar in size to Flanders in Belgium. The Finn explained that creation of a new editor's position was planned to handle user input and maintain contacts with contributors, because newspaper managers realized that "online journalists have to devote terribly much of their time to moderating discussion forums."

In fact, the adoption of audience participation in news production had led to the creation of new jobs in every country – including at the other Belgian newspapers in our study. There were two basic types of jobs, although our interviewees used many different labels and job descriptions to identify them. One was a new "community manager" position. The other was "comment **moderator**," a function identified across the online newsrooms we visited.

4.4.1 Community Managers

As mentioned earlier, newspapers believe they must enhance their connection with the public to remain relevant in the Internet era. So the notions of "community" and "interactivity" are at the center of attention in most online newsrooms today. Community "pretty much tops our to-do list," an editor at the *Guardian* (UK) said, adding that the list was a long one.

Confronted with a growing number of users sending in tips, stories, photos and comments, newspapers have decided to dedicate extra resources to managing user interactions. Their most common response has been the creation of a new job profile, which serves the secondary purpose of signaling that the paper is taking interactivity seriously. At some newspapers, whole teams have even been created around user management.

A particularly interesting example came from France, where *Le Monde* had established a separate participatory journalism platform called Le Post and staffed its small newsroom with people whose job was to serve as "coaches" for users. These coaches were responsible for building a kind of mentoring relationship between journalists and members of the public.

Editors at the website of *Le Monde* were watching this development with interest. "It's new, it's a complex but enriching role: He serves as an advisor, an editor, mixed with a personalized relationship with the audience. It's an interesting concept with some excellent results at times," one editor said. Another agreed that the notion of a "link" between journalists and users, someone offering "journalistic guidance for participation," was intriguing.

However, the editors were hesitant about considering a similar formal position at the online newsroom of *Le Monde* itself. "We already do serve a lot of the coach's missions in an informal way," such as emailing a blogger to ask for more specific information about a post, "without it being as structured as it is at Le Post," one editor said.

Interviews in other countries suggested that these ideas can be generalized to virtually all the newspapers we studied. Even journalists at papers that had not created a job title for this new role explained that at least some online editors were fulfilling community management tasks.

Exactly what this "community manager" did varied, however. At *Helsingin Sanomat* (Finland), *FAZ* (Germany) and *USA Today*, for instance, online journalists broadly described the community manager as the person who oversees the daily flow of user contributions across the newsroom.

An editor at The Marker Café (Israel) was a bit more specific, saying the "community director" was in charge of the communities of volunteer citizen journalists with whom the website collaborates. This person's job included appointing community administrators, as well as "making sure the communities are properly managed, handling complaints, merging communities and starting up new ones – that is the main thing."

Community managers also may serve as participatory journalism "evangelists," highlighting successful initiatives and encouraging newsroom colleagues to replicate them.

The most detailed description was provided by one of the community editors at the *Telegraph* (UK), who tried to sum up the many multifaceted tasks for which she was responsible. Day to day, she said, the job includes:

Managing My Telegraph, trying to manage the moderation, communicate with users … talking to them, trying to help them to help us moderate, so ask them what they think about our policies on things or ask them for input on how to manage pictures and how sensitive we should be about [*certain topics or types of content*]. So there's quite a lot of that. And then moderating comments across the rest of the site. … And I have a **blog**, a photography blog, which is trying to encourage a sort of community of photographers. … [*The overall aim is*] to try and spread thinking and knowledge and ideas both with users – and explain to users, show users or encourage users to explore what's possible in terms of inter-action – and also do that internally, with other reporters and journalists right across the company."

At the rival *Guardian*, the "head of communities" was primarily regarded as a strategic role. "It's quite a senior position," one of the editors explained. The person not only oversees a team of in-house moderators but also develops strate-gies for creating a "much greater sense of communities across the site" and looks for partnerships and technological solutions to keep on top of the flood of user-generated content.

In addition, the editor also cited the newspaper's **ombudsman**, saying her duties include ensuring that journalists are sensitive to readers' needs.

Similarly, at *Vecernji List* (Croatia), an editor said that the job description of the newspaper's community editor came close to the role of an ombudsman, who serves as the representative or trustee of the readers within the media organization. This "reader representative" interacts with users and moderates their contributions, along with handling reader complaints – thus fulfilling some customer service roles, as well.

In Belgium, journalists preferred the term "coordinator," though they described functions similar to what others labeled a "community management" role.

"I think the term 'coordinator' suits best," said the online editor in charge of the citizen journalism project at *Het Belang van Limburg* and *Gazet van Ant-werpen*. "I believe that the future task of online editors will not be limited to news making; they will also have to take care of **social networking** and even fulfill some marketing functions." Notably, she admitted taking up a marketing task herself from time to time because of the precarious commercial viability of online newspapers.

Editors at *Het Nieuwsblad* (Belgium) also drew a picture of the future online journalist that went beyond the role of "making news." Professional local reporters at this paper had created a network of citizen journalists around them, users who voluntarily contributed stories about their towns or communities.

"Next to writing stories and processing the local news, [*the professional reporters*] will increasingly have to coordinate and manage their local network of citizens with whom they work," an editor of *Het Nieuwsblad* said. In fact, these people are called "local community coordinators" rather than "local reporters."

At the time of our interviews, the newspaper also was planning to hire a "central coordinator" to work within the newsroom, overseeing the whole user-generated content stream. Editors said this person would be responsible for maintaining contact with the public; evaluating all the incoming user contributions, such as tips, stories, photos and comments; and distributing the newsworthy content to the appropriate print or online journalists.

4.4.2 Comment Moderator

In addition to such community managers – whether they were called "community editors," "coaches," "coordinators" or something else – our interviews identified a second new career track stemming from the adoption of audience participation in news production. This is the job of "comment moderator," whose tasks are almost entirely concentrated on moderating user contributions at the final interpretation stage of the news production process.

In fact, this moderator role already existed in many online newsrooms before such concepts as **Web 2.0**, participatory journalism or social networking grabbed the newspaper industry's collective attention. Most online newspapers have maintained discussions forums since their earliest days on the Internet; by the time of our interviews in 2007 and 2008, journalists were quite familiar with the function of "forum editor."

The job title may have changed to "comment moderator," but the basic tasks remain the same: monitoring and filtering feedback and comments from users. We consider this role, including the work practices and concerns of those who hold it, in more detail in Chapter 6. Here, it is worth quickly mentioning the related function of "chat moderator," which existed at several newspapers in our study, including *The Globe and Mail* (Canada), *Le Monde* (France), *FOCUS* (Germany), *El País* (Spain) and the *Washington Post* (USA).

This person was responsible for setting up live **chats** with users on the newspaper website. At *The Globe and Mail* and *Le Monde*, all online editors filled this role on a rotating basis. "For us, knowing how to moderate a chat is an ability that's common to all multimedia journalists," said the editor at *Le Monde*.

4.5 Outsourcing and Crowdsourcing

While most journalists seemed to agree about what was included in the new job profiles related to audience participation, the ways in which these jobs were filled differed from one newspaper to another.

4.5.1 In-house Solutions

Some newsrooms had shifted people around internally. For example, a journalist had long been in charge of letters to the editor at *Kaleva* (Finland); her print role was simply expanded to deal with user-generated content for the online product. At other newspapers, interviewees also mentioned that jobs within the print newsroom that previously related in some way to reader interactivity had been expanded or reshuffled to include online responsibilities.

Most journalists framed these restructuring initiatives as forming part of their newspaper's broader strategy to integrate print and online efforts. This perception serves as an additional illustration of the way in which convergence accommodates newspapers' constant attempt to do more with less staff, budget and resources (Deuze 2007).

However, the strategy of using old employees to fill new vacancies was not a dominant one. A number of newspapers opted for hiring new employees to do tasks related to participatory journalism.

In the relatively large countries of France, Germany, Spain, the United Kingdom and the United States, newspapers had established separate audience **participation teams**, whose members were responsible for managing and moderating user contributions. While the head of the team, the "community manager," was typically a senior editor with professional journalism experience, comment moderators often were among the youngest or greenest in the newsrooms.

In the smaller national media markets in our study, comment moderation teams tended to be much less structured. In Belgium, Canada and Croatia, as well as at *Kaleva* in Finland, the role of comment moderation commonly was assigned to all online editors. In Israel, moderation was handled by various staff members, depending on availability or expertise.

At *The Globe and Mail* (Canada), for example, "no specific journalist [*is*] tasked with monitoring content from the audience, and no new jobs were created as a result of increased audience interaction," an editor said. "Everyone is expected to monitor the content and look at material flagged by users when they have a chance. The responsibility may fall to whoever is on shift at the time."

In countries where online journalists take on the role of comment moderation, this rarely appeared to be a full-time task. Although time-consuming, the job of moderation was not seen as one that should dominate a journalist's daily responsibilities.

Even at Ynet, the website of the Israeli newspaper *Yedioth Aharonoth*, which received more than 10,000 user comments on an average day at the time of our study, three to four online editors shared the responsibility for moderating those comments. They worked in shifts to manage the workload, and each journalist was expected to combine comment moderation with other news-production activities.

4.5.2 Outsourcing

The belief that moderation is time-consuming, but of lesser importance than some of the other things an online journalist has to do, inspired some of the larger newspapers to consider or implement moderation **outsourcing**. Among the newspapers handing comment moderation off to external companies were those in France and Spain.

At these newspapers, outsourcing was seen as an appropriate way to avoid the problem of user comments becoming an overwhelming burden for professional journalists in the online newsroom. "For some time, we moderated comments ourselves, within the newsroom," said the editor-in-chief of *20 Minutos* (Spain). "But at some point, we were overloaded by these tasks that all in all are very mechanical."

The other Spanish newspaper in our study, *El País*, offered an interesting example of a newsroom that had opted to outsource moderation – but only for comments. The paper's in-house participation team handled all the coordination and moderation of user contributions to audience blogs and to the popular citizen news section of the website, called Yo, periodista. To ensure that these employees could dedicate all their time to managing this user-generated content, the moderation of comments and feedback in news sections of the *El País* website was outsourced.

In other words, the newsroom had ceded responsibility for overseeing user contributions at the post-publication interpretation stage of news production in order to retain control over material in the first four stages described in Chapter 2, including access/observation, selection/filtering, processing/editing and **distribution**. "We outsourced comment moderation because it would be never-ending for us to take care of it," said the online editor at *El País*. "I don't think that newsrooms should take care of moderating comments."

In addition to either handling comment moderation themselves or outsourcing it, most editors were also open to the idea of involving users in the process. One of the leaders in this area was the *Telegraph* (UK), which had undertaken efforts to shift responsibility for moderation to users in its My Telegraph section, despite resistance to the idea from many of those users.

Other newspapers also were exploring ways to at least share the comment moderation task with users, for instance relying on users to **report abuse** or to rate the quality of others' contributions to the comment section.

In other words, these newspapers were attempting to "**crowdsource**," rather than "outsource," the resource-consuming task of keeping a watchful eye on user comments. However, they also acknowledged the risk involved.

"When you give more power to somebody, and they have more responsibilities, they end up committing abuse, trying to transform the community into a place that suits their criteria," said an editor at *El País*. "They may report abuse or censor users far beyond the policies of our company that aim to make forums a diverse space."

4.6 Organizational Structures

Research on the adoption of innovations in professional newsrooms shows the importance of both physical and organizational structure. Case studies have shown that the degree of interactivity on a newspaper website relates to the way in which the newsroom is structured (Boczkowski 2004b).

Boczkowski's work suggested that websites seemed less open to interactivity when print and online journalists worked together in the same newsroom than when print and online staffs worked autonomously. Although the editors we interviewed had different opinions and perceptions about the relationship between newsroom structure and newsroom culture, we would tentatively conclude that what we learned was broadly consistent with his finding.

An online editor at the *Washington Post* (USA), for example, believed the fact that the print and online staffs worked in separate newsrooms (which were merged into a single newsroom subsequent to our study) helped in the development of audience participation. "It would be hard for something like reader engagement to get a foothold in a newsroom dominated by print," he said.

Another example came from the separated print and online departments at the French newspaper *Le Monde*. There, editors said an underlying motivation for establishing the wholly participatory LePost.fr website was to create a lab where journalists could "experiment with new tools, new formats and new rhythms for news. We try to be the most 'porous' possible, the most flexible [*and*] hyper-reactive," as the editor of Le Post put it. He explained that even though the editorial teams of Le Post, *Le Monde* and the Le Monde.fr website were completely independent, they had "regular contacts" and "cordial exchanges," enabling each newsroom to learn from the others.

Partly because of their smaller staff size, online newsrooms generally tend to have a flatter organizational structure than their print counterparts, which means that responsibilities are shared among the journalists.

In such newsrooms, all the editors commonly are involved in managing user contributions and exploring new ways of integrating audience participation in the news-production process. "Everybody kind of does it," said an online journalist at *The Globe and Mail* (Canada), adding he would be "shocked" if other online newsrooms were structured in a less linear and more top-down manner.

In fact, some newspaper managers drew on the experiences in these "flattened" newsrooms to argue that such a structure should be expanded to the whole news operation. They suggested that centralization and integration of print and online activities should foster collaboration, involving everybody in a collective journalism effort.

A journalist at the *Guardian* (UK), for instance, said that having a separate staff for participatory journalism is "probably not a model we'll favor." Rather, their aim was to encourage interactions and foster collaboration between print and online journalists on the one hand, and between journalists and users on the other.

By increasing these interactions, the editor argued, the newspaper might succeed in changing newsroom culture, generally seen as necessary to thrive in a twenty-first-century participatory media environment. He believed print and online journalists should all be involved as much as possible in participatory efforts: "Just by being exposed to it, hopefully they might understand a bit better what it all means."

The biggest perceived advantage of the **integrated newsroom** in meeting the goal of encouraging participatory journalism, then, may be its potential to accelerate the newsroom cultural change discussed earlier in this chapter.

The lack of consensus about which newsroom structure is most suitable for the development of participatory journalism indicates that organizational structure may influence editors' perceptions more than it shapes newsroom practice itself.

On the one hand, editors working in an integrated newsroom were likely to focus on the possibilities it offers for fostering closer collaborations between print and online journalists, which they perceived as beneficial for implementing participatory news-making practices. On the other hand, journalists working in an online newsroom that was not integrated with the print newsroom praised their autonomy, seeing it as enabling them to more fully explore new opportunities offered by the Internet.

"In my opinion, the online department is more dynamic and future-oriented than the print department," said the community manager at *Het Belang van Limburg* and *Gazet van Antwerpen* (Belgium).

Indeed, the idea that people in online newsrooms might be more open-minded about innovation recurred in many interviews. In fact, some online editors were quite excited about opportunities to experiment with audience participation and user-generated content. That observation brings us to the concluding section of this chapter, which considers the role of technology as a facilitator of change or a barrier to it.

4.7 Conclusion

The technological infrastructure available to journalists also has a significant effect on the adoption of innovative practices in professional newsrooms (Paulussen and Ugille 2008). Boczkowski (2009) and Domingo (2008) both describe the mutual relationship between journalism and technology, a concept they refer to as the "materiality" of work.

What they are basically telling us is that although technology does not determine editorial practice, tools do influence practice, sometimes in subtle ways. Technology can foster journalistic innovation, but it also can hinder innovation or even reshape efforts to change in an unforeseen manner.

Again, the editors in our study had different and occasionally contradictory opinions about the role of technology in shaping newsroom adoption of audience participation. That said, a general feeling among our interviewees was that newspapers, like all media, have to keep pace with the socio-cultural changes associated with the Internet.

This belief suggests journalists must experiment with the participatory options that new technologies offer. A Canadian editor, for example, argued that the main reason for embracing new technologies is simply "because we can" – and because it would be a useless and losing game to "fight the technology."

However, other interviewees sounded much more enthusiastic about technological opportunities for opening up the news-production process to user participation, such as the editor at *Kaleva* (Finland) who said that "even without declining circulations," his newspaper would be experimenting with the interactive features of the Internet.

Further, a few editors also put faith in technological solutions for automating the process of filtering user-generated content, or at least making that process semi-automatic. At the time of our interview in 2008, for example, *Le Figaro* (France) was already working with an IT company that had software for "filtering comments by keywords and the like," an editor there said.

Other editors emphasized the limitations of available technology. This concern was especially striking among the Belgian journalists.

At all the Belgian newspapers in our study, interviewees said they would extend participatory options once the technology allowed them to do so. At the time of the interviews, they all referred to their news organization's imminent plans to implement a new **content management system (CMS)** enabling them to take advantage of all the Web 2.0 "bells and whistles."

In the meantime, journalists at *Het Nieuwsblad* said, they were forced to use blogging software to enable local citizen reporters to send in their stories, a solution the managing editor described as "certainly not ideal." (At the time of writing this chapter, almost two years after the interviews were conducted, *Het Nieuwsblad* was still using the blogging software for its local citizen journalism project, having encountered problems with implementation of the new system.)

Perhaps one could argue that these Belgian editors were expecting too much of the technology. That is what an editor at the *Washington Post* (USA) seemed to suggest. "You can spend a lot of time trying to figure out what the next big thing would be and then pour everything into it," she said. "But I think it's more important to be agile, and when you see something that looks like something, [*you*] ought to move quickly enough to experiment with it."

With that good summation, which nicely captures the cautious and pragmatic step-by-step approach of most newspapers toward participatory journalism, we conclude this chapter. We turn next to a closer investigation of journalists' practices, workflows and strategies for offering and managing participatory journalism options on their websites.

Participate!

1. Why is it important for newspapers to find a good balance between economic and journalistic motivations for investing in participatory journalism? What do you see as the main economic motivations for doing so? From a journalistic point of view, what opportunities does involving users in the news-production process afford?

2. Many organizational challenges accompany the process of changing a newsroom culture and making it more "adaptive" to the participatory character of the new media environment. Among other things, it requires restructuring the newsroom. If you were a newsroom leader, would you opt for an integrated or separated newsroom? Why? Would you consider the outsourcing of certain editorial tasks? Why or why not?

References

Boczkowski, Pablo J. (2004a) *Digitizing the news: Innovation in online newspapers,* Cambridge, Massachusetts: MIT Press.

Boczkowski, Pablo J. (2004b) The processes of adopting multimedia and interactivity in three online newsrooms, *Journal of Communication* 54 (2): 197–213.

Boczkowski, Pablo J. (2009) Materiality and mimicry in the journalism field. In: Barbie Zelizer (Ed.) *The changing faces of journalism: Tabloidization, technology and truthiness* (56–67), New York: Routledge.

Deuze, Mark (2007) *Media work,* Cambridge, Massachusetts: Polity Press.

Domingo, David (2008) Interactivity in the daily routines of online newsrooms: Dealing with an uncomfortable myth, *Journal of Computer-Mediated Communication* 13 (3): 680–704.

Gade, Peter J. (2004) Newspapers and organizational development: Management and journalist perceptions of newsroom cultural change, *Journalism and Communication Monographs* 65: 3–55.

Gade, Peter J., and Earnest L. Perry (2003) Changing the newsroom culture: A four-year case study of organizational development at the *St. Louis Post-Dispatch, Journalism & Mass Communication Quarterly* 80 (2): 327–347.

Gans, Herbert J. (1979) *Deciding what's news: A study of CBS Evening News, NBC Nightly News, Newsweek, and Time,* New York: Pantheon.

Lewis, Justin, Andrew Williams and Bob Franklin (2008) Four rumours and an explanation: A political economic account of journalists' changing newsgathering and reporting practices, *Journalism Practice* 2 (1): 27–45.

McLellan, Michele, and Tim Porter (2007) *News, improved. How America's newsrooms are learning to change,* Washington D.C.: CQ Press.

Paulussen, Steve (2004) Online news production in Flanders: How Flemish online journalists perceive and explore the Internet's potential, *Journal of Computer-Mediated Communication* 9 (4).

Paulussen, Steve, and Pieter Ugille (2008) User generated content in the newsroom: Professional and organisational constraints on participatory journalism, *Westminster Papers in Communication and Culture (WPCC)* 5 (2): 24–41.

Pew Research Center's Project for Excellence in Journalism (2008) *The changing news-room*. Accessed 16 January 2010: http://www.journalism.org/node/11961.

Preston, Paschal (2009) *Making the news: Journalism and news cultures in Europe*, London: Routledge.

Quinn, Stephen (2005) Convergence's fundamental question, *Journalism Studies* 6 (1): 29–38.

Ryfe, David M. (2009) Broader and deeper: A study of newsroom culture in a time of change, *Journalism* 10 (2): 197–216.

Singer, Jane B. (2004) Strange bedfellows? Diffusion of convergence in four news organizations, *Journalism Studies* 5 (1): 3–18.

World Editors Forum (2008) *Trends in Newsrooms 2008*, Paris: World Association of Newspapers / World Editors Forum.

5

Managing Audience Participation
Practices, workflows and strategies
David Domingo

Research on making news, or the process of news production, shows that over the decades, journalists have developed and streamlined a set of standardized practices to deal with the uncertainty of current events (Schudson 2003, 2000; Tuchman 2002; Manning 2001). Decisions that define the news **agenda** and determine the space and resources devoted to any given story are based on shared values and assessments of newsworthiness, which broadly form part of the culture of journalism.

For instance, reporters develop a network of institutionalized sources to try to guarantee a trustworthy and constant input of information. In general, newsroom staff responsibilities, roles and procedures are structured to address various parts of their news production task, including making news judgments, gathering information, writing and editing.

Media companies tend to be cautious in approaching innovation. Journalistic culture is a very strong force shaping the adoption of new technologies and trends (Domingo 2008; Paterson and Domingo 2008), and the law of inertia means that existing practices resist change. A number of studies of newsroom **convergence** in the mid-2000s demonstrated just how strong that cultural resistance can be (Avilés and Carvajal 2008; Silcock and Keith 2006; Singer 2004). Yet at some point, the implications of change become so far-reaching that they must be addressed.

Participatory Journalism: Guarding Open Gates at Online Newspapers, First Edition.
Jane B. Singer, Alfred Hermida, David Domingo, Ari Heinonen, Steve Paulussen, Thorsten Quandt, Zvi Reich, and Marina Vujnovic.
© 2011 Jane B. Singer, Alfred Hermida, David Domingo, Ari Heinonen, Steve Paulussen, Thorsten Quandt, Zvi Reich, and Marina Vujnovic. Published 2011 by Blackwell Publishing Ltd.

As this chapter describes, user input unavoidably challenges newsroom production practices that previously were stable and internally controlled. **User-generated content (UGC)**, unlike material from official sources, is wildly diverse as well as uneven in quality, focus and reliability. Many of our interviewees felt overwhelmed by the idea of managing this material – of "opening the floodgates," as one journalist at the *National Post*, in Canada, put it. But once the gates are in fact open, journalists in each of our newsrooms realized the need to find an appropriate strategy and define a new set of practices for handling these user contributions, as well as a way to embed those strategies and practices into existing news production workflows.

Although the desire to protect journalists from the burden of managing user contributions was widespread, the response to it varied. As other research into newsroom innovation has shown, broad trends affect many organizations, but decisions about how to address those trends are made locally based on specific circumstances (Boczkowski 2004a, 2004b). In our study, different attitudes toward the potential use and value of **audience** participation resulted in different ways of addressing the need to manage that participation.

This chapter analyzes the processes through which user contributions are received, filtered, sorted and published in online newspapers – through which, in other words, they fit into the various **news production stages** described in Chapter 2. These processes vary depending in large part on the nature of the content and on the tactics that media professionals employ to engage and motivate active **users**. These diverse approaches raise a number of questions.

We want to know, for instance, whether elite and popular newspapers have different ideas about the best way to manage participation. More broadly, what sorts of workflows enable different individuals to make decisions, and at what point in the news production cycle are those decisions made? We look at the involvement of reporters to see how audience participation is connected with newsgathering. We also ask if users are being invited to assume the role of managers or co-managers of the content they produce – and if they are, how journalists are coping. The chapter ends with a summary of best practices in managing **participatory journalism** and a consideration of the implications of our findings.

5.1 Different Materials, Different Management Strategies

As we saw in earlier chapters, participatory journalism takes various forms, and newsrooms treat those forms differently. Providing facts is different from providing opinion; user photos from the scene of a breaking news story are different from photos that have nothing to do with news at all. The designated position on the website for publishing a specific type of **user-generated content** influences management strategies and practices. So do journalists' motivations to develop participation options and encourage their use, especially the extent to which user contributions are seen as journalistically relevant.

The diversity of management strategies can be highlighted through a series of contrasting examples of how journalists in our newsrooms handled various categories of user input, such as facts and opinions, or hard news and non-news. Again, different newsrooms took different approaches; indeed, a specific participation feature might be managed in many different ways, as explored further below. But we'll start with a variety of examples to illustrate how disparate those alternatives for managing audience participation can be.

5.1.1 Facts vs. Opinion

The management of facts and opinions submitted by users to Ynet (Israel) provides our first example. The nature of the contribution was used to justify its delegation to journalists at opposite ends of the newsroom hierarchy: editors for facts and junior reporters for opinions.

The website's "red email" was an explicit call for story tips from the audience, and a very successful one. When an earthquake hit, for example, the newspaper got the story first because it received what one interviewee described as "thousands of emails" from users. Despite the challenges created by the high volume of user input, this participation channel was considered so important to the newsroom that online editors were responsible for sifting through it to determine what might be relevant. They emphasized that this process altered the usual workflow through which facts enter the newsroom at the **access/ observation stage** of news production. "I notified the reporter that something happened – he did not notify me," explained one editor.

On the other hand, **comments** on news items were managed by five junior reporters at Ynet, all of whom – of course – had other tasks, too. The volume of opinion-based comments was also high, but the main aim when filtering them was to avoid legal trouble, as discussed further in Chapters 6 and 7. Although "it is a lot of work reading all these materials," one interviewee said, it is necessary because of the risk of being sued for defamation.

The complexity of managing each type of user contribution also varied, requiring the mobilization of different resources. While facts submitted by users were assigned to a reporter to be checked and developed into a story if they were deemed newsworthy, opinions were immediately published unless they were problematic. Decisions about opinion-based contributions seldom involved anyone other than the junior journalist who was **pre-moderating** them.

Another example comes from *20 Minutos* (Spain), where comment management was completely separated from the newsroom. Comments on news stories were **post-moderated** by an external company, and the newsroom was not involved at all in the management process. "Reporters may check the comments in their own story to complement their story or correct it, but not to moderate them," explained an interviewee at *20 Minutos*.

The Spanish journalists argued that systematic oversight was necessary – but it could not be guaranteed if left to reporters, whose priority is to produce news. Instead, news tips and materials such as photos reached a centralized database, where a **participation team** consisting of four full-time journalists sorted them. These staffers systematically forwarded relevant material to the appropriate section editor, who assessed whether it could be developed into a story.

5.1.2 Newsworthiness of Images

Helsingin Sanomat (Finland) treated users' hard news photos and feature or non-news images very differently. The newspaper's website offered a non-news section called "Oma maailma" (My World), where users could recommend places to visit and share pictures from their holiday trips. Photos submitted by users for this section were published automatically and only reviewed afterwards by a **moderator** from the marketing department.

However, if a picture reached the newsroom email inbox, it was evaluated before being published, typically by a photojournalist and sometimes also by news editors, who considered its newsworthiness and reliability. It might end up being used in a story for the website or even for the print newspaper. Journalists at *Helsingin Sanomat* said they received many more news-oriented photos than travel photos.

In the Finnish newspaper, then, the way an item reached the newsroom and its perceived relevance to the news-production process influenced how it was treated at the **selection / filtering stage**, where on the website it was published at the **distribution stage** and who took responsibility for it. Non-news content was circumscribed within a separate section, clearly labeled as a space produced by users. But potentially newsworthy pictures were more strictly filtered. These entered the professional news production cycle and might eventually be posted alongside journalists' work. Such pictures would still be identified as submitted by a citizen, but journalists felt their location made it more crucial to impose strict journalistic **gatekeeping** procedures.

5.1.3 Placement within the Website

Position within the website was itself a key factor that defined different management strategies for the same kind of user contribution. At the *Telegraph* (UK), for example, management of comments posted on news items produced by the professional journalists, which were accessible through the main *Telegraph* website, was different from management of those posted on user **blogs**, which were in a separate area called My Telegraph.

The separation contributed to the belief that a largely hands-off approach to moderation in that area was appropriate. Journalists intervened there only when users reported abuse. "One of the key things is to recognize that it's their space rather than ours," explained a community editor.

In contrast, user comments in news sections were pre-moderated, and journalists were becoming increasingly active in managing contributions to the stories they had produced. At the time of our interviews in late 2008, *Telegraph* journalists mainly tried to filter abusive comments. But the community editor hinted that differences between journalistic participation in the user community and in other sections of the website would increase over time:

> What I think we're going to do increasingly with the parts of the site that we own is shape the debate much more actively so that it is more constructive. So we can say to people, 'My Telegraph is the space where you can have a conversation any way you like.' But the conversations on the main part of the site, that's our realm, and we'll shape it, and we'll moderate that discussion very actively.

5.1.4 Attitudes and Motivations

Newsroom attitudes toward participatory journalism also shaped management practices. The same kind of participation feature might be dealt with differently in different organizations depending on journalists' motivations in establishing the option in the first place.

USA Today and *El País* are good examples. User comments at the U.S. newspaper's website were post-moderated, while those at *El País* were pre-moderated. This would seem to suggest that the Spanish website oversaw audience commentary more closely. But understanding the newsroom rationales for affording the opportunities for user input goes further to explain the actual management strategy of each paper.

At *USA Today*, comments were regarded as an opportunity for journalists to take advantage of the potential for audience members to become valuable sources, a role you learned more about in Chapter 3. "There can be a lot of good information coming from people. If they're talking about their experiences and information they have, we'll try to, at the bottom of the story … mention 'share your story and tips,'" explained the **community manager**.

In response to this perceived value, the responsibility of overseeing comments on news items had been spread throughout the newsroom. All journalists were encouraged to read user comments attached to their stories and to be on the lookout for ideas for new stories. Users, who had to register in order to participate, were encouraged to provide a contact phone number so journalists could get in touch if they wanted to follow up on a tip or a description of personal experience with the topic of a story. Reporters even published stories under development, issuing "calls for action" to request information from users – a form of **crowdsourcing**.

In contrast, journalists at *El País* believed they got few "journalistically valuable" comments. Although they did pre-moderate comments, they did so mainly because of a desire to protect their brand, not to develop stories or ideas. They opted to **outsource** the management of this form of participatory journalism in order to keep tight control over the legal validity of contributions without putting a burden on the audience participation team. Members of that team therefore could devote time to dealing with user contributions the journalists felt were more relevant, such as citizen-produced stories.

Expectations about the content thus help explain the different strategies at these two papers. But the varying approaches turned into something of a self-fulfilling prophecy: *USA Today* users contributed relevant data because they knew they might end up the protagonists of the next print story, while comments to *El País* tended to include a huge volume of useless ranting. Users fought among themselves over a topic much as they would do in a bar, with no sign of the journalists in the debate whatsoever.

5.2 Workflow Trends in News Production Stages

While these examples show how diverse the management of participatory journalism can be, some general trends were common across the online newspapers in our study. The logic was not necessarily tied to the news production stage at which participation occurred; different newspapers applied different solutions in any given stage. However, we'll use those stages, as described in Chapter 2 and summarized in the glossary, as an organizing tool here to help us present what we learned more clearly.

5.2.1 Access / Observation Stage

The greatest amount of consensus could be found in handling input in the initial observation stage. Any contribution that might end up being used in newsroom reporting tended to be pre-moderated, evaluated by journalists and integrated into the news production cycle as another source to be fact-checked.

There was generally no space on the websites for raw news tips. *USA Today* was a rare exception, using comments as a space for users to share story ideas. In this way, the newspaper website transformed a public debate space into a collaboration tool for journalists and users.

Some newsrooms made systematic monitoring of user-submitted news tips and other material, such as photos or video, part of the duties of the audience participation team or other online staff. Among the newspapers taking this approach were *24 Hours* (Croatia); *Yedioth Aharonoth*, the publisher of Ynet, and NRG (both Israel); and *20 Minutos* (Spain).

Other newsrooms found it more fruitful to issue specific calls for input when they believed citizens might have had the opportunity to collect information that journalists could not. Examples ranged from local accidents to riots in foreign countries. *De Standaard*, for example, tried to get Belgians living abroad to send in photos and narrations in these situations. As indicated earlier, however, journalists found that it took concerted effort to get users to contribute this material: "People will not do it automatically," as one editor explained.

Nonetheless, journalists in the newsrooms of *De Standaard* and *Het Nieuwsblad* agreed that a more systematic approach to user input would be beneficial. "What we learned is that we need to coordinate the UGC (user-generated content) stream more actively and more effectively," said the editor-in-chief of the two papers. "The steering and coaching will require investments, for more people and more resources. But once you have this, you can have a big advantage over your competitors." An online editor at *Het Nieuwsblad* said the newspaper planned to hire a "central coordinator" to handle all the UGC and assign it to the appropriate journalists.

Collective interviews or "**chats**" provided another clear instance of strict filtering in the access/observation stage. In all the websites analyzed, a journalist coordinated these chats, selecting the most appropriate questions from the hundreds posed by users. Citizen blogs and **forums** were at the other end of the spectrum, as journalists only loosely monitored those. Only a few websites that did not enable comments on news items, instead channeling all their participation through forums, pre-moderated user contributions there. In the rest, newspapers expected users themselves to **report abuse** by flagging posts that broke participation rules.

5.2.2 Selection / Filtering,
Processing / Editing and Distribution Stages

At the production stages of news creation, citizen stories tended to be pre-moderated and carefully fact-checked before publication. This was the case at *El País* (Spain) and in the historical narratives section of *Der Spiegel* (Germany), which devoted a team of around ten staff journalists and freelancers to evaluate the contributions.

However, in newsrooms with a more active approach to **citizen journalism**, more open publishing policies were being developed. In the Belgian newsrooms and at LePost.fr (France) – the user-dominated spin-off of *Le Monde* – journalists managing citizen stories were considered coaches for citizen reporters and developed relationships with them. At *Het Nieuwsblad* (Belgium) local reporters assumed the task of coordinating groups made up of citizen contributors and freelancers, with whom they had regular contact. At the time of our interviews, journalists anticipated allowing these users to publish without moderation, with the journalist selecting the better stories to display on the local homepage.

Le Post already had transformed moderation into **curation** by spring 2008. All citizen stories were immediately published, and journalists labeled those that they deemed particularly interesting or relevant. Beyond editing and fact-checking, the website staff worked closely with users who provided these stories. The editor-in-chief, who also served as the main "coach," described his work this way:

I call up people and sometimes spend two hours with them. There's an emotional link that is created. What's interesting for users is not only **Web 2.0** but to have a human contact, to bring their relationship to news. ... So we have a newsroom that is very close to our posters, to the audience. We work daily in close relationship with the readers.

5.2.3 Interpretation Stage

The most variation across newsrooms came in the way different newspapers managed comments, at the **interpretation stage** of news production. As we saw in the previous section (and will discuss more in the following chapter), rationales for enabling user participation were crucial to defining comment-handling strategies. Sites that pre-moderated comments tended not to require **registration**, while post-moderation commonly relied on registration to temper abusive contributions.

However, online newspapers with different moderation principles might share a rationale. The allocation of resources to oversee comments in news was determined largely by whether the medium sought top quality in the contributions, ideas for reporters or just sheer volume that boosts traffic statistics.

At *Focus* (Germany), journalists carefully picked the comments to be published. One journalist was devoted full time to this job, with the help of a freelancer; at times of high input, as many as seven other online journalists might assist, as well.

These German journalists regarded the comments as letters to the editor, placing high demands on their structure and arguments. The main comments moderator engaged in "educating" users to improve the quality of their contributions: "If you take these five minutes more time in order to explain, instead of saying 'your account has been deleted,' and you react and explain why a comment has been deleted, and that the user needs to word it in a different way so that it can be re-published, then you instantly get positive feedback. They [*users*] stay, don't make the same mistake again and everything works fine."

A different consideration regarding the quality of comments was the desire to ensure they are legal and thus to avoid damage to the newspaper brand, as discussed further in Chapters 7 and 8. In this case, the profile of moderators was usually not journalistic. "We want that our readers can trust that what comes through us is somehow legal content, fit to publish," said a journalist at *Helsingin Sanomat* (Finland), where a team of five, led by a journalist, pre-moderated the news forums.

Süddeutsche Zeitung (Germany) had the same aim but used post-moderation to achieve it. Interviewees there stressed the importance of having the moderators in-house – a team of six part-timers without journalistic background, led by a journalist – "so that they have the direct contact to the editors" to decide criteria and provide ideas in newsroom editorial meetings.

Editors at *El País* (Spain) expressed the same rationale of protecting the brand, but they admitted that obtaining a high volume of comments was also their aim. In this case, management was outsourced, but online journalists retained a large measure of control by deciding which stories to open to comments in the first place.

Journalists at other newspapers in our study said they saw comments as discussion spaces for users, limiting their own role to the deletion of inappropriate contributions. An example was the *Washington Post* (USA), where the newsroom had no involvement in moderation. Instead, the *Post* had five full-time staffers post-moderating comments to allow "a full and vibrant discussion rather than one that is closely edited and controlled by somebody," as the website's participation team leader said. In newsrooms with similar philosophies but fewer resources, such as the Croatian and Belgian newspapers, online journalists dealt with post-moderation along with their other tasks.

Those newspapers that saw comments as a good source of ideas for reporters tended to have the whole newsroom involved in managing comments, guaranteeing that everyone was exposed to the audience input. Some newsrooms dealt with this responsibility at the section level, while others expected all journalists to read the comments in stories they had written.

We already presented the case of *USA Today*, which reduced the burden on journalists by having them report abuse when they detected it without actually deleting problematic comments; this was instead the task of the community manager, who oversaw the queue of reports of abuse created by journalists and users alike.

At both *Focus* (Germany) and the *Telegraph* (UK), reporters managed comments on their blogs; *Telegraph* staffers were increasingly being urged to engage in discussions with audience members, as well. Journalists at the *Guardian* (UK) were not yet managing their own user communities at the time of our interviews, but editors saw that engagement as necessary in the future: "The only way you can possibly make use of all that vast flow of stuff is to have individual journalists looking at what's being said in their individual areas," said an editor there.

In some newsrooms, top editors emphasized the idea of using the comments as a source for news tips, but reporters explained they were too busy to really do so. An example was *Haaretz* (Israel), where every journalist had to manage comments in his or her stories because resources did not allow for a dedicated person.

At *Le Figaro* (France), despite outsourcing moderation in an effort to prevent journalists from being overwhelmed, journalists were still expected to read comments for inspiration – though there were indications that seldom happened. The editor-in-chief, who was considering hiring a full-time user-generated content coordinator when we talked with him, admitted having doubts regarding the best management strategy. "If a journalist were to read all 300 comments, he wouldn't be able to do anything else, so there's a middle path that we must find," he said.

Journalists at *The Globe and Mail* (Canada) and *FAZ* (Germany) also admitted being uncertain about the right strategy for comment moderation, and in fact were unable to describe their motivation for offering this participation feature. In some newsrooms where journalists had to juggle moderation tasks among their other duties, such as the *National Post* (Canada), some interviewees suggested user comments took too much time relative to the value they produced. "I hope that when they're doing the budget, they never have to decide between a comment moderator and a journalist because that would be silly," a *National Post* interviewee said.

5.3 Playground or Source:
Two Approaches to Managing User Contributions

At many newspapers in our study, management strategies for audience contributions were not clearly defined or justified, and journalists admitted they were seeking appropriate solutions by experimenting.

Our interviews revealed a lot of uncertainty, especially at papers that had not developed many participatory journalism features or did not have a passionate discourse about the benefits of audience participation. "I don't know what the next new thing is," said a top *Washington Post* (USA) editor. "We're always willing to experiment."

However, the management strategies of online newsrooms that had thought a lot about, and invested resources in, fostering user participation fell into two main categories (see Table 5.1).

One group included newspapers that created specific sections or even separate websites for user participation beyond news story comments. *El País* (Spain) was one of the first to offer a section dedicated to citizen stories and establishment of a blog community; the *Telegraph* (UK) developed a similar strategy with My Telegraph. *Haaretz* (Israel) created The Marker Café, and *Le Monde* (France) set up Le Post, both separate and distinctly branded places dedicated primarily to user contributions. The *Washington Post* (USA) also explored (unsuccessfully) the possibilities of **hyperlocal** journalism with the since-discontinued *LoudounExtra*.

Dedicated staff managed these spaces, with little or no involvement (at the time of our interviews) by reporters producing news for the website or print newspaper. We refer to this as a "playground" strategy: Journalists set up a separate space in which users were invited to play.

5.3.1 Source Material

A second strategy was to integrate UGC into existing newsroom practices, primarily with an eye toward capitalizing on user contributions as source material for journalists, as we have seen in Chapter 3. Examples of newspapers pursuing

Table 5.1   This chart shows examples of the two approaches to participatory journalism management among the online newspapers in our study that were providing extensive user participation options.

Participatory journalism as playground	Participatory journalism as source
Le Post (*Le Monde*, France); *Haaretz* (Israel); *El País* (Spain); *Telegraph* (UK); *Washington Post* (USA) – Designated space, separate from rest of the website, for user contributions other than comments in news – Loose moderation	*Gazet van Antwerpen* (Belgium); *Het Belang van Limburg* (Belgium); *Het Nieuwsblad* (Belgium); *24 Hours* (Croatia); NRG (Israel); Ynet (*Yedioth Aharonoth*) (Israel); *20 Minutos* (Spain); *USA Today* – UGC input feeds the news production – Relatively strict moderation and fact-checking

this strategy included *24 Hours* (Croatia), *Yedioth Aharonoth* (publisher of Ynet) and NRG (both in Israel), *20 Minutos* (Spain) and *USA Today*.

These newsrooms had different configurations for managing user input, ranging from a dedicated participation team to a group of online editors to even the whole newsroom. But all had systematic mechanisms for treating users as sources for stories that journalists would produce. "Citizen are like little springs of clear water," said a top editor at *20 Minutos*. "Put all together, they can be a significant source."

Other editors used different metaphors to express a similar idea. "To some extent we're going fishing," said the community manager at *USA Today*. "We're hoping we can pull out of that some comments that lend themselves to an informed dialogue that we can either pull out and highlight in a story or use for a later story. So again, our reporting resources are expanding greatly."

Journalists in several Belgian newsrooms emphasized the value in this closer relationship between journalists and citizens, through their network of local reporters described earlier. "If you can build a marriage between user-generated content and the professional content from journalists, you can create something strong," said the community manager at *Het Belang van Limburg* and *Gazet van Antwerpen*.

This is not to say that the journalists in this second cluster of online newspapers were giving up the core definitive values of journalism. However, they were particularly eager to engage in a dialogic relationship with the audience, as we discussed in Chapter 3, because of a perceived potential to use that input to inform their own reporting.

But they still underlined the importance of the role of journalists as gatekeepers, as indicated in these comments from an online journalist at *20 Minutos* (Spain):

> That is why it is so important to have someone with journalistic criteria [*in the participation team*] to judge if behind some input there is a good story or not. ... I don't think that citizen journalism or audience participation implies any change in the routines of professional journalists. Because in the end, readers and the content [*they contribute*] are just another source – a source that had been neglected or at least not acknowledged. ... What happens to many journalists, even if they don't dare to say so, is that they fear that citizen journalism will take over their jobs. And that's ridiculous, because there will always be a need for a filter, and that's a function for the professional journalist: He has to be there to fact-check the information.

These journalists thus regarded user input as necessary for the success and even the identity of their newspapers. What they were seeking was a sort of equilibrium between the value they saw in audience participation and the need to keep journalistic standards. "Of course, all user-generated news needs to be double-checked," said the online editor at *Het Nieuwsblad* (Belgium). "But I think we should publish as much as we can on our local news pages."

5.3.2 A Place to Play

Newspapers in the first group, those moving toward creation of distinct places for user content and community-building, tended to be more relaxed about moderation of user contributions in these audience-only spaces. One key rationale for the separate spaces seemed to be protecting the core newspaper brand from the possible loss of quality that visitors might perceive if audience contributions were mixed with professionally produced content.

The creation of a separate "playground" area for users thus eased pressure on the newsroom, which was not directly involved in management of that area. This strategy allowed them to explore participatory journalism extensively, but with relatively little risk. Online editors might select content from the participatory spaces for the homepage of the online newspaper – or they might not. The decision was entirely up to them.

At *El País* (Spain), retention of the right to make this internal judgment call actually was an ongoing source of frustration for the participation team, as the newsroom showed little interest in user contributions that team members selected as relevant. A UGC manager said they had to put a lot of effort into their pitches. "If we don't sell it well, they [*the online editors*] won't buy it, and whatever you have produced won't be successful" in terms of traffic numbers, he said.

Overall, journalists on *El País*' participation team were dissatisfied with the workflow. They felt the conscious separation of news production and participation management prevented the optimal use of user contributions, resulting in what they saw as inefficiency and a missed opportunity to enhance journalistic quality.

In contrast, journalists at newspapers that were more apt to look at users as sources regarded stories produced with the help of citizens as valuable and tried to make them as visible as possible, with an explicit acknowledgement of the user contribution. "The participation team proposes and we [*the online editors*] decide. But usually what they propose is accepted," said a journalist at *20 Minutos*, the other Spanish newspaper in our study. "The criterion is to protect citizen content to the maximum."

5.3.3 Tensions and Contradictions

The tensions underlying both these strategies can be at least partially explained by the way journalists define themselves and their media product in relation to audiences. The mechanism may be similar to what Boczkowski (2004a: 175) identified as the "representation of the intended user" in US online newspapers in the late 1990s.

In shaping interactivity options at that time, journalists in his study thought of users as technically savvy or not, and as either primarily consumers or primarily producers of content. For example, *New York Times* developers thought of their online users as similar to the broad, general audience of the print newspaper. Seeing these users mainly as consumers at those early stages of online news development, the *Times* developed a technologically simple website with no space for user contributions.

In our study, the origin of the two distinct sets of UGC management highlighted in this section also may be rooted in the ways that journalists in different newsrooms imagined their audiences, stemming from relationships established when the only product was a print one. Many of the newspapers pursuing the development of separate spaces for users are elite products; those in the second group, which seemed more open to the idea of users as sources, are generally less traditional news organizations or even more populist in nature.

Elite newspapers see their role as constructing news narratives for the record; the work of professionals at these outlets is regarded especially highly. This self-perception creates a context in which there is little room for a dialogical news-production relationship with the audience. More popular newspapers, on the contrary, define themselves more overtly as reflecting the interests and preoccupations of the public.

These two different rationales resonated in the strategies of the newspapers that were among those in our study most heavily involved in developing user participation options. Other newspapers may fit into these categories, as well, but their initiatives at the time of our interviews were still too hesitant or too few in number for us to draw any conclusions. If our categorizations do hold up as more newspapers become involved in extensive participatory journalism efforts, however, it may be possible to predict how participatory management strategies will evolve at different news outlets.

5.4 Best Practices: Reporters' Involvement in Management

In both the "playground" and "source" conceptualizations of user contributions, and to an even greater extent in online newspapers with fewer participation features, newsroom managers sought to protect journalists from actual hands-on management of most user input. They generally did this by outsourcing the oversight responsibilities, by setting up a dedicated participation unit (which might be as small as a single person) or by limiting the involvement of reporters to specific tasks.

For instance, reporters might be urged to develop stories out of user tips but not asked to do the initial work of sorting the newsworthy tips from all those received every day. Interviewees repeatedly referred to journalists' resistance to active engagement with user-generated content. "News editors have been asked to read the discussions about their areas, but in reality no one has time for that," said an online journalist at *Helsingin Sanomat* (Finland).

Nonetheless, as highlighted earlier, there were several ways in which journalists whose main responsibilities involved producing news also ended up assuming audience participation management tasks or at least being exposed to user material – often with very positive outcomes, according to the interviewees.

5.4.1 Highlighting User Contributions

Many online newspapers systematically selected what journalists considered worthy user contributions for prominent posting on the website or in the print newspaper. In doing so, they enhanced the visibility of these contributions, created a motivation for user participation and provided an incentive for high-quality input.

Eight of the newspapers in our study also included content from users in the print product. Typically, online editors were the ones who selected the content, such as comments or photos, and print editors made the final decisions about what to include and how to play it.

In other cases, the website homepage was the final destination, with citizen items or blog posts featured there if online editors considered them worthy. For example, *Haaretz* (Israel) regularly featured several user blog posts and discussion threads each day.

5.4.2 Curation and Coaching

The concept of curation as an alternative to moderation was regarded as a fruitful evolution by those community managers who were exploring or considering it. In curating content, the journalist concentrated on highlighting the best instead of deleting the worst, and our interviewees saw this approach as boosting the effectiveness of participatory journalism management.

For example, *USA Today* applied the philosophy of curation in its topical communities, such as the one on cruises. Similarly, the *Guardian* (UK) used it in the "Been There" section for travel photos and tips. "That's not something you have to moderate so tightly," explained an online manager at the *Guardian*. "The curation model is one we're really keen to move towards for a lot of stuff. Actually, quite a lot of filtering happens almost automatically. You're promoting the very best."

The risk of losing control over the quality of contributions with this more open approach could be minimized through closer relationships between reporters and citizens, interviewees said. Examples from our study included the use of local citizen reporters in Belgium, as well as contributors to LePost.fr in France, who are patiently coached by journalists, as described earlier.

Other sites – including *Focus* (Germany) and both British newspaper in our study – also took this approach in comment moderation, with the goal of helping users improve their contributions. "We're trying to do more positive moderation, if you like, so engaging with them rather than just shooting down things we don't want," explained a community manager at the *Telegraph* (UK). The *Washington Post* (USA) also involved journalists in citizen debates through its long-standing discussion boards led by experts.

5.4.3 Systematic Oversight and Direct Interaction

We have already presented the two main ways for journalists to become exposed to users' ideas: through calls for news material and tips, and through comment management or oversight. In both cases, structural arrangements that provide a systematic way to deal with user input had been designed to enhance the quantity and quality of the contributions, thus seeking to ensure a more effective use of citizens as sources.

At *20 Minutos* (Spain), for instance, journalists gave technological innovations a lot of credit for improved workflow efficiency, and they were committed to continued improvement of the tools. Interviewees there were very proud of the management strategy of a centralized newsroom database for user contributions, which enabled content to be sorted and distributed to the appropriate journalists or participation spaces.

Print journalists in some newsrooms had additional spaces in which to experience direct interaction with the audience. Examples included **collective interviews**, in which journalists served as experts responding to the questions of motivated users who connect to a chat at a scheduled time, and the increasingly popular **journalist blogs**, with writers typically encouraged to engage in discussions with commenters.

More broadly, journalists were being encouraged to monitor what users said about their stories. "Rather than having audience specialists, we consider that a journalist working on a certain beat should read the reactions to have feedback on the editorial content," explained the online editor of *Le Monde* (France).

5.4.4 Newsroom Evangelization

In some newsrooms, the person or team in charge of audience participation management had an additional crucial task: to evangelize the newsroom into a dialogical attitude toward users.

At *Le Monde*, for example, comment moderation was outsourced, but three community managers helped foster interactions among users and journalists. Similarly, at the *Telegraph* (UK), the community managers were active in helping journalists develop good strategies for user interaction. And at *USA Today*, a community manager communicated across the newsroom any successful participation initiative of a given section.

5.5. Best Practices: Users' Involvement in Management

When we conducted our interviews, user participation in managing their own contributions to these newspaper websites was limited, although there has since been increasing use of recommendation tools and other **reputation systems**. However, a growing number of newspapers at the time of our study did enable, and even encourage, users to flag problematic comments or other audience contributions – though as a *Telegraph* (UK) community manager said, users tend to have "very subjective views about what's allowed and what isn't."

That said, many interviewees not only were comfortable having users reporting abuse, particularly in comments, but also appreciated their help. The community manager at the *Washington Post* (USA) said it was "absolutely critical to get users involved in moderating and rating comments," and an editor at the *Guardian* (UK) agreed that user assistance was vital in order to "keep the standards of debate high." An online editor at *USA Today* explained:

> There are things that can be quite inappropriate without being profane, and that's where we rely on the community to police itself. And sometimes you'll get comments that are borderline abusive, and someone will come in and say "you're over the top here," and then the conversation levels off. But we rely on them to report that so we can remove them as soon as possible.

5.5.1 Voting

At the time of our study, five online newspapers allowed registered users to vote on the comments made by other users. That is a less aggressive option than allowing them to delete others' contributions, and it helps in sorting out the best content.

"This is a very interesting and important option," said an online editor at *20 Minutos* (Spain). "We need to tend toward this self-regulation of users by other users, because it is the more logical thing to do. It is them, in the end, who know what they want, what information is more useful and what is less, and what bothers them."

This strategy of having users essentially vote on their own contributions was also applied to many of the non-news sections where journalistic oversight was less systematic, such as the travel section of the *Guardian* (UK) or the historical narratives of *Focus* (Germany). In Israel, *Haaretz* editors relied on user recommendations of blog posts at The Marker Café, their blogs community, to help them identify the best posts to be promoted to the homepage of the online newspaper.

5.5.2 Moderation

Only in long-standing online forums had user moderation been fully developed – but these forums were rarely if ever included in journalists' routines, as newsroom resources were being devoted to comments and other more newly created participation features. For example, forums in *Focus* (Germany) and the *Guardian* (UK) were largely ignored by the newsroom; they relied on veteran users to post-moderate abuse.

Among the newspapers in our study, the *Telegraph* (UK) was an innovator in actively seeking to encourage user moderation and feedback on the website's user-generated content policies, "trying to help them to help us moderate." However, their experience suggested that many users feel uncomfortable with managing the participation of other audience members, as a *Telegraph* community manager explained:

> Maybe the solution is to have them moderating their own blogs a bit more, so they could at least remove comments on their own blog, but then I think they would upset each other by taking, you know, if somebody took a comment down on somebody's thread, it would very quickly inflame it. ... So you want them to have as much ownership as possible, but equally, you don't want these spats that break out and then run and run. And we have a few people who report content by a particular blogger because they don't like that blogger, so every time they post anything, they hit the 'report' button. And that of course takes time for us to look into, but if they took it off every time, then we'd really have problems. So it's very difficult!

5.6 Conclusion

The extremely rich diversity in UGC management solutions of the online newspapers in our study is hard to capture and summarize, but this chapter has tried to highlight diverse examples to suggest that there are no universal audience participation practices, workflows or strategies. This finding is consistent with research on innovation in newsrooms (and technological innovation in general). New developments are shaped by local actors and their circumstances, which in turn are part of the historical practices of a given news organization (Weiss and Domingo 2010; Boczkowski 2004a, 2004b; Lemonnier 1993).

Nevertheless, there were commonalities in the management of some user contributions, such as news tips and material that journalists perceive as newsworthy. Our study also identified two general models that online newspapers were using to deal with participatory journalism.

Many outlets that consider themselves their country's "newspaper of record" were creating "playgrounds," generally very loosely moderated, as safe places to test out options for user input. Such separate places helped protect the overall newspaper brand, as well as newsroom routines designed to preserve the integrity of that brand, from the interference of user-generated content.

Other newspapers, including some of the less traditional or more "populist" ones in our study, were more likely to embed user material in their news production practices. In particular, they were more open to the idea of user input as a potentially valuable source for journalists' stories, and they tended to overtly acknowledge the positive contribution of the audience to their products.

Other researchers have connected such differences in participatory journalism approaches to the ways in which journalists imagine or "represent" their audiences in relation to the overall mission or identity of the newspaper itself. But competition within national media markets also may play a role, creating the sort of "mimicry" detected by Boczkowski (2009) in Argentinean media. Newsrooms try to keep up with the new developments of their direct rivals.

That could help explain why the two Spanish and two French newspapers outsourced comment moderation; why two Israeli online newspapers used identical labels for user news tips; or why the two competing media groups in Belgium had both developed local networks of citizen reporters.

Interviewees spoke openly and honestly when they were dissatisfied with management strategies they had designed. In many cases, they accepted that they were still searching for the best solution to meet their goals. But they also highlighted their victories and were proud of those strategies that worked well.

A reasonable way to boost the quality of contributions and their usefulness for journalists' production seems to involve spreading the responsibility for managing those contributions. Although many of our interviewees believed it was desirable for reporters to be more responsive and sensitive to user wishes and needs, they also recognized the risk of transforming this opportunity into a burden.

To avoid that happening, four strategies stood out:

1) Having a leader with the mission of coaching journalists in participation management and users in the creation of meaningful contributions.
2) Having systematic participation channels that are clear for the users, with specific newsroom roles designed to manage the input.
3) Shifting the focus from moderation to curation of user contributions, devoting more energy to highlighting the best content rather than hunting for the bad apples.
4) Involving the audience in UGC management, reinforcing the curation strategy but without eliminating the oversight by professional moderators or journalists.

The other big lesson in an examination of management strategies and processes is that active audiences appreciate it when journalists make the effort to blend user contributions with professional content. Doing so does seem to encourage users to improve the quality of their submissions.

Labeling the elements in a story that have been produced or suggested by a citizen also seems to be a good strategy, both to protect the brand of the newspaper and to acknowledge the important collaborative role that users can play in creating a better journalistic product.

Management strategies are not neutral. They actively and demonstrably shape the kind of content that online newsrooms get from their users, its relevance to the news and its overall quality. In the process of developing audience participation, newsrooms have lots of decisions to make, and they are continually adapting their strategies to find the most appropriate approaches.

The key to success is probably to thoroughly understand the aim in providing participation opportunities to the users – that is, to clearly define the motivations behind the strategy. Online newspapers actually get what they are looking for.

We turn next to a more intensive look at the issues raised here and in earlier chapters, with a chapter devoted to the most common user participation option we encountered: comments.

Participate!

1. What factors shaping management strategies for participatory journalism in the cases discussed here do you consider most important? Why?
2. What do you see as the pros and cons of the two models of UGC management – as playground and as source – for a user who is eager to share information about a social issue important in her community?
3. Think about the different ways UGC is managed in the different newsrooms described here. Which newsroom would you feel most comfortable working in if your job primarily involved reporting the news? Writing feature articles? Working with users?

References

Avilés, José Alberto, and Miguel Carvajal (2008) Integrated and cross-media newsroom convergence: Two models of multimedia news production – the cases of Novotécnica and La Verdad Multimedia in Spain, *Convergence* 14 (2): 221–239.

Boczkowski, Pablo J. (2004a) *Digitizing the news: Innovation in online newspapers*, Cambridge, Masssachusetts: MIT Press.

Boczkowski, Pablo J. (2004b) Books to think with, *New Media and Society* 6 (1): 144–150.

Boczkowski, Pablo J. (2009) "Materiality and mimicry in the journalism field." In: Zelizer, Barbie (ed.) *The changing faces of journalism: Tabloidization, technology and truthiness*, London and New York: Routledge.

Domingo, David (2008) Interactivity in the daily routines of online newsrooms: Dealing with an uncomfortable myth, *Journal of Computer-Mediated Communication* 13 (3): 680–704.

Lemonnier, Pierre (1993) *Technological choice: Transformations in material culture since the Neolithic*, London and New York: Routledge.

Manning, Paul (2001) *News and news sources: A critical introduction*, London: Sage.

Paterson, Chris, and David Domingo (2008) *Making online news: The ethnography of new media production*, New York: Peter Lang.

Schudson, Michael (2003) *The sociology of news*, New York: Norton.

Schudson, Michael (2000) "The sociology of news production revisited (again)." In: Curran, James, and Michael Gurevitch (eds.) *Mass media and society* (3rd edn.), London: Edward Arnold.

Silcock, B. William, and Susan Keith (2006) Translating the Tower of Babel? Issues of definition, language and culture in converged newsrooms, *Journalism Studies* 7 (4): 610–627.

Singer, Jane B. (2004) More than ink-stained wretches: The resocialization of print journalists in converged newsrooms, *Journalism & Mass Communication Quarterly* 81 (4): 838–856.

Tuchman, Gaye (2002) "The production of news." In: Jensen, Klaus A (ed.) *Handbook of media and communication research: Qualitative and quantitative methodologies*, London and New York: Routledge.

Weiss, Amy Schmitz, and David Domingo (2010) Innovation processes in online newsrooms as actor-networks and communities of practice, *New Media and Society* 12 (7): 1156–1171.

6

User Comments
The transformation
of participatory space
Zvi Reich

Once upon a time, when the only form of **user-generated content** was a letter to the editor, journalists were desperate for feedback. Publishing a news story without any feedback, as the historian Robert Darnton recalls in his brilliant journalistic retrospective – be it from peers, superiors, news sources, friends or even mom – could be "like dropping a stone in a bottomless pit: you wait and wait, but you never hear the splash" (Darnton 1975: 185).

Today, as the threads of user **comments** are spun instantly from almost every online news item, journalists can only yearn for the quiet old days when there were no splashes. Those comments create a variety of interesting ripples in the newsroom, and this chapter explores them in some detail. We use comments as a specific case study here, unlike in our other chapters that address **participatory journalism** more generically.

Why pay specific attention to comments from **users**? They are typically written by only a small fraction of the people who visit a news website, and it appears that only a minority of site visitors even read comments (see Bergström 2009; Tausig 2009). Moreover, they appear at the tail end of the news production process, at the **interpretation stage** after most if not all of the journalistic decisions have been made and tasks performed.

However, there are at least five major reasons for examining this form of participatory journalism:

Participatory Journalism: Guarding Open Gates at Online Newspapers, First Edition.
Jane B. Singer, Alfred Hermida, David Domingo, Ari Heinonen, Steve Paulussen, Thorsten Quandt, Zvi Reich, and Marina Vujnovic.
© 2011 Jane B. Singer, Alfred Hermida, David Domingo, Ari Heinonen, Steve Paulussen, Thorsten Quandt, Zvi Reich, and Marina Vujnovic. Published 2011 by Blackwell Publishing Ltd.

1. *The evolution of participatory spaces.*

   User comments represent a new stage in the evolution of user participation in media-provided spaces. The number of people wanting to make their voices heard is unprecedented; precursors to comments, such as letters to the editor or radio call-in programs, attracted far smaller percentages of the overall **audience**. Online user comments, which typically are not edited, open up a public forum for more informal, spontaneous, and even aggressive and impulsive authorship, most of it by people who hide behind the anonymity of assumed screen names.

   In addition, media **gatekeepers** turned older participation channels into exclusive spaces: Only those citizens whom the gatekeepers decided were worth hearing were allowed a public voice. Comment threads, in contrast, are inclusive spaces; most comments that do not break explicit rules of participation are included. The former spaces were governed by journalistic logic, while user comments are governed by broader social standards such as considerations of decency, civility, taste and legality (Williams, Wardle and Wahl-Jorgensen 2009; Thurman 2008).

2. *The responsiveness of news.*

   Comment functions have been a product of trial and error. Media websites initially tried to steer users to more traditional channels, such as online letters to the editor, special "have your say" sections (which drew relatively little traffic), or opinion columns and **blogs** (Örnebring 2008; Thurman 2008).

   It took time and experimentation to arrive at the idea of comment threads, which have proved far more appropriate to the responsive nature of online news. The surprising success of story-specific comments indicates what was not clear before: The desire of people to express themselves is often topical and item-oriented. Despite the old anecdotal image of a reader so amazed by an item in the morning newspaper that he spits out his coffee in the middle of breakfast, most journalists seem to have been unprepared for the widespread desire among users to let off steam about specific pieces of information.

3. *The hybrid nature of online news.*

   Web designers usually separate user comments from journalistic content in one or more ways, such as by their physical placement on the page, their hierarchical relationship to news items or their typographical presentation. But in reality, the two types of content are inseparable. Online items without comments are becoming rare and starting to look awkward, even suspicious. For some users and some items, comments may be no less interesting and informative than the main journalistic texts to which they relate or respond.

4. *Their great popularity.*

   Comments were the most popular and widely used forms of participatory journalism among a majority of the websites in our study and in other studies, as well (Bakker and Pantti 2009; Singer and Ashman 2009; Örnebring 2008; Hermida and Thurman 2008). The tsunami of user comments surprised many of the journalists we interviewed.

The popularity of comments can highlight the characteristics of successful journalist-audience collaboration. For users, they offer the immediate satisfaction of getting published and having a part in the day's **agenda**, without demanding a lot of involvement or creativity to produce (Örnebring 2008); users posting a comment do not even have the burden of finding their own topic. From the journalists' perspective, comments can be ego-gratifying. Unlike other user contributions, comments leave the journalist in the traditional position of the lead singer, while audience members generally play the minor, faceless and reactive role of the chorus.

5. *The controversy they create.*

As we will see in this chapter and the next, user comments have proved to be quite controversial, not least within the newsrooms that enabled them. Areas of contention include their low quality, uncertain origins and frequently dubious contribution to the public discourse. Journalists also have expressed concerns about the malicious inclusion of profanity or even libel (Sayare 2009; Singer and Ashman 2009; Haner 2006).

Journalists in our study expressed varying degrees of support for comments. Their views can help us identify how open media practitioners are to the inclusion of non-journalistic voices and how eager they are to exploit new deliberative possibilities to enable those voices be heard. Such an exploration can also lay foundations for suitable editorial, ethical, legal and regulatory policies regarding this new form of *vox populi*.

Despite their many intriguing aspects, user comments are still in their infancy and have received only limited attention from scholars so far. Although there were early adopters in Israel and a few other countries as early as 2000, the comment phenomenon only began to be widespread in the second half of the decade. To take examples from the newspapers we studied, comments appeared in 2005 on the website of *Le Monde* and two years later on French rival *Le Figaro*, around the same time in the British press (Hermida and Thurman 2008) and, in 2008, at two of the Belgian newspapers in our study.

This chapter investigates how journalists at leading newspaper websites across different democracies perceived and managed user comments at the time of our study. Covering both attitudes and practices helps us see the match between what journalists said about comments and what they actually did, as well as understand the connections between individual and organizational factors.

But first, we need to step back and provide more context for looking at this phenomenon.

6.1 The Legacy of Participatory Media Spaces

Allocating journalistic space for citizen voices to be heard is not an obvious thing to do. Professions in general are mainly interested in unilateral communication, in which they do the talking while lay people mainly listen or reply to their queries.

Even in rhetorical contexts outside the realm of journalism, audiences generally are not given a substantial voice – if they have a voice at all (Zoran 2009; Levinson 1988; Goffman 1981). Except for limited cases, such as when they perform as members of a jury or bidders at an auction, audience opportunities for self-expression do not range much beyond applauding what they like and booing or heckling what they dislike.

6.1.1 Journalists and Citizen Voices

News people were never passionate about ordinary citizens' voices, neither as news sources (Dimitrova and Strömbäck 2009; Reich 2009; Gans 1979), nor as audiences whose characteristics, views and preferences matter in making editorial decisions (Gans 2009, 1979; Schudson 2003; Bogart 1991). Yet beyond their core role of observing and informing, journalists also are responsible for "providing a channel, forum or platform for extramedia voices" (Christians *et al.* 2009: 116). Journalists and the media organizations that employ them offer a public forum for audience opinion (Charity, 1995), "making readers count in the discussion of public questions" (Leonard 1999: 91).

This role incorporates the notion of communication as a ritual "directed not toward the extension of messages in space but toward the maintenance of society in time, not the act of imparting information but the representation of shared beliefs" (Carey 1989: 18). "In a ritual definition, communication is linked to terms such as 'sharing,' 'participation,' 'association,' 'fellowship' and 'the possession of common faith.'"

As a practical matter, journalists always have preferred their audiences "imagined" (Reader 2007; Wahl-Jorgensen 2002; Anderson 1983; Goffman 1981). Public voices have largely been confined to the post-publication interpretative stage described in Chapter 2 and to "symbolic participatory spaces," such as the letters to the editor and studio call-in programs mentioned above. These spaces belong to the public only symbolically, since they typically display just a tiny selection of audience voices – and even those are constrained by rules laid down by the journalists who remain in control.

Letters to the editor, for example, are chosen for publication according to criteria similar to those used to select news sources for a story (Ericson, Baranek and Chan 1989), with every letter assessed for relevance, entertainment, brevity and authority (Wahl-Jorgensen 2002). Other positive criteria include fairness, newsworthiness, humor, novelty and quality of the argument; letters that correct an error made by the newspaper are likely to be published, as well.

Criteria for deciding not to publish a letter also are basically journalistic ones. For example, editors reject letters judged to be incomprehensible, stylistically poor, untrue or unfair, among other problems. Letter-writers seen as being too emotional or, at the other end of the spectrum, too theoretical also are denied publication. And someone who writes frequently would be less, not more, likely to have his or her letter appear in the print newspaper (Ericson, Baranek and Chan 1989).

In fact, many of the issues that seem to have arisen when newspaper websites opened their articles to user comments actually were issues in earlier participatory media spaces. These issues include the overall quality of audience input; the application of journalistic standards in managing that input; the use of anonymous, fake and orchestrated contributions; the motivations of contributors; and the degree to which contributors represent the overall audience (Richardson and Franklin 2004; Wahl-Jorgensen 2002; Hollander 1996; Herbst 1995; Rothenberg 1946).

Media organizations had mixed motives for providing older participation spaces, just as they did for enabling newer ones, such as comments spaces. In the older spaces, they wanted to encourage public debate and foster a sense of a community, but they also were very interested in attracting audiences, boosting their revenue, and fortifying their social and political legitimacy (Reader 2007; Wahl-Jorgensen 2001; Herbst 1995; Ericson, Baranek and Chan 1989). We return to these themes in Chapter 8.

6.1.2 Thinking About Comments

Most of the scholarly research related to the still-new phenomenon of comments also discusses other forms of user-generated content or participatory journalism (Hermida and Thurman 2008; Örnebring 2008; Thurman 2008). There are five approaches to the topic.

- First, analysis can focus on the rhetorical aspects of an item, or the way it is framed, in an effort to identify what will evoke more or fewer comments (Kabalyon 2009; Abdul-Mageed 2008; Kohn and Neiger 2007; Melamed 2006).
- A second approach concerns the people behind the comments – both readers and writers – and their characteristics (Bergström 2009; Tausig 2009).
- The ethical issues raised by comments are a third area of interest (Singer and Ashman 2009; Kim and Her 2008).
- The fourth perspective focuses on the evolution of comments (Thurman and Hermida 2010; Hermida and Thurman 2008).
- And a fifth, suggested by the current study, explores the perception of comments among journalists, including their management procedures.

One promising framework for understanding all these aspects is rhetorical theory, which emphasizes the spontaneous or "oral" nature of comments (Kohn and Neiger 2007; Kogen 2005). We use another rhetorical framework here: Goffman's (1981) model of "production format roles."

Goffman's model considers three entities involved in the production of utterances: the "author" who originates the text, the "animator" who decides whether

Table 6.1 This table shows the different roles played in creating three kinds of content.

Production format role	News story[a]	Letter to the editor[a]	User comment
Author	Reporter	Reader	User
Animator	Copy or sub editor/ news staff	Copy or sub editor/ news staff	Journalistic moderator or user
Principal	Editor	Reader	Editor or user

[a]The first two columns are suggested by Scollon (1998: 199), based on Goffman (1981).

and how to play the author's texts, and the "principal" who takes social (though not necessarily legal) responsibility for the whole utterance. The model has helped researchers explore letters to the editor (Scollon 1998), and we take it one step further to look at comments.

Table 6.1 shows how Goffman's ideas can be applied here.

As our table shows, the *author* role moves outside the newsroom with letters to the editor and remains an external role with user comments. Essentially, only what we call the author – a "reader" or a "user" – has changed.

In a traditional environment, any input designated for publication in journalistic spaces – including material that originates outside the newsroom – is the exclusive jurisdiction of editors, who in their role as *animators* select and edit it. Research suggests many journalists think this animation role should be extended to cover user comments, as well (Singer 2010). However, an open network, with its unlimited space and empowered users, enables the role to be more widely shared (Amichai-Hamburger, McKenna and Samuel-Azran 2008).

The *principal* is the person or entity with responsibility for the content. According to Scollon (1998: 199), the principal of the news item is the news organization that "sponsored the text to appear within its editorial spaces." The principal of a letter to the editor, for example, is the newspaper reader who signed it. The news item carries a journalist's byline; the letter carries a signature.

Comments, on the other hand, are likely to carry a pseudonymous screen name, making the responsible party harder to identify or trace. This results in a combination that is intolerable in news organizations: an "author" without the responsibilities that go along with authorship. Changing this situation would involve assigning responsibility to someone, either members of the audience or a newsroom designee – for example, as various organizations in our study have determined, a reporter, an editor or a **moderator**.

At the time of our interviews in late 2007 and early 2008, only one of the newspapers in our study – *Het Nieuwsblad* in Belgium – did not enable comments on stories. Users wanting to express an opinion about *Het Nieuwsblad* stories could use the website's **forum** section – where discussions were **premoderated** by the same editor responsible for letters to the editor.

All the other organizations in our study allowed user comments but kept them clearly separated from the stories themselves, using graphic, typographic and placement cues.

Three distinct placement options signalled different degrees of journalistic distance from user comments. A little more than half the newspapers used "integral placement" of the comments, typically beneath the news item. The rest employed one of two techniques to distance themselves from comments. Six papers used "separate placement," in which comments and news items are placed in different spaces. And five used "selective placement," in which a few selected comments (or their headlines) are displayed beneath the story but the rest have to be accessed separately.

These placement decisions may provide clues to journalists' attitudes toward user comments. In the next section, we look at those attitudes.

6.2 Journalists' Attitudes

Comments pose less of a challenge to journalists' self-perceptions than some other forms of participatory journalism. As we have seen in earlier chapters, commenters remain essentially audiences for journalistic work rather than more threatening co-producers of content.

Nonetheless, most of our interviewees were ambivalent about comments, acknowledging upsides but also describing downsides. Particular individuals, of course, were more (or less) positive than others.

Those with relatively favorable views tended to highlight the potential contribution of comments to journalism or to the public discourse. Interviewees from the British and American newspapers were especially likely to portray user comments as vehicles for accomplishing deliberative ideals, particularly engaging the audience in discussion of public issues.

Those whose views were relatively unfavorable focused principally on the actual nature of user input, often citing as examples the worst of the contributions – and, not uncommonly, the work needed to deal with them.

At nine of the 25 news organizations in our study, at least one interviewee highlighted the benefits of comments. One such benefit was the diversity of views that comments represent. For example, an editor at the *Guardian* (UK) explained: "We are a liberal voice. We believe in diversity of opinion. We want lots of voices to be heard. That's precisely what we can do [*through opening up items to user comment*]. We can make lots of voices, including ones we don't agree with, heard. I think that's a central plank of the liberal thought."

However, another *Guardian* editor expressed reservations. "You're dealing with the interests of a group of obsessives, really," he said. "Most people don't want to comment. And actually, most people don't want to read other people's comments."

6.2.1 Perceived Problems

In general, the view that comments were at least somewhat problematic found broader support among our interviewees. People who write comments "just prattle on, babble on at everybody," said a *Globe and Mail* (Canada) editor. "Mostly the comments you get on individual stories on the website are not terribly well-thought through or just vitriolic. … Very few of them make intelligent comments or have intelligent things to say. It's very deceiving, because it essentially makes you look like your readers are idiots, to be quite honest." Despite this criticism, *The Globe and Mail* website at the time of our study allocated unusually prominent space to user comments, displaying them parallel to newsroom-generated material in the page hierarchy.

Many interviewees supported use of comments as long as their quality was tightly controlled, minimizing risks to the organization's reputation. This view was expressed by journalists at *De Standaard* (Belgium), *Focus* and *Der Spiegel* (both Germany), the Israeli websites and the French ones, among others.

"It's true that for now on Figaro.fr, we don't yet exploit comments enough," said an editor at that French paper. "But then again, there's 180 years of tradition at *Le Figaro*. The seriousness of the newspaper shouldn't be hindered by unbridled comments."

Some journalists at much less long-standing news organizations also expressed a similar view. "The tone of your paper can really suffer from reader comments," said an editor at the *National Post* (Canada), a newspaper founded in 1998. In Germany, an editor at *Focus*, which was founded in the early 1990s, said comments were comparable to letters to the editor; he added that users looking for a more freewheeling conversation could go instead to the website's discussion forums.

Some journalists described comments as a necessary evil. Comments, they felt, were necessary to attract audiences and thus survive financially. But comments also were evil because their standards of expression were seen as intolerable.

In fact, as we explore in more detail in the following chapter, many of our interviewees said the greatest challenge posed by comments stemmed from their low quality: Comments not infrequently contain defamation, incitement, abusive content, and even racism and hate speech.

The quality issues also have a commercial side effect, journalists said. Other users can be put off, and the organization's reputation and perceived legitimacy can be damaged. "One comment like that," suggested a *Washington Post* (USA) editor, "can cast a negative image on 50 others that are legitimate commentary."

"If it's very negative, nasty commentary" said an editor at the *Guardian* (UK), "you do think, 'why would people be coming back?'" An editor at the *National Post* (Canada) went further: "It sounds almost blasphemous for me to say it, but I wouldn't be unhappy to see comments disappear from a lot of newspaper sites. I don't think they add too much to it."

Some interviewees suggested specific reasons related to national culture for the abrasive tone of comments. For example, research has shown that a straightforward and even aggressive tone is part of the discourse ethos in Israel (Kohn and Neiger 2007), and the French are renowned for what one *Figaro* editor termed a national "taste for debate."

However, psychologists who study online behavior suggest a more universal explanation. They propose that the anonymity of the online user creates a "disinhibition effect," causing "a reduced sense of responsibility and less pressure to conform to societal norms" (McKenna and Green 2002). Many of our interviewees concurred.

"Writing under pen names" lowers both the "intellectual level" of comments and user responsibility for them, said an editor at *Helsingin Sanomat* (Finland). At *El País* (Spain), an interviewee said comments can enrich a story "if they come from people with substantive opinions, but they are not the most abundant. Then you find the extremists and those who use the anonymity that the net allows, and they sadly outnumber the former."

However, an editor at Ynet (Israel) pointed out that anonymity has its advantages: "There will always be people who wish to remain anonymous since they want to report something they do not wish others to know they have reported."

6.2.2 On the Plus Side

Other interviewees gave more prominence to the benefits of comments. The most commonly cited upside, mentioned even by those who perceived comments as primarily a necessary evil, was their commercial value. Comments help increase traffic to the website and strengthen loyalty to the brand, as we explore further in Chapter 8.

An editor at *Der Spiegel* (Germany) said the organization was "certainly using the possibilities of the Internet for attracting adolescents to the brand," adding: "Needless to say that we make a pile of money, but initially the idea has been to tie … people to the brand."

Another commercial motivation for using comments was their ability to serve as an additional ratings system, or at least as proof that a story resonates with audience members. Journalists "appreciate people commenting a lot on their stories," said an editor at *El País* (Spain). "'I have 300 comments,' you hear them say." Receiving critical comments is not the worst thing that can happen to a journalist, said an editor at the *Guardian* (UK): "The worst thing that can happen to a journalist is they're ignored."

At the time of our study, fewer than half the websites of these leading national newspapers highlighted the total number of comments associated with a given story, perhaps suggesting that journalists saw such information as of more value inside the newsroom than to other users.

Another value of user comments stemmed from their ability to help journalists detect sources, story ideas and material, and leads to be followed up, as discussed in Chapter 3. However, as we already have seen, not all interviewees agreed about their news value.

"In many stories, quality information in comments is zero," said an editor at *El País* (Spain). "To some extent we're going fishing," said a *USA Today* editor. Journalists, he said, look for "some comments that lend themselves to an informed dialogue that we can either pull out and highlight in a story or use it for a later story."

Of course, such practices predate the Internet, as an editor at *Le Monde* (France) pointed out. "To seek more sources of information in the audience or opening a debate in the wake of news, that's still doing fundamental activities of journalists' work," he said. It involves "using new tools, on a new media, with a new relationship to the audience. But it's still answering to traditional and fundamental missions of the journalistic job that have already existed. It's simply new ways of doing it."

Comments also may serve as a source of information about users and their preferences, both critical and positive, giving journalists additional tools for making and assessing editorial decisions.

Comments can confirm that the website is doing a good job, showing that people "care about articles and the newspaper as a whole," explained an editor at *24 Hours* (Croatia). Comments "are a good instrument for testing the gut feeling of the journalist," said an editor at *FAZ* (Germany). An emotional topic or controversial topic, one that "animates" people to discuss it, can receive validation through the extent of user engagement.

Comments, which typically are attached to specific stories, also are useful in helping journalists identify errors and typos; in general, they can help improve accuracy, particularly with topics that require distinctive expertise. A beat journalist "should read the reactions to have feedback on the editorial content, perhaps to get new ideas from users, especially because our subscribers have some expertise on a variety of domains but also to have a sense of which areas engage the audience in the most vivid debates," said an editor at *Le Monde* (France).

Similarly, an editor at *USA Today* emphasized the human capital provided by readers: "If someone mentions in passing that they have expertise in a certain area, or are living in a certain place or in a certain situation – if you can re-aggregate all the people who have that same thing in common at a different point in time for a different story, there may be value there to come back to them."

A small subset of interviewees suggested one of the most interesting upsides of comments: their potential as a deliberative forum. New technologies afford new opportunities for journalists to fulfill long-standing aspirations, as a *Telegraph* (UK) **community manager** explained:

> News has always been a conversation. But we were never able to take part in the conversation before. And so it happened without us. Suddenly there's this realization that, 'Wow, we can actually talk to these people now! And

they can talk to us! And this is great!' We've been trying to stimulate debate, we've been trying to get people to have conversations around the breakfast table and in the pub and in the office, and now we can take part.

Journalists are indeed a part of this debate, particularly in the role of negotiator. "If you are able to create a forum space and bring together specialists and users debating about actual and crucial topics," said an editor at *FAZ* (Germany), "you really can create a platform. That's an expression of democracy, and in my view is bringing forward society."

However, some journalists see comments as a separate territory inside the one that they create. "We have a discussion policy that [*states*] that this is the user's area," said an interviewee from the *Washington Post* (USA). "We don't say that certain topics are off limits, or we don't remove a comment if we think it's wrong or we disagree with it, even if it's critical of our reporting. It belongs to users."

Journalists, then, have a range of diverse attitudes about user comments. In the next section, we look at how they actually handle those comments.

6.3 Comment Management Strategies

How open are the gates of online news organizations to user comments? One way to begin to answer that question is to look at how open they were to earlier forms of user input.

6.3.1 Rejection Rates and Reasons

A review of earlier research suggests journalistic gatekeepers dismissed far more contributions in the past. The Internet is inherently a more open and less selective medium. Leading national newspapers such as those studied here, for example, published between five and 50 percent of letters to the editor (Wahl-Jorgensen 2002; Ericson, Baranek and Chan 1989). Radio call-in programs aired fewer than a third of the calls they received (Aucoin 1997; Hapogian 1993; Times Mirror Center 1993).

In our study, not all interviewees provided an estimate of how many comments were rejected. Among those that did, the *Guardian* (UK) and the *Washington Post* (USA) let the greatest proportion of comments through; journalists at those papers estimated that fewer than ten percent were rejected. Journalists at *Der Spiegel* (Germany) said 80 to 90 percent of the comments the newspaper received were posted, while interviewees at *20 Minutos* (Spain) estimated a publication rate of 70 to 75 percent.

Comments were more likely to be rejected at *Focus* (Germany) and the Israeli publications Ynet and NRG, but even the most restrictive of those still published at least 40 percent of its user comments, interviewees said.

These rates are affected by a variety of factors, including story topics, management strategies, political climate, journalistic culture, and prevailing newsroom norms and standards – as well as the standards set by the comments that *are* published.

Of these, story topic appears to be a primary factor. Comments with the highest dismissal rates tend to be associated with stories about sensitive issues such as religion, ethnic tension and conflicts, particularly the conflict between Israelis and Palestinians.

Such topics attract impassioned and often aggressive discourse, some of which crosses the line into hate speech. One explanation for the relatively high rejection rate for comments on the Israeli websites is the prevalence of problematic topics in the news that the country's journalists must cover. As an editor at Ynet said, comments depicting all Arabs as murderers are simply not going to be published.

As discussed further in the next chapter, other normative issues also come into play when journalists decide whether a comment should be published or deleted. For instance, the principle of separating commercial and editorial messages leads journalists to reject comments that are clearly intended to promote a product or service. The principle of even-handed political coverage means comments instigated by political parties will similarly be barred.

6.4 Giving Comments the Green Light

Again, though, our interviews suggest that a majority of comments received were published at most of the newspapers in our study. This increased openness, especially in comparison with participatory forms in more traditional media outlets, indicates a shift in journalists' gatekeeping strategy. That shift has three interconnected dimensions:

- The strategy for gatekeeping comments shifted from exclusion as a default to inclusion as a default.
- The specific criteria for assessing comments were transformed from positive to negative ones. That is, comments were dismissed because they violated rules rather than published because they were notably "worthy." As discussed further in Chapter 7, racism is a common violation. Others include both ethical problems, such as sexism and abusive comments, and legal ones, such as sedition, defamation and invasions of privacy.
- The criteria for assessment also shifted from journalistic ones, such as perceived interest value, to non-journalistic ones, such as a desire to build traffic.

To protect their websites from abusive comments, journalists at the websites in our study employed variable sets of practices. Comment management was shaped primarily by two important, and typically interrelated, decisions: whether submissions were moderated before or after publication, and whether users had to register in order to comment. The identification requirements for users, the types of moderators used and, again, the sensitivity of the topic also were key factors.

6.4.1 Moderation

News organizations that used pre-moderation tried to assess – or control – every comment before it was published. Journalists taking this proactive approach basically followed the logic of traditional participatory spaces, even though moderation typically carries extremely high financial and editorial resource costs.

On the other hand, **post-moderation**, or moderation after a comment already had been published, was a more relaxed and open approach. It was reactive rather than proactive. Users' comments could be published freely, but journalists would intervene if there were a reason to do so, such as a complaint about a specific comment or a particularly sensitive item. Serial violation of the terms of participation provided by the website also resulted in comments from a particular user being blocked or deleted.

Many of the websites used pre-moderation for most or all of their comments at the time of our study. The newspapers opting for post-moderation included all four of those in North America (the *Washington Post* and *USA Today* in the United States, and *The Globe and Mail* and *National Post* in Canada), along with *Het Belang van Limburg* (Belgium), *20 Minutos* (Spain) and the *Guardian* (UK).

The complexity of making moderation choices was well illustrated by the German websites in our study. These websites insisted on pre-moderation, not only because of their legal liability for published comments but also because of their cultural and political sensitivity to comments related to Nazis.

German interviewees said they were reluctant to limit pre-moderation to sensitive topics, explaining that problematic comments were submitted regularly even for stories completely unrelated to politics or historically sensitive issues. Community editors cited "trolls" who tried to circumvent moderation and deliberately add comments that violate the rules.

However, some news organizations in stereotypically more permissive national cultures also had opted for pre-moderation. Pre-moderation is "quite an innovative strategy, and it demands a big effort. But we try to keep it because we are really convinced that posted comments under the elpaís.com brand are our responsibility," said an editor at *El País* (Spain). "We need to filter comments. We can't publish anything we get."

An editor at the *Washington Post* (USA), on the other hand, believed that pre-moderation distorts the public discourse. "I don't think it works to pre-screen comments," he said. "You don't get enough comments to make the conversation worthwhile. I think it's possible to get comments and then get rid of the bad ones and still have a good conversation. I don't think you can do the opposite."

Interestingly, some of the post-moderating organizations – including larger ones, such as the two U.S. newspapers and the UK's *Guardian* – initially had tried pre-moderation. However, journalists said, they quickly realized they could not cope with the volume, which at the time of the study amounted to tens of thousands of comments every day (Hermida and Thurman 2008; Tsoref 2006). The opposite shift (from post- to pre-moderation) was much more rare, although *Kaleva* (Finland) did go that route.

USA Today, for example, had switched from pre-moderation to post-moderation shortly before our visit. "When you're getting one comment every 'x' seconds instead of 'x' minutes or 'x' hours, we have to be able to scale," an editor there said. Before the change, "we read every single comment we posted. I probably read about 40,000 comments for On Deadline and probably hit the publish button for every single one of them. It was an experience."

He said the solution combined "collaborative moderation," with both users and journalists reporting abusive comments; incorporation of user **registration**; and "smart, up-front filters" to encourage as many people as possible to get involved while still keeping quality at "an acceptable level."

At the *Guardian* (UK), which made a similar move away from pre-moderation, an editor said the change had paid off "in terms of numbers going through. I think that's what probably stifles debate most on a lot of other [*websites*]. You can't really beat hitting 'submit' and seeing your comment there before you go away. It encourages you to come back. You feel you've engaged."

6.4.2 Registration

At the time of our study, post-moderation strategies were nearly always accompanied by mandatory prior registration. Users had to submit their personal details in order to be accredited as commenters.

If anonymity has what academics call a "disinhibition effect," registration goes a long way to counter it, our interviewees said – in essence creating what might be termed a "reinhibition effect."

"The first step is registration," said a *USA Today* editor. "I have to give some information. I'm not going to do that if I'm just going to screw around. And then if you choose to do that, screw around, there's the profanity filter." An editor at the *National Post* (Canada) bluntly described registration as a barrier for "crazy commenting."

However, registration is not without its costs. Although registration reduces moderation time and thus expense, it also reduces the size of the participation community. Some people will be deterred by the need to register and will decide not to comment at all.

"We are having another interesting internal debate, in fact a permanent debate: Whether it is convenient or not to require users to register in order to comment on news stories," said an editor at *20 Minutos* (Spain). "We have been very open until now, we have let them say whatever they wanted, even nonsense! I think we will evolve in forthcoming months [*to more structured comment management*]. But I still don't know which will be the strategy."

The reaction to commenters who violate the rules despite the registration is typically instigated not by journalists but rather by other users, who press a "**report abuse**" button to alert the moderation team. A *Telegraph* (UK) community manager said this approach worked pretty well. "There's far too much for us to read. So we don't read it. We rely on them [*users*] to read it and police it for us, which they're very good at. They're very happy to tell us when they don't like something, and when they're quiet, we know that they're happy," he said. "That model probably is going to be used increasingly across the site."

The other British newspaper in our study, the *Guardian*, employed an additional strategy. Moderators kept an eye on users with abusive track records, using special procedures for these "risky" people suspected of sending spam, trolling or posting abuse. Their comments were pre-moderated or even blocked, temporarily or permanently, even though most submissions were simply post-moderated. Abusers could be "reinstated" if, after a suitable amount of time, the moderation team became convinced they would "contribute reasonably and sociably to the conversation in the future" (guardian.co.uk, 2009). In such cases, then, the *Guardian* monitored the people commenting, instead of the comments posted. By paying close attention to people who violate the rules, the newspaper sought to encourage and increase self-control.

Some newspapers at the time of our study were exploring a middle ground between required registration and none at all: voluntary or "light" registration. Typically, users who register voluntarily are then offered an assortment of privileges. These include double-long comments (*Focus*, Germany), un-moderated posts (*Telegraph*, UK), an aggregation of previous posts by the individual user (Ynet, Israel, and *USA Today*) and the ability to vote for or against others' comments (*Gazet van Antwerpen*, Belgium; *The Globe and Mail*, Canada; and *20 Minutos*, Spain).

An additional benefit of this last perk, a *Gazet* editor said, is that it provides an incentive for higher-quality comments: "The reactions will be ranked in an hierarchical order with the best comments on top."

6.4.3 Identification

Although journalists tended to say that users identify themselves when they register, websites typically required no more than a valid email address. The real identity of the commenter generally remained unexamined.

An editor at *USA Today* said websites cannot do more. Ensuring that a person is who he or she claims to be "is almost impossible, and it would take a number of resources to go in and verify that. You're always exposed to that risk of that person not being real anyway," he said. "The other issue is that if you require [*the use of real names*], you're going to reduce your community greatly."

Many online users choose screen names or pseudonyms, and they often are quite colorful. "We often get 'Zorro' and other 'cowboys' posting their reactions," said an editor at *Gazet van Antwerpen* (Belgium). An editor at the *National Post* (Canada) was bothered by the asymmetry between users and accountable journalists. Reporters' bylines are their real names, "whereas bob23bc can throw out anything he wants to just to inflame the crowd."

To avoid this jungle of fake pen names, *FAZ* (Germany) asks its users to register under their real names, using a verifiable email address. The newspaper also "locks" the comments of users who do not provide precise names.

At Ynet (Israel), journalists have identified a technological solution to the anonymity problem. "We do not expose it, but during the filtering, we see the IP number in order to avoid [*situations, such as*] if I suddenly see 20 comments from the same user, and every time he signs with another name."

6.4.4 Moderators

Journalists served as moderators at most of these websites at the time of our study. Some newspapers used moderators who were not journalists, such as producers, administrative workers or dedicated moderation staffs; *Focus* (Germany) used both journalists and non-journalists, along with users. Other papers, such as those in France and Spain, outsourced their comment moderation altogether.

Regardless who does it, pre-moderation is a heavy burden. **Outsourcing** was one response. Another widely used practice involved the development of dedicated filtering software, which helps the human moderator detect (among other things) racist, profane and hate speech keywords, problems mentioned by journalists at many of these newspapers, as we'll see in the next chapter.

Perhaps the most interesting solution is enlisting users to monitor other users' commentary. This approach provides a rare case in which users are allowed into the **selection or filtering stage** of news production, as described in Chapter 2, bringing the websites that employ it closest to the idea of a public forum with minimal journalistic intervention.

This can be done on a basic level by inviting audience members to use "report abuse" buttons or to vote for or against comments, as mentioned above. "I think the community handles [*abusive comments*] often better than we do, as users themselves tell trolls to stop distorting the discussion," said a *USA Today* editor. "There are things that can be quite inappropriate without being profane, and that's where we rely on the community to police itself. And sometimes you'll get comments that are borderline abusive, and someone will come in and say 'you're over the top here,' and then the conversation levels off."

A more unusual but arguably more sophisticated way of involving users in moderation is to embed them in the website's moderation teams, as was done by *Focus* (Germany) and, at the time of our study, was being considered by the *Guardian* (UK). Such "super-users" can help the newspaper staff tend the garden, as a *Guardian* editor said in describing the idea. Subsequent to our interview, the *Guardian* invited audience members to apply for "community member" positions, working closely with editors to share the moderation duties.

Journalists at other newspapers were weighing similar approaches when we talked with them. "This is a very interesting and important option," said an editor at *20 Minutos* (Spain). "We need to tend towards this self-regulation of users by other users because it is the more logical thing to do. It is them, in the end, who know what do they want, what information is more useful and what is less, and what bothers them."

6.4.5 Sensitive Items

Abusive content can be predicted to appear in highly sensitive topics, as discussed above, and a number of the newspaper organizations at the time of our study employed specific gatekeeping arrangements for these items.

The most effective, yet extreme, remedy is total closure of the sensitive item for comments. A *USA Today* editor rejected this procedure, saying "There's never been one story we've shut comments off."

In contrast, an editor at *El País* (Spain) said online editors were sometimes asked "not to open a story for comments because we foresee people will fight over it." At *FAZ* (Germany), an editor said any item related to Islam created "big problems" and had to be censored to avoid potential lawsuits.

Some websites, including *USA Today* and the *Telegraph* (UK), gave sensitive items extra attention or added a second round of moderation rather than closing topics off completely. "When we're about to publish an article, we know we'll have to monitor it because it discusses religion, immigration," said an editor at *Le Figaro* (France). "Those are topics that can lead to polemic so we're very careful with them. So we add a second level of reading of the comments. The journalist who wrote the stories takes care of reading the comments. But we haven't had any major mishaps."

Several newspapers that generally post-moderated comments – including the British newspapers, Canada's *Globe and Mail* and at least one of the Belgian ones – switched to pre-moderation when sensitive topics were involved. "There are certainly some things where we know the issue's going to be quite contentious. So we want people to have the debate, but we know there's a possibility for them to go off the rails," said a community manager at the *Telegraph* (UK). "There are some stories that come up where you know that you're kind of setting a legal trap for yourself."

This solution is a creative complement to post-moderation, enabling newsrooms to minimize their intervention with the vast majority of comments and yet act responsibly with particular subject areas susceptible to causing trouble.

Journalists' attitudes about comments did not necessarily correspond with their moderation strategies. Some who were generally favorable toward comments still pre-moderated them. Some others who took a more negative view allowed comments to appear as soon as the user hit the "send" button. The explanation may be that attitudes are personal, while management strategies generally are set at the organizational level. It will be interesting to see how both attitudes and strategies evolve, as comments become a more mature phenomenon and are increasingly homogenized across diverse news organizations.

6.5 Conclusion

User comments mark a new stage in the evolution of participatory spaces, representing a dramatic change from more tightly controlled antecedents such as letters to the editor and studio call-in shows. No other forum has been so open, offering such an immediate and unedited access to any citizen wishing to express a view about specific news as it unfolds. Comments have become nearly ubiquitous on major newspaper websites, with comment threads woven beneath a large majority of items.

However, as our interviewees pointed out, comments are less thoughtful and more impulsive, shallow and aggressive than earlier forms of audience participation. More openness seems to produce a lower common denominator for expression (Aucoin 1997: 131).

Although journalists have expressed some ambivalence about the inclusion of audience voices, several also explicitly described them as having the potential to fulfill deliberative ideals in their democratic societies.

In order to handle comments, news websites have developed two main strategies. An interventionist strategy insists on pre-moderation of every comment despite the heavy financial and editorial tolls. Organizations employing this strategy sought direct control of user comments.

In contrast, other organizations used a relatively autonomous strategy of post-moderation; some of those newspapers had tried the former strategy but were overwhelmed by the flood of comments. This more hands-off strategy reflected more optimistic assumptions about the public and the ability to enhance accountability among commenters.

Some supporters of this second strategy additionally perceived comments as separate from the territory controlled by journalists. They saw these participatory spaces as belonging to their audience and hence sought to minimize their own involvement. They employed a combination of technology and regulations, including pre-registration and *ad hoc* post-moderation, to facilitate the ability of users who abided by the ground rules to comment without intervention.

Paradoxically, the journalists and organizations convinced of the need for intervention may find themselves on a slippery legal slope, as discussed in the following chapter. They are closer to becoming "principals" (Scollon 1998) with at least some responsibility for user comments, a potentially problematic position given the ambiguity surrounding the real identity of commenters who hide behind the anonymity that screen names afford.

We end this chapter with a forecast. We anticipate that the relatively autonomous model has a better chance to become dominant in the future. There are several reasons:

- Prior registration can effectively counterbalance some of the disinhibition effect created by online anonymity.
- This model is more in line with the attitudes held by journalists who are generally favorable toward comments and thus perhaps more likely to cultivate them in innovative ways.
- Post-moderation is much cheaper in terms of staffing, budget and editorial attention. It releases news organizations from the growing burden of pre-moderating an endless flow of comments around the clock, allowing them instead to focus on sensitive topics, on comments reported as abusive and on serial violators of participation rules.
- The more hands-off approach is more attuned to the inherently participatory nature of the Internet, in which audience members have access to spaces that go well beyond the merely symbolic participation options of more traditional media.
- Finally, the organizations that typically adopt pre-registration and post-moderation strategies tend to be large ones with strong reputations – large enough and strong enough to legitimize the strategies and enhance their appeal for smaller news outlets, at the time of our study, were still able to pre-moderate the relatively small number of comments they received. Among the organizations in our study that had changed their strategy over time, almost all shifted from pre-moderation to post-moderation rather than the other way around. This adjustment underscores the growing legitimacy of a more open, and not coincidentally less expensive, approach to participatory journalism.

This chapter has touched on many of the legal and ethical issues raised by participatory journalism. In the first of our Section III: Issues and Implications chapters that follow, we look at these concerns in more detail.

Participate!

1. In what ways do user comments mark an evolution of user participatory spaces compared to letters to the editor and studio call-in programs?

2. To what extent do the different attitudes among journalists and the different management strategies employed by their websites show openness to users' voices? Do both attitudes and strategies work together, or are they at cross-purposes?
3. Where is the appropriate balance between the website's right to select proper comments and the public's right to comment without interference?
4. Why do you think comments have been so much more popular than other forms of participatory journalism? What lessons can journalists take away from that popularity?

References

Abdul-Mageed, Muhammad M. (2008) Online news sites and journalism 2.0: Reader comments on Al Jazeera Arabic, *tripleC-Cognition, Communication, Co-operation* 6 (2): 59–76.

Amichai-Hamburger, Yair, Katelyn Y.A. McKenna and Tal Samuel-Azran (2008) E-empowerment: Empowerment by the Internet, *Computers in Human Behavior* 24 (5): 1776–1789.

Anderson, Benedict (1983) *Imagined communities: Reflections on the origin and spread of nationalism*, London: Verso.

Aucoin, James (1997) Does newspaper call-in line expand public conversation? *Newspaper Research Journal* 18 (3): 122–140.

Bakker, Piet, and Mervi Pantti (2009) Beyond news: User-generated content on Dutch media websites. Paper presented at the Future of Journalism conference, Cardiff, Wales, September.

Bergström, Annika (2009) The scope of user-generated content: User-contributions within the journalistic online context. Paper presented at the Future of Journalism conference, Cardiff, Wales, September.

Bogart, Leo (1991), *Preserving the press: How daily newspapers mobilize to keep their readers*, New York: Columbia University Press.

Carey, James W. (1989) *Communication as culture: Essays on media and society*, Boston: Unwin Hyman.

Charity, Arthur (1995) *Doing public journalism*, New York: Guilford Press.

Christians, Clifford G., Theodore L. Glasser, Denis McQuail, Kaarle Nordenstreng and Robert A. White (2009) *Normative theories of the media: Journalism in democratic societies*, Urbana: University of Illinois Press.

Darnton, Robert (1975) Writing news and telling stories, *Daedalus* 104 (2): 175–194.

Dimitrova, Daniela V., and Jesper Strömbäck (2009) Look who's talking, *Journalism Practice* 3 (1): 75–91.

Ericson, Richard V., Patricia M. Baranek and Janet B.L. Chan (1989) *Negotiating control: A study of news sources*, Milton Keynes, UK: Open University Press.

Gans, Herbert J. (2009) "Can popularization help the news media?" In: Barbie Zelizer (ed.) *The Changing Faces of Journalism*, New York: Routledge: 17–28.

Gans, Herbert J. (1979) *Deciding what's news: A study of CBS Evening News, NBC Nightly News, Newsweek, and Time*, New York: Pantheon.

Goffman, Erving (1981) *Forms of talk*, Philadelphia: University of Pennsylvania Press.

www.guardian.co.uk (2009, 7 May). Frequently asked questions about community on guardian.co.uk. Accessed 19 February 2010: http://www.guardian.co.uk/community-faqs

Haner, Lior (2006, 4 December) Users will be required to register their name before posting comments for articles. The Marker Café. Accessed 23 January 2010: http://www.themarker.com/tmc/article.jhtml/tmc/article.jhtml?ElementId=skira20061204_796519

Hapogian, Arthur (1993, spring) Sound off turns readers into participants, *The masthead*: 16–17.

Herbst, Susan (1995) On electronic public space: Talk shows in theoretical perspective, *Political Communication* 12 (3): 263–274.

Hermida, Alfred, and Neil Thurman (2008) A clash of cultures: The integration of user-generated content within professional journalistic frameworks at British newspaper websites, *Journalism Practice* 2 (3): 343–356.

Hollander, Barry A. (1996) Talk radio: Predictors of use and effects on attitudes about government, *Journalism and Mass Communication Quarterly* 73 (1): 102–13.

Kabalyon, G. (2009) Ilan king of Israel. In: Shoham, Shlono Giora, and Uri Timor (eds.) *Penology issues in Israel*, Kiriyat Bialik, Israel: Ach Publishers.

Kim, Jin Woo, and Eun Ja Her (2008) Inducing journalistic values from grass-root level discourse on journalism: An explorative analysis of user comment replies posted on online news articles. Paper presented at the International Association for Media and Communication Research, Stockholm, Sweden, July.

Kogen, R. (2005) The rules of discourse in Israeli news sites. Unpublished MA thesis, submitted to the Department of Communication Studies, the Hebrew University, Jerusalem.

Kohn, Ayelet and Motti Neiger (2007) "To Talk and TalkBack: Analyzing the rhetoric of talkbacks in online journalism." In: Swartz Altshuler, Tehila (ed.), *Online newspapers in Israel*, Jerusalem: Israel Democracy Institute: 321–350.

Leonard, Thomas C. (1999) "Making readers into citizens – the old-fashioned way." In: Glasser, Theodore L. (ed.) *The idea of public journalism*, New York: Guilford Press: 85–96.

Levinson, Stephen C. (1988) "Putting linguistics on a proper footing: Explorations in Goffman's concepts of participation." In: Paul Drew and Anthony J. Wootton (eds.) *Erving Goffman: Exploring the Interaction Order*, Cambridge, Massachusetts: Polity Press: 161–227.

McKenna, Katelyn Y.A., and Amie S. Green (2002) Virtual group dynamics, *Group Dynamics* 6: 116–127.

Melamed, Orly (2006) The talkback in Israel: A reflecting and intensifying mirror or a pendulum that balances and corrects the journalistic discourse. Unpublished MA thesis, submitted to the Department of Communication Studies, the Hebrew University, Jerusalem.

Örnebring, Henrik (2008) The consumer as producer – of what? *Journalism Studies* 9 (5): 771–785.

Reader, Bill (2007) Air mail: NPR sees "community" in letters from listeners, *Journal of Broadcasting & Electronic Media* 51 (4): 651–669.

Reich, Zvi (2009) Weaving the thread: Gatekeeping and filtering strategies for user comment. Paper presented to the conference of the International Communication Association, Chicago, May.

Richardson, John E., and Bob Franklin (2004) Letters of intent: Election campaigning and orchestrated public debate in local newspapers' letters to the editor, *Political Communication* 21: 459–478.

Rothenberg, Ignaz (1946) *The newspaper: A study in the workings of the daily press and its laws*, London: Staples Press.

Sayare, Scott (2009) As Web challenges French leaders, they push back, *The New York Times*. Accessed 20 February 2010: http://www.nytimes.com/2009/12/13/world/europe/13paris.html

Schudson, Michael (2003) *The sociology of news*, New York: W. W. Norton.

Scollon, Ronald (1998) *Mediated discourse as social interaction: A study of news discourse*, Reading, Massachusetts: Addison Wesley.

Singer, Jane B. (2010) Quality control: Perceived effects of user-generated content on newsroom norms, values and routines, *Journalism Practice* 4 (2): 127–142.

Singer, Jane B., and Ian Ashman (2009) "Comment is free, but facts are sacred": User-generated content and ethical constructs at the *Guardian, Journal of Mass Media Ethics* 24: 3–21.

Tausig, Shuki (2009) Journalism 2010: The survey, The Seventh Eye. Accessed 24 December 2009: http://www.the7eye.org.il/articles/Pages/241209_Journalism_2010_Israeli_Media_Consumption_Poll.aspx

Thurman, Neil (2008) Forums for citizen journalists? Adoption of user generated content initiatives by online news media, *New Media and Society* 10 (1): 138–157.

Thurman, Neil, and Alfred Hermida (2010) "Gotcha: How newsroom norms are shaping participatory journalism online." In: Monaghan, Garrett, and Sean Tunney (eds.) *Web journalism: A new form of citizenship*, Eastbourne: Sussex Academic Press: 46–62.

Times Mirror Center for the People and the Press (1993) The vocal minority in American politics. Accessed 20 February 2010: http://people-press.org/reports/pdf/19930716.pdf

Tsoref, Ayala (2006, 9 September) The national sorter of user comments. The Marker Café. Accessed 3 March 2010: http://www.themarker.com/tmc/article.jhtml?log=tag&ElementId=skira20060909_760371

Wahl-Jorgensen, Karin (2002) Understanding the conditions for public discourse: Four rules for selecting letters to the editor, *Journalism Studies* 3 (1): 69–81.

Wahl-Jorgensen, Karin (2001) Letters to the editor as a forum for public deliberation: Modes of publicity and democratic debate, *Critical Studies in Media Communication* 18 (3): 303–320.

Williams, Andy, Claire Wardle and Karin Wahl-Jorgensen (2009) "Have they got news for us?" Audience revolution or business as usual? Paper presented at the Future of Journalism conference, Cardiff, Wales, September.

Zoran Gabriel (2009) *Beyond mimesis: Text and textual arts in Aristotelian thought*, Tel Aviv: Tel Aviv University Press.

Part III

Issues and Implications

7

Taking Responsibility
Legal and ethical issues in participatory journalism
Jane B. Singer

In the traditional media, journalists are the ones who "make news." They decide what to cover, what sources to use, what to write or say or photograph, and what "play" the item should get when it is ready (by their reckoning) for public consumption. In short, they control everything about the story. They are the **"gatekeepers"** who see to it "that the community shall hear as fact only those events which the newsman, as the representative of his culture, believes to be true" (White 1950: 390).

Being a gatekeeper, then, is not just about the quantity of what makes news on any given day – how many items fit into the pages available in the newspaper or the minutes in the news broadcast – but about its quality. Journalists feel responsible not simply for how much information they provide to the public but for how good, especially how truthful, that information is.

As information has moved online and the space constraints of traditional media forms have vanished, quality issues have become even more important. Journalists weigh two interconnected aspects of quality in deciding what makes news. One has to do with assessments of how valuable something is as a piece of information; those are decisions about "news judgment."

The other has to do with how well it meets legal and ethical standards. Is it verifiably true, and are we willing to stand behind it once it's "out there"? Is it one-sided or does it fairly represent diverse views – without unfairly pushing

Participatory Journalism: Guarding Open Gates at Online Newspapers, First Edition.
Jane B. Singer, Alfred Hermida, David Domingo, Ari Heinonen, Steve Paulussen, Thorsten Quandt, Zvi Reich, and Marina Vujnovic.
© 2011 Jane B. Singer, Alfred Hermida, David Domingo, Ari Heinonen, Steve Paulussen, Thorsten Quandt, Zvi Reich, and Marina Vujnovic. Published 2011 by Blackwell Publishing Ltd.

our own? Will it harm innocent people? Is it defamatory or a form of hate speech, or a violation of copyright?

None of those questions has changed. What has changed, radically, is the amount of control the journalist has over the answers.

Participatory journalism means that what the journalist creates is only one part of the story, literally as well as metaphorically. As we have seen, people outside the newsroom are adding **comments** and other bits to journalists' stories, as well as creating all manner of their own online content from scratch and publishing it on media websites.

All well and good … except that journalists now feel legally and ethically responsible for those user contributions. In response, they are attempting to control not just their own output but also the ensuing conversation about it (Hermida and Thurman 2008), as well as all manner of other **user-generated content**.

Earlier chapters have highlighted the pressures that user contributions exert on journalists' work routines and newsroom resources. Here, we look in more detail at the issues of law and ethics that journalists believe this content raises, as well as the pressures created by a perceived need to ensure it meets their own standards for legal and ethical quality.

Do they continue to feel, as they have said in the past, that they are failing to fulfill their responsibility to the public if they allow articles to appear online without checking them for "decency and taste" (Thurman 2008: 145) – or libel or copyright violation? If so, how are they coping with the enormous volume of material that **users** submit to these national websites day in and day out? Are new perceptions emerging about ways to enhance the quality – as journalists define it – of these contributions?

After a brief discussion of the difference between law and ethics, this chapter has four main parts. The first looks at how user input affects journalists' own ethical behavior. The second considers journalists' perceptions about how well material provided by people outside the newsroom meets the ethical standards recognized within it; the third takes a similar approach to legal standards. And the fourth section looks at journalists' gatekeeping attempts to ensure user contributions break no laws and breach no ethical boundaries.

7.1 Law and Ethics

Law and ethics are different animals. Laws are a form of external restraint; they are rules imposed from outside the immediate social or occupational environment, typically by the government.

Nations with a free press, including those in our study, generally seek to minimize the external restraints on the media in order to safeguard that press freedom. Democracies protect speech and press because both are seen as essential for advancing knowledge and discovering truth, a well as for enabling widespread participation in civic decision-making (Emerson 1970).

However, all these countries do have media laws, and the limits they place on the press vary. Libel laws, for instance, are nearly universal. But in the United States, it is difficult to win a libel case because successive judicial interpretations of the First Amendment to the U.S. Constitution afford broad legal protection for the press. Although as we write, there are efforts afoot to reform British libel law (BBC News 2010), plaintiffs historically have had a much easier time in the United Kingdom, whose national laws more severely restrict what journalists can publish.

"One straightforwardness to being based in the UK is that you have the most inhibiting libel laws in the world," an editor at the *Guardian*, whose website has more readers outside Britain than within it, told us. "So actually, as long as you're corresponding with them, you don't really have to worry about the rest of the world!"

Ethics, on the other hand, are primarily internal restraints. Although ethical guidelines may be written down and even organized into formal codes available to the general public, adherence to those guidelines is monitored mainly from the inside – by individual journalists, by their editors and by other members of the profession.

Although researchers have found national variations in ethical guidelines and journalists' responses to ethical situations, studies also have indicated significant consistency in the importance of core normative concepts such as accuracy and truth-telling (Hafez 2002; Weaver 1998; Laitila 1995; Cooper 1990; Kocher 1986).

7.1.1 Professional Oversight

One of the hallmarks of any profession is a claim by its members that they are uniquely responsible for their own self-regulation (Larson 1977). Esoteric debates about whether journalism is truly a profession rage on, but most journalists see themselves as professionals – and share nearly universal norms related to such ethical precepts as truth-telling and fairness.

Many, though not all, of the nations included in our study have formal "press councils" or other organizations with ethical oversight of the media. However, their rulings generally are advisory rather than legally binding, and they typically include members of the press, as well as the public.

Neither media law nor journalism ethics change fundamentally when information is disseminated online rather than in a more traditional way. Truth-telling and fairness, to use those same two examples, are as important as ever; libel and copyright violation are just as unacceptable.

But as you have already seen, the medium does change the nature of the interaction between journalists and **audiences** in various ways. It also has raised the issue of just who is responsible for user contributions – as well as when that responsibility kicks in and how it is enacted.

The answers are not yet clear, and they vary from nation to nation. However, though still far from definitive, an emerging legal consensus holds that news organizations that "**post-moderate**" user contributions – that is, enable them to be published without prior review, as described in Chapter 6 – are not legally responsible for the content of those contributions the moment they appear.

The organization, however, is responsible – legally and ethically – for responding to post-publication concerns raised by users or anyone else. Failure to do so, within a reasonable but not very lengthy amount of time, could result in legal liability. Actual court cases have been extremely rare, though – "touch wood," every journalist reading this sentence is saying right now – and the metaphorical jury is still out on how things will ultimately shake out.

As law and ethics are about our behavior in social spaces, the precepts underlying both external and internal restraints come in for fresh interpretations and present fresh challenges in an open, networked environment.

7.2 The Effect of User Contributions on Journalists' Own Legal and Ethical Practices

Observers outside the newsroom – and some inside, as well – have highlighted two primary benefits of a more open and inclusive media space for the practice of journalism that relate to the media's overarching norm of serving the **public interest**.

One benefit is a broadly social one: In democratic nations, such as those included here, enabling more citizen voices to be heard is seen as an inherently good thing (Jenkins and Thorburn 2003).

"When presenting 'fair and balanced' news can be just another way to limit voices and disguise a corporate or political agenda, bloggers are the dam-busters of the media world," the *Christian Science Monitor*'s Tom Regan wrote back in 2003, as software for creating **blogs** – since followed by successive waves of increasingly sophisticated **social media** tools – was just beginning to be widely used. "Long may they blow open holes in the gatekeepers' firewalls so that all the voices that are being ignored or silenced can find ways to be heard."

User participation in creating media content of various kinds has indeed spurred journalists to draw on fresh perspectives from outside society's traditional power structures. However, as we have seen, journalists at least at the time of our study remained somewhat reluctant to allow users access to the **news production stages** where such participation would arguably be most valuable: the stages that involve the actual creation of content.

The other ethics-related benefit of an open media environment involves user input in the after-the-fact **interpretation stage,** where our interviewees tended to feel users more appropriately belonged. This benefit is narrower in scope, but also seen as crucial: Citizens can serve as the "watchdog on the watchdog," a check on the power of an institution that, as described above, is left relatively unfettered by formal laws. Citizens have chronicled perceived evidence of bias, censorship, inaccuracies and more, serving as a corrective mechanism for sloppy or lazy reporting (Andrews 2003; Bowman and Willis 2003).

In foregrounding transparency as a dominant ethical principle online, they have sometimes shocked thin-skinned journalists unused to being scrutinized the way they scrutinize others (Gillmor 2006). But the result over the past decade has been a perceptible shift away from the aloof (and, some would say, arrogant) journalistic stance that typically characterized traditional media in the past (Robinson 2007; Mitchell and Steele 2005).

7.2.1 Journalists' Reactions

Journalists who have talked to researchers about participatory forms of journalism have acknowledged these strengths of an increasingly participatory news environment – even if they have tended to focus mostly on perceived drawbacks, including the ones discussed in the remainder of this chapter.

For example, online journalists at the *Guardian* in the UK highlighted the comments section of their website as a platform for a healthy democratization of the media conversation, recognizing that "the old model of top-down, from-the-pulpit editorializing just doesn't do anymore," as one editor said (Singer and Ashman 2009: 13). Local journalists also have expressed strong support for the value of user-generated content in bringing diverse voices into the newspaper – although, as one added, "debate is a core role; hosting mindless abuse and self-publicity shouldn't be" (Singer 2010: 134).

In general, researchers have found that although journalists see the value of a more open media in theory, in practice those participatory ideals "do not mesh well with set notions of professional distance in journalism" (Deuze, Bruns and Neuberger 2007, 335).

Our interviewees also gave a nod to the civic potential of participatory journalism, though most considered it in the relatively narrow context of the democratization of news (or of the newspaper itself) rather than as a central component of democratic society in general.

The editor of LePost.fr (France), for instance, highlighted the goal of democratizing news content and breaking down barriers to its production, while an editor at the *Guardian* (UK) said user contributions were integral to the mission of a newspaper that believes in diversity of opinion. An editor at *Vecernji List* (Croatia) also gave journalists the central role: "By allowing citizens to participate, journalists behave ethically, and hence they democratize journalism and the web," he said.

This benefit is not always an easy sell in the newsroom. "There are still tensions with our professional journalists, who ask whether we are really going to invite anyone and allow anyone to participate," said a Belgian editor.

"Yes, that is exactly what we want, and that is different than what we used to do."

A different editor at the same Croatian paper said some journalists "believe that users are unprofessional, that they don't know professional standards and that the quality of journalism is under threat."

However, despite lingering concerns, our interviewees indicated most journalists do recognize that user input can result in improved reporting, as we have seen throughout this book already. So while the broader social implications of a more open and participatory media space were not something the journalists in our study dwelled on if they considered it at all, they did acknowledge its potential utility in a narrower sense – enhanced democracy once removed, if you like.

They were a bit more likely to consider new forms of journalistic accountability – that is, the ethical implications of being the subject of users' scrutiny, a second key benefit of participatory journalism outlined by outside observers.

In particular, user feedback was seen as useful to the extent that it led to a more accurate news account. As they become more comfortable in a world of give-and-take with users, journalists "start to realize that by saying `actually, I didn't have the piece of information I needed that would have told me I was wrong about that, so-and-so supplied it, thanks very much, now I know where I stand,' that actually leaves you looking better than if you just pretend that you didn't make a mistake," a community editor at the *Telegraph* (UK) explained. "I don't think anybody expects us to be perfect. They get frustrated when we act as if we are."

7.2.2 News Judgment

In the views of most of our interviewees, however, clear lines remained that they were very reluctant to allow users to cross – particularly, as we have seen, at news production stages involving news judgment, such as the **selection/filtering stage**.

It is one thing to stand corrected on a point of fact within a story you have written; journalists place a high ethical value on accuracy, and they are likely to see anything with the potential to boost that accuracy as a benefit. It is quite another to be told what to write in the first place – and yet another to give users a say in shaping the actual newspaper contents. On issues related to news judgment, our interviewees were generally united in the belief that they should be the ones making the decisions, as we saw in the discussion of user roles in Chapter 3.

Other studies also have shown that journalists remain fiercely protective of their own right to decide what goes in the news product – and those at leading quality newspapers, such as the ones in our study, are particularly wary about anything they believe might drag them down market (Singer and Ashman 2009).

"There is a danger here, we need to be aware of it, we need to fight it – we cannot fight it entirely, but we need to minimize it – not to be overly populist or pulp," said an editor at Ynet (Israel). "It is wrong for [*users*] to have impact at the expense of my judgment as a journalist," he added. "Let us consider the users, listen to them, consult them – but not at the expense of your ethics and your work principles."

More broadly, our interviewees expressed concern at the effect of user contributions on their overall brand as a news outlet, a topic we return to in the next chapter. If nothing else, the participatory environment has prompted newspaper journalists to think in new ways about who they are – and who they might become.

"By being a traditional media organization, we do have to balance who we are because we have readers who really like who we are," said an editor at *USA Today*. "And there's a whole other group of readers who loves who we need to be. I think we have to strike a balance there. ... We have to be recognizable to the people who want us to stay the same and the people who want us to move ahead."

7.2.3 Ethical Interactions

How to respond to what readers have to say – not all of which is polite, level-headed or even noticeably cogent – has been one of the biggest ethical issues for journalists whose working relationships now extend well beyond their comfort zones, to people who are neither colleagues nor traditional sources. Striking the right note to make unfamiliar, and in some cases uncomfortable, relationships work can be difficult, as an editor at the *Guardian* (UK) explained:

> It's a cultural thing more than a set of rules. ... I actually think being robust, engaging in all the rough and tumble with users is absolutely fine at the *Guardian*, and we've kind of got the mission to do that. But you have to also be careful you're not perceived as jumping on individuals from your very high pulpit. So a balance needs to be struck. But culturally, if we get the culture right, and give credit to a lot who are knowledgeable about the world they're entering, then we should have fewer problems.

Journalists expressed a sometimes conflicting need for guidelines to encourage consistency in navigating those relationships, as discussed further below, and flexibility in dealing with specific situations and personalities – their own as well as those of users.

One interesting response was developed by the *Telegraph*. The British newspaper took the position that journalists can define what's acceptable in comments on their own blogs, with the understanding that different journalists will have different tolerance levels for everything from anonymous comments to personal abuse. On the other hand, consistency was important in moderating the My Telegraph community section, a space devoted to user contributions, and editors sought to be responsive to what users said they wanted to be allowed and disallowed there.

"You can get into a mess quite early on if you treat it as 'this is our space, and you must behave yourself' because they see it as theirs, and they're very happy to tell us that," said the paper's community editor. At the same time, he added, "simply policing the community is not enough. You have to do stuff to encourage the kind of behavior you do want, as well as just stamping out the kind of behavior you don't."

What sorts of user behavior made journalists particularly uncomfortable? The next two sections take a closer look at some of the specific ethical and legal concerns about participatory journalism expressed by people in the newsrooms we visited, followed by an examination of the actions journalists were taking to address the concerns.

7.3 Ethical Issues

The journalists we interviewed characterized user contributions as ethically problematic in two main ways. One cluster of issues stems from the difficulty of knowing much if anything about where information comes from, a concern related mainly to journalistic norms of accuracy and truth-telling. The other relates to the abusive nature of too many user contributions.

More broadly, journalists expressed considerable angst about the potential of user material to debase the quality of the newspaper website. A few took a more benign view, such as the editor of *De Standaard* and *Het Nieuwsblad* (Belgium), who stressed that user contributions were complementary to material produced by professional journalists and need not be held to the same norms. As long as the latter adhered to high standards, he said, "it doesn't matter that facts and opinions get mixed" in user contributions. But most of our interviewees seemed to feel it did matter, a lot.

7.3.1 Unknown Provenance

If a key benefit of user input is its potential to improve the accuracy of journalists' work, a key detriment is the fact that the accuracy of what the user has provided is difficult if not impossible to ascertain.

Some journalists, such as those at *El País* (Spain), said they fact-checked user stories, stressing "journalistic rigor" and "common sense" as selection criteria. But the volume of user-generated content makes such gatekeeping attempts extremely difficult. "We received a fascinating picture of a cargo ship bridge in the North Sea, really very impressive," said an editor at *Der Spiegel* (Germany).

"Then we realized that the picture must have been about eight years old and was taken from some website."

Although the *Spiegel* editors caught the deception quickly, journalists everywhere were bothered by the difficulty of verifying material from users. A Croatian editor at *Vecernji List* said the biggest threat from users was "lies and deceiving of journalists." Another editor at the same newspaper agreed that "you don't know where the story really originated. There is no way to know that this person who brought us a story didn't steal it from somewhere. How can we know for sure?"

Journalists were uncertain how much free rein (and free space) to provide to users whom they do not know and whom they felt could not necessarily be trusted to use the platform as the news organization intended.

"Most professional concerns about the **forum** relate to questions of trust and responsibility," said the same editor at *De Standaard* and *Het Nieuwsblad* (Belgium) quoted above. "To what extent are we responsible for giving a megaphone to the public's voice and the opinion of Jan, Piet or Pol [*John, Pete or Paul*] if we don't know who Jan, Piet or Pol is? That's important, because it might be that these guys are, for instance, politicians who want to use our forum for their own political interests. That bothers us. But we will have to learn to cope with it."

Commercial messages also were a concern. "What might happen if Coca-Cola opens an account tomorrow and starts writing up content?" a community editor in Israel wondered. "What are we going to do with them? How will we take them off or not take them off, charge them, not charge them – what do we do?"

7.3.2 Abusive Content

A number of our interviewees also expressed concerns about abusive content from users. Some of the vitriol is directed at journalists themselves. The *Guardian* (UK) attracted quite a lot of it, as an editor there described:

> A lot of commentators have been very upset by the viciousness of some of the comments, especially if they're writing about the Middle East. If they're a woman writing about the Middle East, God help them. It gets sexist and nasty and vicious and threatening before the moderators can step in. So there has been some savage, real unpleasantness there which we've had to deal with. That's not a double-digit percentage of the comments we get. But it would be impossible to imagine that they're not at least affected by it, that it doesn't cross their minds when they're penning the next piece.

Some abuse was directed at other users. Although virtually all these newspapers publish guidelines that forbid racist, sexist and other ethically problematic postings – and almost all will delete such comments if they discover or are alerted to them – journalists still found themselves constantly having to make difficult judgment calls.

"Almost every day we have to answer to people who claim that their freedom of speech has been violated because we have not published their message. Then we try to explain what freedom of speech actually means," said an editor at *Helsingin Sanomat* (Finland).

"We have developed an approach of distinguishing not between legal and illegal, but between appropriate and inappropriate," an editor at Ynet (Israel) explained. "Some people may know how to express their very categorical point of view appropriately, meaning to refrain from incitement and rough words, so those responses will still get posted, whereas responses that are wild and full of hostility, even though they are legal, will not get posted."

In general, journalists expressed concern about the quality of user comments and their potential to debase the news product. "The Internet has lowered the discourse in general – the brevity, the speed, this sense of 'why should I make an effort?'" another Ynet editor said. "It is problematic for the society, problematic for the democracy, problematic in every sense."

What to do about it is another matter. Some journalists believed they had a responsibility to maintain quality standards for anything that appeared on their websites – even material they did not create. "It's a debate that we're hosting, and we're responsible for that debate. I'm of the opinion that a commentary on a site should uphold journalistic standards," said an executive producer at the *National Post* (Canada).

An editor at *Helsingin Sanomat* (Finland) agreed: "Because the evolution of any discussion anywhere in the world tends to lead toward negative and low-minded [*content*], we want to prevent that in the very beginning. We want to moderate with a heavy hand. And one of the most important guidelines is that discussions stay focused."

But other journalists preferred a more hands-off policy. "We don't accept comments that are unethical, but besides that, we don't use any quality standards. If comments are badly written or plain stupid, we don't remove them because we think the users who post a comment should take the responsibility for their own opinions," said an online editor for *Het Belang van Limburg* and *Gazet van Antwerpen* (Belgium).

Similarly, the community editor at the *Telegraph* (UK) said: "We have a very relaxed attitude to what we let through. Our main goal at the moment is free speech. If somebody wants to say something about a particular topic, we're certainly not going to kick them off because we don't feel it's relevant or constructive. We're not even really going to kick them off if they're just being a bit rude and nasty. Once they get personally abusive, or once they cross legal lines, we will take action. But we allow quite robust debate on our website."

Sometimes, however, that robust debate crosses the line from ethically dubious to legally dangerous. We turn next to some of our interviewees' biggest legal concerns.

7.4 Legal Issues

Concerns about the potential for user contributions to create legal problems for these national newspaper websites were widespread. However, with the exception of one Israeli editor, none of the journalists we talked to said they had actually faced a lawsuit or other legal claim over this material.

The reality was that even with the range of opportunities for getting into hot water offered by the ten different sets of national laws under which our interviewees operated, user-generated content had cost news organizations a lot for **moderation** but little or nothing in actual legal fees at the time of our study. "Considering the scale of the online discussions," said an editor at *Helsingin Sanomat* (Finland), "the problems so far have been really small."

The fear that it could and one day would land them in court, however, was also real, and most had opted to err on the side of caution. "It's still a murky field, so we're treading well below the line, and we cull the ugly stuff," an editor at *The Globe and Mail* (Canada) explained.

In this section, we outline three primary areas of concern about participatory journalism: defamation, hate speech and intellectual property.

7.4.1 Defamation

The word "libel" strikes fear in the hearts of almost every journalist around the Western world, and our interviewees were no exception. "One comment which is not OK is already enough because we are responsible for what is written beneath the articles. If there is only one among them which is legally problematic, in which people are becoming defamed or attacked, then 50 good ones are of no value," said a community editor for *Süddeutsche Zeitung* (Germany).

But most said that – largely thanks to their moderation procedures, discussed further below as well as in Chapter 6 and other chapters – they had been "lucky" so far. They also acknowledged that the vast majority of contributions were fine.

"A newspaper publisher is responsible for everything that it publishes, including the postings that come from the various whackjobs in society. And there are more than a few," said an editor at Canada's *National Post*. "I kind of live in perpetual fear over it, but most of our people are actually surprisingly rational."

A community editor at *Le Monde* (France) acknowledged the risk of illegal comments being published but added: "We spend time making sure that doesn't happen. We've been lucky enough, though. Problematic cases of defamation and such have been very rare, and usually we quickly identify the sources, so often we can act quickly."

7.4.2 Hate Speech

Hate speech is another common problem. Although universally unethical, its legality varies from country to country; for instance, most hate speech is legal in the United States but illegal in Germany.

Ongoing religious tensions create particular dangers. "Always when dealing with Islam-related topics, we had big problems and groups standing irreconcilably facing each other," said an editor at *FAZ* (Germany) "And very often, it reached the realm of criminal law. The only possibility then is to work with the censorship mace."

A community editor at the *Telegraph* (UK) agreed that "two of the big things legally are race and religion. Those are legal lines that it's quite easy to overstep. And often, people can overstep them in good faith, saying something that they just don't realize is something that you shouldn't really be saying publicly. Those are two areas we'd have to be very careful about."

In Britain, as elsewhere, journalists pay closer attention to topics they know have the potential to generate hateful comments. Asked about the percentage of user comments that get rejected, for instance, an editor at Israel's Ynet said: "That really depends on the topic. There are topics where almost everything will go up, and there are ones where almost nothing will go up." Items "with a potential for 'all Arabs are murderers,' 'all Arabs are such and such,'" likely will be rejected, he said, as will those related to news about Arab members of the Knesset, the Israeli Parliament.

7.4.3 Intellectual Property

The law surrounding intellectual property or copyright, for which there are clearer international standards, was a third area of broad legal concern. Here, too, journalists generally felt that users simply did not understand what was and was not permissible.

"It is clear that ordinary citizens don't understand, for instance, copyright issues or ethics," said an editor at *Kaleva* (Finland). But, he quickly added, the resulting problems are more hypothetical than actual; in fact, he said, "I don't remember a single case that would have led to real problems or to compensations."

Some other journalists did offer specific examples of legally dangerous situations, but they too said trouble had been averted. At *20 Minutos* (Spain), for instance, a poem was plagiarized. "Not from a very well-known poet, but the user posted the poem as if he were the author. The real author contacted us to report the infringement," an editor said. "We posted an apology on the website and attributed the poem to its real author." Indeed, he admitted, "in the end, most of the cases are solved with good will, by talking to those involved."

In fact, journalists find themselves taking a range of steps in an effort to assert their control over user contributions. Earlier chapters have dealt with these in various ways; here, we look at journalists' legal and ethical motivations for extending their gatekeeping role.

7.5 Mechanisms for Addressing Legal and Ethical Issues

Essentially, journalists engage in **moderation** or other oversight of user material out of a belief that doing so helps safeguard quality. Poor-quality content may be unethical – abusive or inaccurate, for example – or even illegal. If the latter, it leaves the publication open not only to criticism and cringes from a majority of users but also to more concrete, and potentially costly, penalties.

As a result, journalists at these national newspapers were unwilling to take their hands completely off the reins, as we already have seen in earlier chapters. "Our experience is that, in general, if you just open it up and say, 'well, go ahead,' the debates either fade out or get dominated by five people who are libeling each other," said an editor at *De Standaard* (Belgium). "We are convinced now that you still need to manage user participation online. And we are convinced that you have to manage it differently than in the print newspaper."

7.5.1 Moderation Options

Exactly when and how to perform that management task, however, varied considerably. The variation occurred both country to country – partially in response to national legal parameters, though as mentioned above, those remain less than clear-cut – and newspaper-to-newspaper.

German newspapers, for example, were notably committed to **pre-moderation** as a way to head off any legal problems. One journalist at *Focus* estimated a deletion rate of 40 to 50 percent on some topics. "We don't want disgraceful comments, insults, a coarse lack of objectivity, [*comments that cause*] dishonor, things that could be legally relevant. We had these things, and that's why we intervened," said an editor at *Süddeutsche Zeitung*. "The legal problems were foreseeable."

Another German newspaper, *FAZ*, had moved from a system in which comments appeared live and were checked by the newsroom within 24 hours after publication to one in which everything was looked at before it was published. "That means no squabbles among users are blowing up. Two users playing cat and mouse with each other the whole night has been one of the core problems in the former forum space. And the next morning, the newsroom was confronted with masses of hundreds of postings which had to be banned," said a *FAZ* editor. "As a news website and a quality medium, we can't live with this situation."

Some Israeli news organizations also had become more hands-on over time, as we saw in the previous chapter. "When I first got there, the approach on the site was not to interfere, except in legal cases – say, if someone wrote something that could lead to a libel lawsuit, we would reject that **talkback** [*comment*] and it wouldn't go up. Now over the past year, things have changed. Now we have to be strict not only with legal stuff but also with things that are unpleasant to the eye," said an editor at NRG (Israel).

Moderators at his website "have very clear instructions as to what to post and what not to post, a kind of ten golden rules of what you shall approve and what you shall not approve. But by and large, the main principle is: 'Where there is doubt, there is no doubt.' In other words, whatever looks like something that should not be approved, it is rejected. The tendency is to reject something controversial rather than to approve it."

Other journalists cited legal reasons for taking nearly an opposite, largely hands-off approach. "We feel we are on firm legal ground in that we're opening this up, facilitating this conversation, but we are not manipulating it, affecting it in a way where we're going in and doing something there," said an editor at *USA Today*. "We don't want to put ourselves in the position where we're editing something, and doing it discreetly, because then we have an association with that, and we become a participant. And then we very well could be liable. That's how we determine the court cases to this point, so we try to be very careful in that regard."

Several of our interviewees highlighted different approaches for different types of stories, again as highlighted earlier. The *Guardian* (UK), for instance, pre-moderated only for a small handful of blogs, such as "Blogging the Qur'an." And as described earlier, *Le Figaro* (France) **outsourced** its moderation but enlisted journalists as a second line of defence, having them read comments on their stories about religion, immigration or other topics that "can lead to polemic," as an editor there said.

7.5.2 Legal Liability and Resource Issues

In many ways, journalists are waiting for an external indication of legal liability – or, better, indemnity – that at the time of our study (and subsequently, through the writing of this book) had not yet arrived. The wait is especially trying because it is unclear how legal precedents established in one country might affect journalists and news organizations in another.

"I think there are issues of liability that haven't been fully solved yet," said an online editor at the *National Post* (Canada). "Nobody knows legally who's responsible for those comments. So they've been this gray area that everybody's talking about. Are newspapers responsible for comments?" An editor at Croatia's *Vecernji List* agreed: "The legal system still doesn't have answers to these new challenges. So it is a little bit like the Wild West."

Moreover, it is extremely difficult to head off a user who is absolutely determined to post something that journalists (and lawyers) consider problematic. One of the community editors at the *Telegraph* offered this example of attempts to deal with a user who was incensed that the newspaper was abiding by British "fair trial" laws and thus withholding the names of two adults accused of torturing a toddler to death:

> That case was impossibly difficult because we had a lot of users who were very angry that the family weren't being named. And we couldn't explain why because it was under a court order, so if we'd said anything, we'd have broken the court order. So we were in this impossible position of having to delete everything, not being able to explain to people why that was, and then angering one or two people who just kept recreating accounts and posting the names anywhere they could. Any story that was completely unrelated, they'd just put the names and addresses of the families. And trying to chase this person around the site for three weeks or however long, until they got bored, was impossible. ... We put the names of the family in the profanity filter. ... The problem is if they put the names with different spaces or with a number instead of a letter or something – you can never think of every combination. If somebody's determined enough, there's always a way through. All we can do is try and take it down as soon as we can.

As discussed in earlier chapters, the resources needed for that kind of legal or ethical vigilance – for maintaining the role of gatekeeper over content created by users – can be daunting. Regardless of whether moderation is outsourced or done in-house, it takes considerable amounts of time and money, and the fear that something dangerous will slip through never disappears.

A trio of editors at three different Israeli newspapers each highlighted this issue. "The filterers are doing a great job, but I am certain that when you approve thousands of responses every day, there will be something that will evade you, something that will not be filtered out," said an editor at NRG.

A community editor at another Israeli newspaper website estimated that "if we wanted to review everything, we would need, I believe, a hundred more people that would be sitting there at any given hour, reviewing every account and everything. This does not exist, and there is no precedent for this in the world, either – meaning this just does not exist."

And an editor at the third Israeli newspaper website emphasized that the comments are "subject to libel claims, slander, censorship rules, the ban on publicizing the name of the rape victim – this is tons and tons of work, to read these things, to approve them. So we have added a new person who just deals with this for the most part. At certain hours, in the evening, this is all he is doing."

7.6 Conclusion

There has to be a better way, right? In fact, even at the time of our interviews in 2007 and 2008, there were indications that journalists were beginning to look for alternatives ways to maintain or even enhance the quality of user contributions instead of (or, more commonly, in addition to) these resource-intensive gatekeeping efforts.

For instance, along with moderation, some newspapers at the time of our study were beginning to offer training sessions for users interested in contributing content to the website. We already have discussed, in Chapters 4 and 5, the role of the "coaches" at LePost.fr (France) in working with users to establish a "human contact" to help generate strong content. Journalists at other newspapers also were experimenting with options for user support.

At Belgium's *Gazet van Antwerpen* and *Het Belang van Limburg*, for example, readers had been invited to become local **citizen journalists** and had been provided with a short training and information session. "We try to get acquainted with these people and explain to them some basic rules of journalism, such as how to write an article or how to conduct an interview. We also give them some ethical guidelines," the paper's community editor said. However, they try not to provide too many rules, for fear of "spoiling the pleasure of these volunteers," as the online content manager said.

In the time between our interviews and the publication of this book, many of these newspapers have sought and, in some cases, implemented ways to boost that "human contact" with their contributors. Their approaches may involve increased interaction in blogs, increased emphasis on group conversations rather than on comments from isolated individuals, or other continually evolving strategies, many of them intended to foreground the "good stuff" rather than simply try to stifle the bad.

Ultimately, we believe the quality of contributions will increase only when users feel that they are part of a community that is not just a trendy label but a real (even if virtual) entity. We started this chapter with consideration of the value of self-restraint rather than external controls. That value holds for users, as well as journalists.

We all have grand ideas about what a free and open discourse should look like. Most of the time, though, it doesn't look like that at all. The issue then becomes a consideration of potential effects on stakeholders. So far, we have talked primarily about two groups of stakeholders: journalists and users. But there are others, and some of them hold the proverbial purse strings. It is to some of the more overtly economic issues raised by participatory journalism that we now turn.

Participate!

1. What do you see as the biggest ethical issues related to participatory journalism? Are journalists dealing with those issues appropriately and/or effectively? What would you do in addition – or instead?
2. Although we have considered the ethical issues discussed in this chapter primarily from the perspective of the journalists we interviewed, there is an argument to be made that users bear the main ethical responsibility for what they write. What obligations do users have to other users? To journalists?

What can users do to enhance the overall quality of participatory journalism?

3. Journalists today live in perpetual fear that something a user posts on their website will land them in legal hot water. Should journalists be held legally responsible for content that comes from outside the newsroom? Why or why not?

References

Andrews, Paul (200 3) Is blogging journalism? *Nieman Reports* 57 (3): 63–64.

BBC News (2010, 9 July) Government announces review of libel laws, Accessed 12 September 2010: http://www.bbc.co.uk/news/10580758

Bowman, Shane, and Chris Willis (2003) *We media: How audiences are shaping the future of news and information*, The Media Center at the American Press Institute. Accessed 28 December 2009: http://www.hypergene.net/wemedia/download/we_media.pdf

Cooper, Tom (1990) Comparative international media ethics, *Journal of Mass Media Ethics* 5 (1): 3–14.

Deuze, Mark, Axel Bruns and Christoph Neuberger (2007) Preparing for an age of participatory news, *Journalism Practice* 1 (3): 322–338.

Emerson, Thomas I. (1970) *The system of freedom of expression*, New York: Random House.

Gillmor, Dan (2006) *We the media: Grassroots journalism by the people, for the people*, Sebastapol, California: O'Reilly Media.

Hafez, Kai (2002) Journalism ethics revisited: A comparison of ethics codes in Europe, North Africa, the Middle East and Muslim Asia, *Political Communication* 19 (2): 225–250.

Hermida, Alfred, and Neil Thurman (2008) A clash of cultures: The integration of user-generated content within professional journalistic frameworks at British newspaper websites, *Journalism Practice* 2 (3): 343–356.

Jenkins, Henry, and David Thorburn (2003) *Democracy and new media*, Cambridge, Massachusetts: MIT Press.

Kocher, Renate (1986) Bloodhounds or missionaries: Role definitions of German and British journalists, *European Journal of Communication* 1 (1): 43–64.

Laitila, Tiina (1995) Journalistic codes of ethics in Europe, *European Journal of Communication* 10 (4): 527–544.

Larson, Margali Sarfetti (1977) *The rise of professionalism: A sociological analysis*, Berkeley: University of California Press.

Mitchell, Bill, and Bob Steele (2005) Earn your own trust, roll your own ethics: Transparency and beyond. Paper presented to the Blogging, Journalism and Credibility Conference, Harvard University, Cambridge, Massachusetts, 17 January. Accessed 28 December 2009: http://cyber.law.harvard.edu/sites/cyber.law.harvard.edu/files/webcredfinalpdf_01.pdf

Regan, Tom (2003) Weblogs threaten and inform traditional journalism, *Nieman Reports* 57 (3): 68–70.

Robinson, Sue (2007) "Someone's gotta be in control here": The institutionalization of online news and the creation of a shared journalistic authority, *Journalism Practice* 1 (3): 305–321.

Singer, Jane B. (2010) Quality control: Perceived effects of user-generated content on newsroom norms, values and routines, *Journalism Practice* 4 (2): 127–142.

Singer, Jane B., and Ian Ashman (2009) "Comment is free, but facts are sacred": User-generated content and ethical constructs and the *Guardian, Journal of Mass Media Ethics* 24: 3–21.

Thurman, Neil (2008) Forums for citizen journalists? Adoption of user generated content initiatives by online news media, *New Media and Society* 10 (1): 139–157.

Weaver, David H. (1998) *The global journalist: News people around the world*, Cresskill, New Jersey: Hampton Press.

White, David Manning (1950) The "gate keeper": A case study in the selection of news, *Journalism Quarterly* 27 (4): 383–390.

8

Participatory Journalism in the Marketplace
Economic motivations behind the practices
Marina Vujnovic

For well over a decade, the newspaper industry has been struggling to find some way to prosper in a media environment increasingly dominated by the Internet. During that time, advertising revenue has plunged precipitously for many of the newspapers in our study, particularly since the recession of the late 2000s, and circulation numbers have continued to melt, as well.

As more and more people have turned to the Internet for news, most of which is available for free online, the already worrisome economic trends have become downright alarming. While traditionalists may still buy a conventional print paper, many of those readers are supplementing their news diet with online information (Pew Project for Excellence 2009). Growing numbers of other readers, particularly younger ones, never see a print newspaper at all.

In a number of the countries in our study but most notably in the United States, media companies have responded with deep cuts in spending. An estimated 13,000 U.S. newspaper jobs were eliminated in just three years, from 2006 to 2009, leaving 25 percent fewer journalists employed by newspapers than at mid-decade (Pew Project and Edmonds 2010). Those who remain not only must pick up the slack left by departed colleagues but also must take on new responsibilities associated with the ongoing transition to a multimedia environment –

including developing and overseeing the user contributions you have been reading about.

The employment situation in other nations in our study varies, but nowhere in the print world does the future look bright. The nature of media work is changing everywhere (Deuze 2010), and the concerns of many observers have shifted from profitability to survival. "The accountants appear to be guiding the transformation," Philip Meyer wrote in his recent book titled *The Vanishing Newspaper*. "If they continue to slash and burn their existing businesses, all they will end up with are slashed, burned, obsolete businesses" (2009: 2–3).

This chapter examines the effects of this multi-faceted economic crisis on the ways in which journalists think about **participatory journalism**. We start by looking more closely at the economic challenges facing media companies and workers in an online environment. We then consider the economic motivations for an ongoing redefinition of media and journalistic roles, as user contributions become a larger part of news websites – and consume, at least potentially, a larger share of the remaining journalists' time and effort.

8.1 Market Forces

The pressures described in previous chapters can be viewed as part of a broader ideological or cultural battle. Journalists are taught to provide and to value timely, accurate and verified information, which – as described above – many see as vital for the proper functioning of democracy (Gans 2003). Market forces, however, have a strong tendency to give more weight to increased profits instead.

Journalism, some say, has shifted from being a public good to another cog in the market-based economy (Nichols and McChesney 2010) – and at least in economic terms, an increasingly ineffective cog at that. The resulting tension is hardly new. But the rise of the Internet and, more recently, of a wholly open **social media** environment exacerbates the pressure.

In this section, we look at commercial and other economic motivations that have helped prompt the development of online news, considering how these contemporary financial concerns relate to historical and cultural definitions of professional journalistic roles.

8.1.1 Information as a Commodity

Information is one of the most economically significant commodities in our postmodern world (Drucker 1969), and twentieth-century media became very, very good at selling information. Newspaper industry consolidation throughout the latter part of the century (Bagdikian 2004), along with other strategies aimed at increasing the cost-effectiveness that shareholders like to see, meant annual profits for many news corporations were reliably high year after year after year. In the eyes of some observers, the quality of news during the period soon took a back seat to its ability to bring in the money that kept those share-holders happy.

Some of the revenue underlying those profits came from selling information directly to people who wanted to read it and were willing to pay for the privilege. But a far larger chunk of newspaper revenue came from information *about* those people – particularly how many of them were reading the newspaper and how much disposable income those readers were likely to have.

That sort of information was very valuable indeed to advertisers hoping to reach buyers for their goods or services, and advertisers were a major source of newspaper revenue throughout the twentieth century, especially in the United States.

This structure has been particularly entrenched in the U.S. newspaper indus-try, which in 2008 relied on advertising for 87 percent of its revenue, according to a report by the Organization for Economic Cooperation and Development (Associated Press 2010). This figure compares with less than 60 percent of the revenue for newspapers in, for example, Germany and Spain, which rely more heavily on copy sales to contribute to their bottom line.

And advertising, of course, includes both display ads and classified ads. Here, too, American newspapers have been more vulnerable than their European counterparts to a combination of the economic downturn and the encroachment of the Internet. The Internet has brought an end to their near-monopoly on local classified ads, notably including those for sales (think eBay), real estate and employment; the economic crisis of the late 2000s made both of the latter kinds of ads dramatically scarcer anyway. Rising production costs and declining readership have further exacerbated the economic problems (Albarran, Chan-Olmsted and Wirth 2006).

8.1.2 Public Discontent

The old economic system has long been one that tended to please shareholders and industry executives more than it pleased media observers. Critics said that what they saw as excessive loyalty to advertisers compromised journalism as a profession that was supposed to be loyal primarily to the public it ostensibly served by providing information promptly and accurately (Kovach and Rosen-stiel 2007; Curran 1997). While money is needed to underwrite that social goal, the augmentation of media revenue should not be the goal in and of itself, according to observers both inside and outside the newsroom.

Nor were members of that public very happy with the news product they were getting. In the United States, more than 60 million people regularly bought a newspaper in the mid-1980s. By 2008, total national newspaper circulation had fallen below 50 million (Newspaper Association of America 2010), although the overall U.S. population had swelled by more than 25 percent.

Again, European markets have suffered a bit less – but they still have suffered. The OECD report mentioned earlier indicated a 30 percent decline in the U.S.

newspaper publishing business between 2007 and 2009. But Britain was not far behind, losing 21 percent of its market in the same period; between mid-2009 and mid-2010, circulation among quality papers such as those in our study dropped another 12 percent (McAthy 2010). Among other nations in our study, the market in Spain fell by 16 percent, in Germany by 10 percent, in Finland by 7 percent and in France by 4 percent (Associated Press 2010).

The factors are not only economic, of course. Journalists routinely hover near the bottom of the list of the "types of people" who can be trusted to tell the truth; for years, considerably more than half the respondents in a periodic U.S. poll have said they would not trust a journalist to be truthful (Harris Poll 2006).

The low levels of trust in the media affect their ability to exert a positive influence in their communities, whether geographical or interest-based (Meyer 2009). Indeed, Entman (2010) suggests that lack of trust in the media and an overall decline in the quality of hard-hitting political news are major reasons readers have turned away.

These long-term trends and economic prerogatives – which are more pronounced in some of the countries in our study than in others, though they are having at least some impact everywhere – predate by many years the emergence of the Internet as a popular media platform. Nonetheless, it is safe to say that the Internet has not helped matters. On the contrary.

8.1.3 Digital Economy

As digital networks have grown, media organizations have found it harder and harder to find an economic model to sustain their own growth or even prevent their slide. Online profitability levels have never been high (Boczkowski 2004), and newspapers companies have never found it easy to accommodate either the Internet's global reach or its "information wants to be free" zeitgeist. Free access to online information has accelerated what already was a steady erosion of print circulation.

As indicated above, the recession of the late 2000s made the existing problems much worse. In 2009, one analyst estimated that advertising revenue for that year, adjusted for inflation, would be the lowest it had been since the mid-1960s (Chittum 2009); advertising revenue in some US markets was estimated to be down 30 percent and more in 2009 alone (Kilman 2010).

Although signs pointed to slightly better news in the early part of the new decade, it was abundantly clear that the advertising model that had paid most of the bills for 150 years – a model in which the cost to an advertiser was based largely on how many people were likely to see the ad – was not going to migrate effortlessly to the Internet (Singer 2010).

The belated response from the industry in recent years has been a rather frantic search for alternative revenue streams. Convincing audience members to pay for online information is one option (Pérez-Peña 2010; Isaacson 2009) – and by 2009 more and more newspapers were considering it quite seriously, or had already begun putting at least some of their content behind a "**paywall**" – despite the fact that online users have long been extremely resistant to the idea (Chyi 2005; Chyi and Sylvie 2001).

Even if users agree to dip into their pockets for online news, their contribution toward the newspaper's profit margin is certain to be far below what advertising once provided and, by itself, unlikely to be enough to keep the industry alive (Herbert and Thurman 2007). Other publications – including various start-ups focusing on in-depth or investigative journalism – have begun exploring non-profit business models, which proponents say can enable journalism to sustain its watchdog function while engaging mass audiences in the news (Entman 2010).

8.1.4 Tradition and Change

All these trends contribute to what Mitchelstein and Boczkowski call "the tension between tradition and change" (2009: 562), created by overlapping concerns about the media's role in the democratic process and its survival as a market-driven industry at a time when that market is evaporating.

The concerns about the validity and sustainability of a profession whose goal is to inform a democratic public add up to what many have proclaimed to be a crisis for journalism and the news. Some observers doubt practitioners' ability to ever regain the far-reaching public influence they had before the emergence of the web. Princeton University Professor Paul Starr, for instance, argues that "journalism – or at least some parts of it – may find new sources of financing. It may be reconstructed in imaginative ways. But it is unlikely to have the broad public reach it once had" (Starr 2009).

Journalists, then, are under enormous economic pressure in addition to the cultural and occupational pressures created by the transition to a more participatory news environment, as described throughout this book.

As we have seen, some journalists react defensively, highlighting the benefits of traditional approaches and remaining resistant to change until forced by internal or external demands to adapt their work practices (Allan 2006; Boczkowski 2004). Others are more open to innovation and experimentation, which they see as necessary for their industry's survival.

We now turn to a look at the economic context and motivations for participatory journalism, as identified by interviewees across the newsrooms in our study.

How do economic considerations feed into the ongoing redefinition of traditional journalistic roles, as participatory journalism becomes an increasingly dominant feature of news websites? The journalists we talked with identified three economic benefits of **user-generated content**, each related to the others: building brand loyalty, boosting website traffic and remaining competitive. In framing the value of participation at least partly in economic terms, our interviewees draw user contributions into the sphere of commodity culture that also includes information produced within the newsroom.

8.2 Building Loyalty to the News Brand

In describing what he called "**convergence** culture," Jenkins (2006) stressed consumer loyalty to a media brand as crucial in an era of increasing market fragmentation. Across all our interviews, in fact, the importance of the newspaper's brand, and the perceived need to build user loyalty to it, were dominant themes.

Newspaper websites compete in a marketplace where a rival news source is simply a click away, so gaining and retaining the attention of readers is more important than ever. "It's not just getting the eyes on your site," an editor at the *National Post* (Canada) pointed out. "It's getting them to stay on your site."

8.2.1 User Communities

Creating or strengthening a community of online **users** – both as active **audience** members and as more or less traditional news consumers – was therefore seen by our interviewees as a crucial benefit of participatory journalism. In general, both news managers and lower-level journalists in our study lent support to the argument that "collaborative culture" and the related ideas of "mass creativity" and content co-creation are "contagious buzzwords that are rapidly infecting economic and cultural discourse on Web 2.0" (Van Dijck and Nieborg 2009: 855).

Building a "community of loyal consumers" is a primary goal of participatory journalism initiatives at *Vecernji List* (Croatia), for example. "Our whole strategy for UGC is developed with the idea that we need to build the site to which our readers will return daily if not hourly," explained at online editor at that newspaper. "We can't risk losing more readers to our competition."

An executive at the *Telegraph* (UK) similarly argued that the lack of attention to maintaining the online community could put the whole business "in peril."

Maintaining or increasing the quality and quantity of opportunities for participatory journalism thus was seen as crucial to the economic survival of the newspaper. Another example came from Belgium, where journalists at *Het Belang van Limburg* and *Gazet van Antwerpen* saw creation of an economically sustainable brand through development of **hyperlocal** communities as a prerequisite for industry success. Journalists at these Belgian newspapers, and elsewhere as well, appeared less concerned about the quality of the information created by such communities than about their ability to engage people (including younger people) and extend technological development.

The **community manager** at these Belgian outlets also described the newspapers' marketing department as a driving force in the move to focus on different communities and to brand the news product based on specific user interests – in other words, creating interest groups or stakeholders around particular news brands.

8.2.2 Brand Loyalty and Brand Management

In academic terms, this perspective reflects the need of an economic elite – represented here by the newspaper – to turn publics into consumers of an information commodity. In this view, a desire to build brand loyalty is the real motive behind efforts to create a sense of community among website users.

The community editors at the *Telegraph* (UK), for example, described the **blog**-hosting section of the website as a way to give users not only an audience but also a sense of connection based on shared allegiance to the newspaper brand.

Brand loyalty and brand management, in service to the goal of gaining and retaining audiences, also were clear themes in the interviews with North American journalists – particularly senior editors. The editor of the *National Post* (Canada), for instance, said online news production in a **Web 2.0** environment was about marketing and building relationships with audiences rather than simply delivering information.

Importantly, however, these audiences were not the passive ones of traditional media, whose value lay primarily in attracting advertisers. Rather, these users were members of a more explicitly active audience and of niche online communities.

Marketing strategies therefore revolved around drawing such users together around particular interests – and in doing so, creating a sense of loyalty to the website itself. In Israel, for example, an editor of *Haaretz* explained the need to encourage users to feel connected to the newspaper and its online communities in order to prevent "web surfers" from migrating to other sites.

Some journalists, however – including interviewees in Finland, France and Spain – were reluctant to assign economic motivations to their decisions to offer or expand participatory journalism options. "Good marketing" does not overshadow the importance of journalistic roles or functions of the media, the editor of *20 Minutos* (Spain) argued.

That said, even among interviewees who tended to view marketing and other economic motivations as having a broadly negative impact on journalism, a majority still believed that strategic attention to economic imperatives was necessary for survival in the fragmented online world.

8.3 Boosting Website Traffic

One effect of the ongoing extension of what scholars call commodity culture into more and more spheres of social life is the creation of economic relationships among people who previously had different sorts of relationships or even none at all (Mosco 1996: 153). As they continue to add opportunities for user input, newspaper websites are creating new venues for such economic relationships, what Coté and Pybus (2007: 89) call "immaterial labor."

Fostering user communities based on brand loyalty, as we have just seen, is one example. Another closely related approach involves relying on various forms of participatory journalism as a tool for boosting website traffic.

8.3.1 Using Users

The economic value of drawing more users to a website derives from a traditional media revenue model. At least in theory, more users make the site more attractive to advertisers. If nothing else, traffic figures represent a language that advertisers (as well as newspaper executives and investors) understand, one that deals in concrete numbers: of users, of time spent on a website or a section of it, of **comments** posted or recommendations made.

This is arguably a highly exploitative use of the medium. The newspaper creates controlled spaces that entice citizens, wearing their "website users" hats, to contribute unpaid labor in the form of comments or other input.

Users get, perhaps, a sense (real or not) of democratic, or at least civic, participation. The newspaper gets their "eyeballs" – traffic figures it can then sell to advertisers or sponsors; the greater the traffic, the greater the amount of unpaid labor that has been expended to generate it (Coté and Pybus 2007).

Interviewees in our study identified an increase in traffic as a "strategic goal" for their websites. At both *Vecernji List* and *24 Hours* (Croatia), for example, the pressure to increase website traffic was a major concern for journalists and a motivational force for the development of more participation opportunities intended to attract and keep more users, for longer periods. Indeed, media managers at those newspapers made it clear to newsroom staff that more traffic was what they wanted, and they saw user contributions as a way to get it.

In Spanish and U.S. media organizations, increasing traffic also was seen as a specific strategy for industry survival. And editors at the *Guardian* (UK) stressed the importance of keeping users on the site as long as possible – which they said benefited everyone. "In cold commercial terms, it's [about] page impressions," said an online newsroom executive, though he immediately added that engaging users "does improve journalism. You can see why that kind of debate and discussion is an interesting proposition."

Interviewees typically linked the desire to increase website traffic with building loyalty to the news brand, as described above. At the *Telegraph* (UK), for instance, community editors described the My Telegraph section, which housed user blogs, as a way to foster that loyalty through social interaction.

By taking advantage of users' need to establish their own online identities and connect with others through content production, the website not only keeps users coming back and staying longer but also relies on those users to bring their friends into the online community – thus increasing traffic from multiple directions. "Once we can make My Telegraph the central area for all the community stuff that we do, we're going to see UGC representing a huge chunk of traffic, I think," the site's community editor said.

8.3.2 Market Lingo

Similarly, a marketing executive at *Le Figaro* (France) connected search engine indices to ways in which participatory journalism works as one of the most useful tools for generating website traffic. Indeed, online news sites – with their specific, detailed and readily available hit logs – speak better, more direct market lingo than the print newspaper ever could.

The numbers allow journalists and their bosses to know exactly what appeals to users. Thus, a story about a caravan fire on a camping site in a small town in Flanders could be identified and highlighted by Belgian journalists as a successful story because it attracted considerable traffic for the website – even though it was, in journalists' eyes, a minor event that never would have made it into the print newspaper at all. An online news manager at *Het Belang van Limburg* and *Gazet van Antwerpen* explained that it was an appealing way to do relevant journalism.

The high traffic volume of U.S. media websites was cited with admiration by other journalists in countries including Britain, Croatia and Germany – and was seen as the most significant indication of online success by editors at *USA Today* and the *Washington Post*, as well. These editors also connected increasing traffic to what they saw as the larger goal of building brand loyalty, described above.

In particular, they cited the need to maintain the interest of a larger audience, which Entman (2010) identifies as a good strategy for online news production. Appealing to a "mass public," Entman suggests, works in tandem with building and strengthening smaller niche communities, with which it is possible to engage at a more specific and deeper level.

Canadian interviewees were particularly articulate about the usefulness of participatory journalism in addressing strategic marketing goals. Several described online news sites as part of an overall business strategy and viewed the various approaches to engaging audiences as indicators of a good business. An editor at *The Globe and Mail*, for example, argued that attracting readers and then keeping them faithful to the news product had always been good business, in print no less than online.

In general, Canadian interviewees saw maintenance of the community as vital, both for attracting new users and keeping existing ones. Strong numbers that can be presented to advertisers and media executives are what truly matter in the end, a *National Post* editor explained. A "tangible number," he said, "that becomes a business thing."

Website traffic also was a particularly salient economic issue for journalists in Israel and Spain. Spanish journalists invoked U.S. success stories but also depicted website traffic as important to the popularity of individual journalists;

in addition, they cited goals of satisfying market demands and remaining competitive.

This view of participatory journalism as beneficial in competing with other newspapers and other websites was the third key economic motivation identified by our interviewees, and we turn to it next.

8.4 Competing Effectively

Competition is a hallmark of capitalist economic systems, and online competition has played a major role in driving the development of newspaper websites. In their initial forays online, news organizations were arguably more concerned with protecting the competiveness of existing products than with taking risks to explore the medium's new possibilities (Allan 2006; Boczkowski 2004).

8.4.1 Innovation Incentives

In our study, journalists described competition – both with other major newspapers and with non-newspaper websites – as an incentive for innovation. An editor of the *National Post* (Canada), for example, highlighted media competition as driving the development of participatory journalism, which he saw as crucial to survival in a Web 2.0 world.

Among the more problematic competitors for interviewees were aggregator sites such as Google News, which were seen as essentially stealing the work of traditional news gatherers. These "unfair competition strategies," as a Croatian editor described them, underscored the perceived need to protect the business – and to battle vigorously for users' attention. However, interviewees also saw aggregation sites as essential tools for indexing and ranking websites.

Several journalists said their news organizations became involved in participatory journalism for the very pragmatic reason that they did not want to get left behind. "Everyone is doing it," said an Israeli editor. "We need to join the competition."

This bandwagon effect, or the desire to keep up with the competition, also was in evidence elsewhere. At the *Guardian* (UK), for instance, an online news manager described what he called the widespread motive of "Me-Tooism." Rather than taking the time to analyze exactly what should be done with user contributions or why, he said, "there's been a great deal of fear about missing out – there's a scramble to get this stuff up and running."

Our interviewees' comments suggested that the fast-moving, unpredictable developments in the online environment challenged traditional approaches to dealing with the competition. For example, **social networking** sites such as Facebook were emerging as new competitors at the time of our study, and journalists were uncertain how to compete with them. But as the editor of *Kaleva* (Finland) pointed out, user-generated content was seen as one logical option.

Other journalists also felt that news organizations could and should try to replicate the participatory functions of such sites, with which users are increasingly familiar and comfortable.

8.4.2 Does Size Matter?

In the smaller markets we studied, including Belgium and Croatia, the sense of competition was especially heightened. Winning the competition for an audience that is small to start with can determine "who will survive and who will die out," as an editor of *24 Hours* said, describing a Croatian media market of just four million people served by four daily newspapers. Croatian newsrooms, in fact, already had experienced layoffs at the time of our study, although journalists there tended to see user-generated content as a way to save time rather than money.

Media executives, as well as some lower-level journalists, in Belgium also were prone to see user-generated content in financial terms, as a cost-saving strategy or at least a way to use limited resources more efficiently. The editor of *De Standaard* and *Het Nieuwsblad* (Belgium), for example, said he tried to convince the newspapers' management committee that they had to invest in UGC as a newsgathering mechanism – "and get rid of the idea that UGC is cost-saving."

However, another interviewee from *Het Nieuwsblad* saw **citizen journalists** as the most cost-efficient way – indeed, perhaps the only way – to cover hyperlocal news.

Although the pressure created by small markets made competition an especially prominent interview theme in Belgium and Croatia, the fact that journalists in larger markets were less likely to explicitly discuss competition does not mean it was not an issue for them. For many, the notion of remaining competitive was implied in their discussion of other topics.

In Germany, for instance, journalists talked extensively about quality – and they saw the search for a new business model that would enable them to keep the quality of German journalism high as a way to succeed in a competitive environment. In fact, most interviewees, especially among the lower-level journalists, stressed that the quality of journalism – and the survival of good journalism – was what mattered most in the end.

8.5 Conclusion

The economic motivations for offering and extending participatory journalism options on the newspaper websites in our study are complex, as well as interconnected with other issues, concerns and motives. However, the perceived commercial imperative of user-generated content is important to understand because it taps into the larger social discourse surrounding the ability of online media to fit within an economic model in which news is one information commodity among many.

As we have seen, the key economic motivations highlighted by our interviewees were the overlapping desires to build brand value, increase website traffic and beat the competition. In two of the smaller markets, Belgium and Croatia, some interviewees also specifically referred to participatory journalism in terms of its contribution to economic efficiency.

It is interesting to note, however, that our interviewees almost always discussed economic motivations in tandem with concerns about how to improve journalism, particularly in terms of its democratic social function. As we said at the start of this book, that perception of journalism as integral to the proper functioning of democracy is central to the professional culture across national borders. But the role of journalism within the capitalist structure, particularly in the current economic and information environment, is more contentious.

8.5.1 Web Workers

Our interviewees, then, saw participatory journalism as a crucial part of their marketplace strategy and even as a key to the organization's survival in the challenging Web 2.0 world. In his recent book, *Journalism Next*, Mark Briggs (2009: 9) suggests that "we are all web workers now." That notion redefines the traditional dimensions of media work, raising new issues related to unpaid labor, the purposes and participants in work, and the shape of the final product (Coté and Pybus 2007; Deuze 2007).

Is online journalism today about creating a news story – or about creating a sense of participation in a production process? If the latter, does participation itself become a commodity in the evolving online environment (Dean 2008)?

New forms of labor in the production of information may threaten traditional ways of doing business, but they pose little threat to the overall capitalist system in which information remains a commodity (Van Dijck and Nieborg 2009). On the contrary, what scholars have identified as a commodity culture has been co-opted and turned into a component of an emerging media business model that incorporates the labor of audiences as well as journalists.

In this model, abstract groups of laborers – call them "users" – contribute their time and effort by voluntarily engaging in the forms of participatory journalism described throughout this book. Their rewards are not wages but rather a sense of being a part of an online community.

Critics would argue that such a sense is false, manufactured by media organizations that are actually pursuing quite different goals, in particular the economic ones that this chapter has described. Whether users agree, or whether they do believe that they gain personal or social fulfilment through their contributions, is a question that our study, with its focus on the perceptions and attitudes of journalists, cannot address.

8.5.2 New Models

The journalists who shared their views with us recognized that old business models no longer work, and they generally agreed with the German editor who said that one of the biggest battles today is to find new models that will sustain journalism economically and, ideally, safeguard and enhance its quality at the same time.

They recognized, too, that they are working in what Mitchelstein and Boczkowski (2009: 563) call "a liminal moment between tradition and change." At this point, the future of participatory journalism is unclear, and so are the motives for encouraging it. Should user contributions be pursued because of their democratic potential to extend civic participation to ever-larger numbers of people? Or is the key issue whether participatory journalism is good business?

Clearly, the benefits could be both social and economic. Many of our interviewees seemed to indicate that although market logic was a crucial factor in exploring and extending participatory journalism options, they also saw and supported its democratizing potential.

American, British and Spanish journalists were especially keen to emphasize the media's role in fostering civic participation, describing user-driven content platforms as places for audiences to be heard or, as a *USA Today* editor said, to exercise their "democratic rights to debate and discuss."

That said, while journalists continued to highlight civic discourse as one of their crucial social roles, some also framed the participatory options on their websites as helping users to "feel" more involved or engaged – not necessarily to actually *be* those things or to otherwise share in fulfilling a collective democratic function. Many acknowledged the pressures, including economic ones, inexorably challenging the civic goals.

Worryingly, then, the potential remains for "participatory journalism" to promise more than it delivers in democratic terms, even to slide into civic irrelevance in the changing environment of what Dean (2008) calls communicative capitalism.

In other words, if users' sense of community engagement or connection through the spaces provided by their media ultimately proves false, then the democratic function of those spaces would be relegated to insignificance. Online user spaces would become a means to encourage people to feel they are part of one thing – a civic community – when the reality is that their primary role is to be part of something quite different, a commoditized media culture with a Web 2.0 upgrade.

Journalists and users share the responsibility for resisting that option and for creating the truly democratic spaces that can effectively counter it.

In our next chapter, we step back a few paces to offer a more conceptual view of what journalism is and the role it plays in our contemporary "hyper-complex" society.

Participate!

1. This chapter discussed three key economic motivations for offering and extending participatory journalism options on newspaper websites: building brand loyalty, boosting website traffic and competing effectively with other online entities. If you were determining your organization's online economic strategic, which of these do you think should get the most attention? Why?
2. Is it possible for participatory journalism spaces to contribute to both democratic and economic goals? In other words, can such goals overlap, or are they inherently at odds with one another?
3. How should media organizations structure participatory journalism spaces to encourage their use as democratic platforms for civic discourse? Would any conflicts with economic goals arise in doing so? If so, how might you address them?
4. Are media organizations merely exploiting users by asking them to engage in participation options, or is there a real benefit to users from doing so?

References

Albarran, Alan B., Sylvia M. Chan-Olmsted and Michael O. Wirth (2006) *Handbook of media management and economics*, Mahwah, New Jersey: Lawrence Erlbaum Associates.

Allan, Stuart (2006) *Online news*, Maidenhead, UK: Open University Press.

Associated Press (2010) Papers in Europe weather crisis better than US, ABC News/ Money. Accessed 29 August 2010: http://abcnews.go.com/Business/wirestory?id=109 09470&page=1

Bagdikian, Ben H. (2004) *The new media monopoly*, Boston: Beacon Press.

Boczkowski, Pablo J. (2004) *Digitizing the news: Innovation in online newspapers*, Cambridge, Massachusetts: MIT Press.

Briggs, Mark (2009) *Journalism next: A practical guide to digital reporting and publishing*, Washington, DC: CQ Press.

Chittum, Ryan (2009, 19 August) Newspaper industry ad revenue at 1965 levels, *Columbia Journalism Review*. Accessed 15 March 2010: http://www.cjr.org/the_audit/ newspaper_industry_ad_revenue.php

Chyi, Hsiang Iris, (2005) Willingness to pay for online news: An empirical study on the viability of the subscription model, *Journal of Media Economics* 18 (2): 131–142.

Chyi, Hsiang Iris, and George Sylvie (2001) The medium is global, the content is not: The role of geography in online newspaper markets, *Journal of Media Economics* 14 (4): 231–248.

Coté, Mark, and Jennifer Pybus (2007) Learning to immaterial labour 2.0: MySpace and social networks, *Ephemera: Theory and politics in organization* 7 (1): 88–106.

Curran, James (1997) "Rethinking the media as a public sphere." In: Peter Dahlgren and Colin Sparks (eds.) *Communication and citizenship: journalism and the public sphere*, London: Routledge: 27–58.

Dean, Jodi (2008) "Communicative capitalism: Circulation and the foreclosure of politics." In: Megan Boler (ed.), *Digital media and democracy*, Cambridge, Massachusetts: MIT Press: 101–123.

Deuze, Mark (2010) *Managing media work*, Thousand Oaks, California: Sage.

Deuze, Mark (2007) *Media work*, Cambridge, Massachusetts: Polity.

Drucker, Peter (1969) *The age of discontinuity: Guidelines to our changing society*, New York: Harper and Row.

Entman, Robert M. (2010) Improving newspapers' economic prospects by augmenting their contributions to democracy, *The International Journal of Press/Politics* 15 (1): 104–125.

Gans, Herbert J. (2003) *Democracy and the news*, Oxford: Oxford University Press.

Harris Poll (2006) Doctors and teachers most trusted among 22 occupations and professions, Harris Interactive. Accessed 28 February 2010: http://www.harrisinteractive.com/harris_poll/index.asp?PID=688

Herbert, Jack, and Neil Thurman (2007) Paid content strategies for news websites: An empirical study of British newspapers' online business models, *Journalism Practice* 1 (2): 208–226.

Isaacson, Walter (2009, 5 February) How to save your newspaper, *Time*. Accessed 15 March 2010: http://www.time.com/time/business/article/0,8599,1877191-1,00.html

Jenkins, Henry (2006) *Convergence culture: Where old and new media collide*, Cambridge, Massachusetts: MIT Press.

Kilman, Larry (2010, 4 March) 20th World Newspaper Ad Conference: Where will the money come from? Shaping the Future of the Newspaper / World Association of Newspapers. Accessed 15 March 2010: http://www.sfnblog.com/advertising/2010/03/20th_world_newspaper_ad_conference_where.php

Kovach, Bill, and Tom Rosenstiel (2007) *The elements of journalism: What newspeople should know and the public should expect*, New York: Three Rivers Press.

McAthy, Rachel (2010, 10 September) National newspaper ABCs show continued decline, Journalism.co.uk. Accessed 13 September 2010: http://www.journalism.co.uk/2/articles/540534.php

Meyer, Philip (2009) *The vanishing newspaper: Saving journalism in the information age*, Columbia, MO: University of Missouri Press.

Mitchelstein, Eugenia, and Pablo J. Boczkowski (2009) Between tradition and change: A review of recent research on online news production, *Journalism* 10 (5): 562–586.

Mosco, Vincent (1996) *The political economy of communication: Rethinking and renewal*, London: Sage.

Newspaper Association of America (2010) Total paid circulation. Accessed 16 March 2010: http://www.naa.org/TrendsandNumbers/Total-Paid-Circulation.aspx

Nichols, John, and Robert W. McChesney (2010, 7 January) How to save journalism, *The Nation*. Accessed 15 March 2010: http://www.thenation.com/doc/20100125/nichols_mcchesney

Pérez-Peña, Richard (2010, 20 January) *The Times* to charge for frequent access to its web site, *The New York Times*. Accessed 15 March 2010: http://www.nytimes.com/2010/01/21/business/media/21times.html

Pew Project for Excellence in Journalism (2009) Newspapers: News investment, The state of the news media: An annual report on American journalism. Accessed 15 March 2010: http://www.stateofthemedia.org/2009/narrative_newspapers_newsinvestment.php?cat=4&media=4

Pew Project for Excellence in Journalism and Rick Edmonds (2010) Newspapers: Summary essay, The state of the news media: An annual report on American journalism. Accessed 12 September 2010: http://www.stateofthemedia.org/2010/newspapers_summary_essay.php

Singer, Jane B. (2010) Journalism ethics amid structural change, *Daedalus: The Journal of the American Academy of Arts and Sciences* 139 (2): 89–99.

Starr, Paul (2009, 19 October) First read: Journalism minus its old public, *Columbia Journalism Review*. Accessed 15 March 2010: http://www.cjr.org/reconstruction/journalism_minus_its_old_publi.php

Van Dijck, José, and David Nieborg (2009) Wikinomics and its discontents: A critical analysis of Web 2.0 business manifestos, *New Media and Society* 11 (5): 855–874.

9

Understanding a New Phenomenon
The significance of participatory journalism
Thorsten Quandt

As we have seen throughout this book, audience participation in journalism has many facets – from the tools used to the way they are managed, from the relationship between readers and journalists to changing roles in the newsroom. Now we need to begin to tie these aspects together by considering the broader impact of user contributions on today's media.

We can do that by looking at the phenomenon as social scientists and asking the big questions about **participatory journalism**. What is its relevance to society? What is its inner logic? Why does it exist at all, and what does its existence mean? The answers will help us understand the significance of the ideas we have presented in our earlier chapters and lay the groundwork for the concluding chapter that follows.

9.1 Public Communication and the Essence of Journalism

Our interviews provide only partial – and frequently conflicting – responses to these big-picture questions. The journalists and web editors, **community managers** and chief editors in the online newspapers we studied diverged in their assessments of and opinions about the meaning of participatory journalism.

Participatory Journalism: Guarding Open Gates at Online Newspapers, First Edition.
Jane B. Singer, Alfred Hermida, David Domingo, Ari Heinonen, Steve Paulussen, Thorsten Quandt, Zvi Reich, and Marina Vujnovic.
© 2011 Jane B. Singer, Alfred Hermida, David Domingo, Ari Heinonen, Steve Paulussen, Thorsten Quandt, Zvi Reich, and Marina Vujnovic. Published 2011 by Blackwell Publishing Ltd.

Some viewpoints seemed diametrically opposed to others. For instance, while some interviewees stressed the democratic benefit of including **user-generated content** in online journalism, others feared that doing so might undermine the very basis of journalism. And many journalists seemed to see at least some merit in both views.

Such oppositional viewpoints do not necessarily highlight contradictory developments in the various countries and media institutions that we selected for this study. Rather, they express two interpretations of the same process – and, within a broadly shared professional culture, two different understandings of journalism and, in particular, its future.

Although journalists' views contained many shades of gray, we will paint the two interpretations here in black-and-white terms in order to highlight the differences between them. Very broadly, one group of interviewees welcomed the changes connected with participatory journalism, while the other rejected or at least was wary of them as a potential threat.

9.1.1 Different Experiences, Different Understandings

At first glance, this seems to be a simple matter of holding traditional or progressive views about what journalism is. Some journalists believed the best times were in the past. Others embraced the **Web 2.0** world and its radically altered message flow, changing what once was almost entirely a top-down form of communication into something that is much less so today.

One obvious factor seems to divide the two camps: age. In general, the younger interviewees were more supportive of the idea of participatory journalism. Unsurprisingly, they also had a more technophile view of their job, online journalism and societal communication in general. Many older journalists seemed more fearful or at least cautious about changes to their profession.

So is it just a matter of older journalists not being able to adapt to a new situation because they have become too inflexible and conservative, too anxious to cling to old habits?

While age does affect attitudes, we are not comparing 20-year-olds and 60-year-olds; our younger interviewees were in their mid-20s, but few if any were past their mid-40s. Online journalists in general are somewhat younger than their print counterparts (Quandt *et al.* 2006), so the age gap tends to be narrower than in a traditional print newsroom. Moreover, *all* online journalists probably have a bit of technophile in them, as they are working in a technology-heavy, continually evolving and relatively innovative area of journalism.

Given these factors, we might expect online journalists to have a much more coherent and uniform perspective on participatory journalism than we actually found. But both our own research and earlier studies have shown that online journalism is still a developing field. People from very different professional backgrounds do very similar jobs, and there are no long-standing work rules or traditions (Paterson and Domingo 2008; Quandt 2005). We talked to journalists with newspaper backgrounds, online backgrounds and backgrounds from other fields altogether.

This diversity of experience partially explains why we encountered such varied reflections on the field *within* the field. The journalistic socialization of its workforce is heterogeneous. Some of our interviewees learned to "do journalism" in a traditional print environment, with next to no contact with **audiences** and a strong focus on in-depth research and exhaustive fact-checking. Others come from news agencies and were trained to work fast under pressure. Others learned journalism in an online environment, doing most of their research through the Internet and engaging in frequent contact with **users**.

These different experiences lead to different approaches to the work of journalism, as well as different understandings of rules, roles and routines.

In fact, these differences do relate to our interviewees' age, in an interesting way. Many of the relatively older journalists began their careers in print and later transferred online. Many of the younger ones, in contrast, are "digital natives" (Prensky 2001). They grew up in an environment where digital technology was not merely present but was regularly used.

These people learned how to be journalists by working online. A difference of just a few years might have a big impact on attitudes. Online journalism in anything resembling its current form dates only to the mid-1990s, and many news organizations waited years to embrace it. Journalists who learned their jobs as few as ten years before when we talked to them, in late 2007 and 2008, were likely digital immigrants from a different field.

9.1.2 Structural and National Variations

The combination of age and socialization thus clearly contributes to the varying orientations. This is still only part of the story, though. An individual's socialization as a journalist might help explain different personal interpretations of the significance of participatory journalism. But structural and national differences also were evident in our study.

Some newsrooms were just generally more pro-participation; the culture of others seemed to mean that everybody was reluctant to embrace user input. Moreover, some countries, such as Germany, seem to foster a more skeptical approach than others, such as the USA or Britain.

Various levels of influence on journalists (Shoemaker and Reese 1996) – individual, structural and systemic – sometimes created a sense of conflict that came across in the interviews. Some journalists said they personally favored user-generated content but said many of their colleagues did not; they described these colleagues as influenced by negative perceptions of user participation, including generally negative views throughout the company. This sort of statement suggested a version of what scholars call the "third person effect" (Andsager and White 2007): People expect others to be more susceptible to the effects (generally negative ones) of a communication message than they think they are themselves. This reaction might be a strategy to handle the contradictions emanating from attitudes that do not mesh well, such as a positive individual attitude in conflict with a more negative one at an organizational level.

The multiple perspectives that many of our interviewees expressed also stem from their connections to different conceptualizations of what journalism is all about. In short, those who supported participatory journalism talked about quite different things than the ones who were more broadly opposed to it.

Opponents stressed the danger to the profession, to professional norms such as accuracy and to the jobs of journalists. On the other hand, supporters of user contributions to the media space usually stressed the democratic aspects of these contributions, the widening of opinions and pluralism they facilitated, and the overall benefits of public discussion. Basically, they felt journalism that incorporated user voices could fulfill its function in a better way than before.

Another way of saying this is that supporters accorded weight to the social function of journalism, which they saw as serving society by offering the means for public debate of relevant issues. The skeptics mainly looked at journalism as a profession, an institutionalized vocational area with a special educational training and a set of rules and structures (Larson 1977).

This juxtaposition of views leads to the more general question about what journalism really is – or should be. Is it a system enabling public communication, a part of public communication or an institutional structure with rules governing the production of content? Or is it simply the sum of what people who are journalists do?

Depending on the answer, user-generated content has a significantly different place and meaning. In order to evaluate the conflicting views of our interviewees, we need to go back in time and examine the emergence of journalism itself.

9.2 The Emergence of Traditional Journalism

The "What is journalism?" question can be addressed in many ways. Historical approaches describe the developments that led to journalism in its current form, portraying journalism as the result of a series of events. Many start with the invention of a rudimentary printing press by Johannes Gutenberg in the fifteenth century or the first newspapers in the early seventeenth century. Other events or inventions of varying impact have continued to change the nature of journalism over the centuries since.

However, recounting key events tells us only about what happened. It does not necessarily help us understand why. Other approaches explore the functions of journalism and seek to explain the rationale behind those functions to provide a coherent, contextual model of how journalism emerged and developed.

9.2.1 Normative Theories

In Chapter 3, we mentioned the work on normative media theories by Christians *et al.* (2009), who propose three different approaches to journalism:

- First, it is the task of journalism to observe and inform.
- Second, journalism participates as an actor in public life when media practitioners comment on the news or advocate particular positions.
- And third, journalism provides a platform for voices from outside the media.

Normative theories put forward certain goals based on theoretical, political, and economic or other broad assumptions. They exist in part outside an observable reality, as these goals can be – and often are – identified before they are tested in the real world. Some normative approaches cannot even be tested, perhaps because they are wholly theoretical or ideological.

9.2.2 Communication Technology and Society

Carey (1989) takes a different approach. He combines a historical perspective with an analytical one, focusing on the emergence of new social paradigms through changes in the media and in communication technology. Carey identifies various broad social changes, particularly in the United States, that led to a shift in how society functioned.

Building on the work of Harold Innis (1951; 1950), who pursued similar ideas in a Canadian context, Carey highlights the introduction of the telegraph and the railway in the early nineteenth century as central to creation of an infrastructure that enabled a modern nation state. With these inventions, time and space could be not only standardized but also effectively shrunk or compressed. Railway transport made distances seem shorter. And information that formerly had to be physically carried from one place to another – no matter how far away – could be conveyed in no time at all thanks to the telegraph.

Carey identifies a similarly fundamental shift from a modern to a postmodern society in the 1970s. Standardized space and time structures were changing once again. In fact, both were being compressed to a point at which they virtually disappeared.

Cable and satellite delivery systems that became available during this time undercut the dominance of earlier communication networks. The Internet, which was developed by scientists beginning in the 1960s and became a public communication medium in the 1990s, extended the range and reach of technologies "that have withdrawn the coordinates of time and space and with it categories of human identity and structures of social relations," Carey wrote (1998: 34).

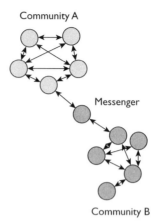

Figure 9.1   Communication in small communities and developing societies

9.2.3 Evolutionary Approach

We believe journalism can best be understood through a framework that links its development to the development of public communication, which in turn is tied to the evolution of society.

Arguably, a society actually consists of communication. A large group of people is not a society if they never speak to or otherwise interact with one another. Without communication, society cannot function or even exist. Some sociologists see communication as more essential to society than the individuals who constitute it (Görke and Scholl 2006).

Journalism is a structured and organized mode of public communication, and that means it is closely connected to the evolution of society. We suggest that the same can be said of participatory journalism, which is a form of communication by the public for the public.

The framework or model we propose here, based on our earlier work (Domingo et al. 2008), is a simple one – too simple to fully reflect the complexity of societal change. But it helps us step back and understand the place of both traditional and participatory journalism in democratic society.

9.2.4 Small, Simple Societies

To trace the roots of public communication, we have to go back to the early stages of societal development, to societies that were small and simple, as shown in Figure 9.1.

These early, developing societies are not typically considered by communication scholars. The members of such small societies communicated directly with one another. Any relevant information was transferred from person to person through direct speech, and there was no need for a large infrastructure to gather, select and exchange information.

Communication in very early human communities was further limited by the difficulty of storing information. Before written language or other durable forms of communication were invented, people had to rely on storytellers and their memory of orally reproduced information.

Even in oral cultures, however, messengers transported information beyond the reach of the directly interacting community members. These messengers were the first "media," in human form.

In Europe, for example, travelling troubadours and monks transferred crucial information from one community to another. They can be seen as weak ties (Granovetter 1973) between different communication networks. While the community networks are densely knit – resulting in a large amount of shared information – the ties to the messengers are weak, as personal contact is rare and sporadic.

However, the messengers did carry and convey important information. Call it "news."

In the terms used by scholars, the communication processes in such societies could be categorized as direct two-way, one-to-one or one-to-few communication in a near-synchronous, reactive fashion. In other words, people talked face-to-face with small numbers of other people, they did it in "real time" and participants in the communication process reacted directly to one another.

This direct interaction thus happened between equal communication "nodes" – that is, individuals. Although the status of particular individuals varied, none would have had anything close to the communications capacity of an organization devoted to that function.

9.2.5 Increasing Social Complexity

Of course, over time, societies continued to grow in size and complexity. The simple, direct form of communication became increasingly ineffective. Face-to-face communication has limited reach, as the information degrades with each step away from the original source. You tell your friend something, but she changes it a bit when she passes it along to another friend; before long, it's a different story altogether. Hearsay and rumors are simply broader examples of the same phenomenon.

In more abstract terms, the information typically becomes distorted if the distance between nodes in the communication network becomes too great or if there are too many intermediaries. Some pieces of information are transformed or go missing altogether, as a message is not simply transferred but also perceived and reconstructed by each person. There also will be a time lag between sending and receiving information.

Another problem is that the people who are central to the communication network – the individuals who are the best-connected to the most other people

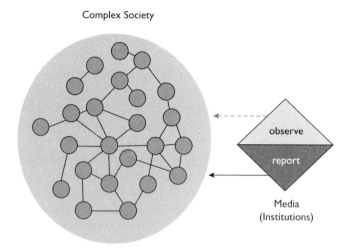

Figure 9.2 Communication in complex societies

– will run into problems selecting, processing and distributing all the information they receive. At a certain point, they simply will not be able to handle the volume of messages or maintain the quality of the information those messages contain.

History offers an unclear view of whether, over hundreds of years, such problems led directly to a solution that took the form of an organized public communication process, later called journalism. Some scholars have argued that the process was essentially reversed. They suggest that a growing formalization of communication processes – including journalistic roles, organizations and working rules – enabled societies to develop in size and complexity (Innis 1951; 1950). Then again, the developments may have occurred in tandem, mutually influencing each other along the way.

Whatever the origin of the process, the outcome is clear. Media institutions solved complex societies' communication problems. Figure 9.2 models how this change looked.

Media are social institutions with organizational structures, working roles and rules on how to select, process and distribute information. Workers within these institutions observe events and consider various aspects of their world, then report these observations back to members of the society. These are among the key **news production stages** we introduced in Chapter 2 and have drawn on throughout this book.

As our simplified diagram suggests, these developments also resulted in a significant change in how public communication was organized. Unlike the more primitive model shown in Figure 9.1, the institutionalized, journalistic communication represented in Figure 9.2 means communication had become one-way, one-to-many and indirect.

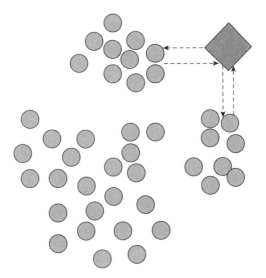

Figure 9.3   Communication in hyper-complex societies

It also was generally non-reactive, meaning that with some exceptions such as letters to the editor, the people receiving the messages had no effective way to react or respond to them.

The nodes in such a communication process were no longer equal. Figure 9.2 depicts a hierarchical system in which significant power and control over that process rest with institutionalized media.

The independent power of journalism in complex democratic societies is generally seen as important, as we described in our introductory chapter. But it also leads to criticism about the potential abuse of that power. Among the concerns are that journalists might manipulate information or take sides as they move through the various news production stages of **selecting**, **processing** and **distributing** information according to a set of rules that are generally inaccessible to members of the public.

Some criticism also stems from the observation that journalism does not serve all parts of society equally. Journalists, critics say, focus too much on political and economic elites. Moreover, the demands of the marketplace, discussed in the previous chapter, mean that journalists may select information based on the potential to attract large audiences – information that does not necessarily have much if any social relevance.

9.2.6 Specialization and Fragmentation

Such criticisms hint at some of the shortcomings of journalism within a mass media structure. Those shortcomings are exacerbated as society becomes still more complex, as Figure 9.3 shows ours has done. If social structure starts to decompose into segregated subgroups, how can media companies address all the diverse voices, interests and communication needs in this newly fragmented society?

Indeed, such "hyper-complex" societies pose a number of new problems. Fragmentation leads to highly specialized topical interests, with individualized information needs. Moreover, such interests might change quickly because of the dynamics of a network structure made up of multiple unstable subgroups.

Journalistic media can try to address the various groups, but they ultimately will lose their focus if they communicate too many different positions at once. Even multiple journalistic voices likely will not reach all parts of society.

Furthermore, critics say, journalists have become detached from the public they ostensibly are serving, fostering a closed professional culture insufficiently responsive to the overall society. The criteria for selecting news, as well as the routines used to gather and process it, have become highly idiosyncratic – a mystery to those outside the newsroom.

Even some inside the newsroom have been baffled. "I have been working 20 years in newspapers, and I never knew for whom I was writing until I got here," said a journalist in our study from *20 Minutos* (Spain). "Many times, I felt I was writing for the sources or for strange beings I did not know."

This is where user-generated content, as well as online communication in general, comes into play. New forms of participatory journalism incorporate elements of the earlier, small communication structure described above, enabling two-way reactive, dynamic communication among equal individuals. At the same time, the general features of indirect communication characteristic of larger societies are retained.

9.3 The Emergence of Participatory Journalism

The incorporation of participatory journalism in the products of media institutions thus can resolve the problems presented by each of the earlier structures, as Figure 9.4 indicates. Communication from the user is added to the traditional journalistic mix.

User-generated communication is situational and contextual, as it usually brings together groups of people based on interest and opportunity. Think of the highlighted network shown in Figure 9.4 as connecting different members based on particular topics of discussion. With each new topic and interest area, that sub-network will be different. So the network is constantly being reconstituted and reconfigured – and on a global scale limited only by the ability to speak a shared language.

This type of participatory journalism is not the same as dedicated **social networking** sites or **blogs**. Most blogs are easy-to-create websites, typically with short items and plenty of links (Lowrey 2006) – and are produced by individuals or small teams. They tend to have a topical, biographical or geographical

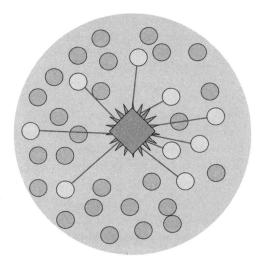

Society 2.0

Figure 9.4 Participatory journalism in hyper-complex societies

focus. Blogs often reflect the personal opinions of their producers, and a single blog rarely offers a wide range of topics.

In their combination as the blogosphere, they do offer a broader range of relevant opinions, following a "long tail" logic (Anderson 2006). The notion of the long tail is based on the assumption that a multitude of sites with minimal impact and focus might form a relevant force in public opinion when added up, equal to the mass audience of relatively few sites with large traffic. However, critics of this idea point out that only the established media offer a clear focus with discernable messages.

Similar criticism has been leveled at social networking sites, where users debate and exchange a wide range of material, including personal updates, ideas, opinions, memories, photos and documents. Social networking sites may concern political topics, and their participants may discuss current affairs in considerable detail. They may even be used as distribution platforms by media organizations. Nonetheless, critics say, they are not focused on reporting in the journalistic sense of the term.

A number of our interviewees echoed this view, especially when they compared participatory and traditional media. They articulated considerable unease with the idea that new forms of **social media** could replace journalism. For example, an editor at *Süddeutsche Zeitung* (Germany) put it this way:

The Internet will provide a crazy richness of voices, opinions and facts. At the same time, the need for orientation and pillars is growing. Journalistic brands … and authors that can be trusted, that you know and that are credible, will develop their very own force. These are contradicting tendencies. It will be more anarchic on the one hand and more centralized on the other. ... The last pillar of credibility ... actually needs to be preserved. That won't be done by Web 2.0. That is not a pillar of credibility but overall adds to the confusion.

The theme also is found in the academic literature. "Instead of uncritically assuming that so-called 'new' media of communication like weblogs represent a radical departure from and challenge to more established (or 'old') communication media, whether for good or for bad," Haas urged, scholars should "carefully attend to both continuity and change as a means of assessing the relationship between them" (2005: 396).

9.4 Perspectives on Participation

A perspective that incorporates online user contributions and other social media elements within the existing framework of journalistic media represents a more careful approach than simply embracing the "new" instead of the "old." In Haas' words, it represents a combination of "continuity" and "change."

Does that mean participatory journalism offers an ideal model that solves all the problems of communication and helps society master the level of complexity it has reached? There are two answers to this question. One answer is a conceptual one, based on the framework illustrated and discussed above. The second is an empirical one, based on our interviews.

9.4.1 Conceptual Framework

From a conceptual level, we might be inclined to argue that a combination of user-generated content and mass media communication offers the best of both worlds. It is flexible yet structured. It is open to the needs of the audience but contained within the context of an institution that values quality and follows journalistic rules.

However, the framework or model depicted in this chapter deliberately simplifies the communication process. By doing so, it might create the false impression that communication involves only transferring information from point A to point B.

On the contrary, mediated communication is a multi-faceted process incorporating the distinct news production stages we have highlighted here. Both the individual and the organization are involved in selecting and filtering, processing and editing, and distributing information. Before the selection can occur, an individual must **access** a source or **observe** an event. And at the end of the process, after the information is published, the receiver of the information **interprets** or reinterprets it.

Moreover, decades of communication research tell us quite clearly that information is never just swallowed whole by receivers and transferred intact to their brain. It is decoded, related to other available information, and interpreted and reconstructed accordingly. As a result, communication is not necessarily successful. That is, the message the sender intended to convey may or may not correspond to the message the receiver takes in.

By including elements of both direct and mediated communication (Figures 9.1 and 9.2), participatory journalism forms reinstate some of the problems that were addressed by institutionalized communication structures – especially the ones related to information overload and communication complexity.

As we saw in earlier chapters, some media companies are creating specialized roles, such as those of "**community managers**," to help deal with the resulting issues. Others, such as the French and Spanish newspapers in our study, are **outsourcing** that task to external companies. We also have seen that most online newspapers have developed strategies and devoted both human and technological resources to protect journalists from the potentially overwhelming task of filtering and choosing among the huge volume of user contributions.

The distribution of user-generated content also raises problems. Technology has addressed earlier online storage issues; enormous amounts of text, audio and visual data now can be easily stored in a digital format. But distribution also involves organizing the transfer of relevant information from the news organization to the user. The greater the volume of user contributions, the harder it becomes to discern what is relevant and what is not.

A universe of unorganized information is arguably no information at all – it is chaos. Information implies structure and relevance. This structure is missing, and relevance is very hard to identify, if media organizations do not organize the material provided by users, making it easily navigable and digestible.

Without an active role on the part of the media, users must shoulder the burden of organizing the information and making sense of it. Many users have no desire to make that considerable effort. But many journalists wonder where the resources to create that structure will come from.

The conceptual framework, then, helps identify some of the pitfalls of participatory journalism content. It also provides some guidance on what both journalism and user-generated content mean in the context of communication in an open network.

This model also hints at the various levels of observation that are useful in evaluating the inclusion of participatory journalism with more traditional journalistic practices and processes. Different perspectives are helpful in exploring how online communication works at these different levels:

- The individual communication process, including the users who provide the information, the community managers and journalists, and the users who receive and interpret the information. These individuals are the nodes and links in our model. Sociologists call this level of observation or analysis the micro level.

- The organizations involved in the process, including organizational structures, rules and roles – the star and diamond shapes in our illustration. This is the meso, or middle, level of observation or analysis.
- The societal level or overall network, including the general function of public communication. This is the macro level of observation or analysis.

Let's look at how those levels apply to what we learned from our interviewees.

9.4.2 Understanding Why

These analytical perspectives are central to a full understanding of what the journalists told us. We have already seen, in earlier chapters, that they discussed their reasons for embracing or rejecting participatory journalism on various levels. With our theoretical framework in hand, it is easier to understand why.

Some comments are based on individual views about, and experience with, user-generated content and the process of handling it, a micro-level perspective. Some are based on the struggle of institutions, both organizations and the profession as a whole, to preserve structural integrity and historic identity; these remarks reflect issues at the meso level.

And some are macro-level concerns, centered on the question of whether user-enhanced journalism can still fulfill its traditional role in society or whether that role has been completely changed by the rising social and communicative complexity.

Unsurprisingly, our interviewees did not explicitly mention these sociological concepts. But references to the three levels of observation and analysis of the phenomenon of participatory journalism could be found in all the interviews in one way or another.

Our interviewees were acutely aware of the deep impact that the Internet and user-generated content has had on journalism. Despite their different perspectives and conclusions, they all reflected on the change in public communication as a process, whether they saw it as evolutionary or revolutionary.

Again, the views of most journalists were nuanced, as we have seen throughout this book. But for simplicity's sake, the two most directly oppositional positions could be described as "journalism traditionalists," who generally opposed the changes, and "participatory evangelists," who generally supported the changes and even sought to advance them.

The people who leaned toward a traditionalist view tended to see participatory journalism at least in part as a threat to traditional journalistic structures. Those with more of an evangelical streak not only welcomed the input from the users but also, in some cases, even framed it as a way to save journalism itself.

As we have seen in earlier chapters, many held positions between the two extremes. For example, journalists who held either a fatalistic or a pragmatic view saw problems with participatory developments but argued that there was very little to be done about them. A German journalist at *FAZ* summed up the fatalist view, describing user-generated content as a destructive and unstoppable "avalanche overrunning you."

Pragmatists, on the other hand, have their metaphorical snowboards ready to carry them along. A journalist at NRG (Israel) described the varying approaches: "There are people who have missed this revolution who fear this, fear information that is decentralized, that anyone can supply," he said. These are journalists who "want to be the one and only pipeline, who want to keep the power for themselves. And then there are those who have joined up with it, who actually see it as a lever. In other words, 'if you can't beat them, join them.' "

Another way of considering these different approaches is to think about journalists as primarily either segregationists or integrationists. In Table 9.1, we use these categories to summarize journalists' views from a micro, meso and macro level.

Those in the first category tend to believe user contributions should be kept apart from journalism. For the most part, they would like journalistic communication to follow the traditional model shown in Figure 9.2.

The integrationists, on the other hand, believe participatory journalism can and should be mixed with professionally produced material. Some, such as the editor of Le Post (France), even advocated the co-creation of content.

9.4.3 The Change Process

In addition to this relatively concrete consideration of specific issues stemming from the growth of participatory journalism, another thread of our conversations with these journalists concerned the struggles and problems created by the process of change itself. The segregationist and integrationist approaches are useful here, as well.

Many journalists expressed concerns not so much about user-generated content in particular but rather about the more general problems of adapting to rapid and dramatic change. Journalists worried not only about their own adaptations but also about how to handle conflict arising from differing degrees of reluctance among their colleagues.

The interviews indicated that journalists were grappling with two key transformations in the communication process: the inclusion of users as new sources of information and as participants in the process of making news decisions.

Nearly all the journalists we interviewed mentioned that users had become new sources, close to what happens in society. "It is important for journalists that they don't miss the users with their writing and publish in the wrong direction, but [*instead*] pick up what is published amongst the citizens," said a

Table 9.1 Views of participatory journalism at different levels of observation and analysis

	Refers to …	Segregationist view	Integrationist view
Change in overall communication process	Positioning of journalists and users; process of control over information	Separating users and journalists: Users as sources, but journalists retain full control	Co-creating content: Users become content producers: Journalists give up at least some control and work with users
Micro level	Effects on personal work process and related experiences	UGC is unorganized input that needs to be structured by journalists: A time-consuming burden, nuisance or distraction that slows down news production	UGC eases and changes production processes: Advocacy of free input and simplified access
Meso level	Structural changes to the organization of journalism as an industry and a profession	Participatory journalism does not follow professional rules and structures: May threaten the profession if not contained or controlled, but can be exploited by journalists in traditional news routines and structures	UGC as rejuvenation, modernizing journalistic production rules: Modification of traditional structures and creation of new user roles in creating journalism
Macro level	Public communication in a changing media environment: Involves issues related to participation, pluralism and democracy	UGC as "pulp communication" lacking public relevance: Threat or competitor that might replace journalism with something worse, resulting in a loss of quality in public communication as well as the loss of valuable journalistic function	Voice of democracy: Pluralism and a better functioning of public communication: UGC helps repair relationships between journalists and users

journalist at *Süddeutsche Zeitung* (Germany). "This is a seismograph for existing societal trends."

Some interviewees also mentioned a heightened social awareness instigated by citizens who, as an editor at *24 Hours* (Croatia) editor said, "are more sensitive to social wrongs."

A minority of journalists criticized user input for not being very useful or interesting. Others pointed out the danger of following users' lead on social issues. "You get pulled into things that are more pulp, populist, the more scandalous things," an editor at Ynet (Israel) said. "You know that they will bring the traffic to you."

Most journalists, even the generally critical ones, had positive things to say about the inclusion of users as a new source. But the effect of participatory journalism on the process of producing journalism – and, in particular, on the process of deciding what is newsworthy in the first place – was a far more sensitive topic.

As we have seen in earlier chapters, even the evangelists were unlikely to support the idea of allowing users to set the news **agenda**. "I don't think we will ever get there. Today we foster a very active participation, but the final decision on the product is taken here [*in the newsroom*]," an interviewee from *20 Minutos* (Spain) said. "Final control, publishing decisions, hierarchy of content – that's something that we logically keep to ourselves with all the material."

Most journalists saw a clear separation between users having some influence on the content and users deciding what that content should be. "If they send things and I publish them, they are going to have an impact," said a journalist at The Marker Café (Israel). "But they are not going to decide, ultimately, whether or not I am going to publish [*what I receive*]. I do not owe it to them."

A number of journalists also mentioned or referred to the traditional **gatekeeping** role of news professionals. For example, a *Globe and Mail* (Canada) editor said:

> We make our editorial decisions based on what we think is news and what we are capable of handling. Because of the comments, there is more reader input [*on the website*] than there is in the newspaper, which has just the letters page, but it doesn't actually affect what we put on the site. ... Basically there's always going to be editors and reporters doing their gatekeeping job, assessing their facts, assembling the facts and writing about them. And the editors will then decide what's going to happen with that information."

At a more micro level, journalists described concerns about their actual work processes and personal experiences with user contributions.

Again, some stressed the positive effects, for instance on individual productivity; a British online editor said being able to generate lots of content on a particular topic without having to actually write it was like "magic." Similarly, an Israeli journalist at NRG pointed out that text is written at no cost to the journalists and the newspaper: "In the end, most journalists are pretty happy about this because ultimately they are the ones who get credited while also getting stories 'for free.'"

However, others only saw minor effects, such as the editor at *El País* (Spain) who conceded that **comments** could enrich a story, but only "if they come from people with substantive opinions."

And some saw a negative rather than a positive effect; for instance, hostile or abusive user comments took time and effort to deal with, making their jobs harder, not easier. Even aside from the nature of some comments, the overall volume of user input demanding to be filtered or fact-checked was a burden. A journalist at *FAZ* (Germany) described the opinionated input by users on free discussion **forums** as "a seven-headed snake that cannot be tamed!"

9.4.4 Rules, Traditions and Structures

Journalists also expressed concerns about change at the organizational or "meso" level of analysis. These concerns focused on the general rules, traditions and structures of professional journalism.

In considering what they saw as the integrity of the profession, most journalists seemed to espouse a strategy that was at least somewhat segregationist – even if they supported the inclusion of user-generated content in general. As another *El País* journalist put it:

> Anyone can do journalism, but not everything that is being done is journalism. Doing journalism requires following some rules, applying rigor. You have to fact-check and try to keep a more or less neutral standpoint. If any person is acting this way, you can surely say they are doing journalism. Which is not the same as saying that whatever people send or whatever a news medium publishes is journalism.

"I think that everyone knows the difference between journalism produced by professionals and user contributions," said a colleague at the same Spanish paper. "Once [*users as content producers*] are here, they are not going to fade away. This does not mean that they are going to replace professional production of content."

A journalist at *Vecernji List* (Croatia) warned that the inclusion of participatory journalism could water down the profession or destroy its image, ultimately reducing trust in the media. "People think now that anybody can produce news. It is less of a profession, but more of ... I don't know what I would call it. Sometimes it looks like a jungle," he said.

And an interviewee at *The Globe and Mail* (Canada) perceived a real threat to the jobs that journalists do, as well as to the traditional idea of a journalistic profession. Overall, she said, journalists feel threatened by user-generated content:

I think there's a certain elitism that goes with any profession, and by pulling more members of the public in to do things – whether it's writing blogs or having their pictures, of which some of them are quite good, added to the mix of the photojournalists – it's a threat to your job, really. … If a company can get just as much out of somebody who's not being paid, then why would they have the paid people? … I think that's always a real threat. It's no different than if they bring in freelance writers to do something or your grandmother to write recipes instead of the food editor. I think that's always been there, but it's a little bit easier now because everybody has a computer.

Finally, on the macro level of overall societal changes, some journalists stressed the positive effect of a more democratic and pluralist public communication. "We're in a position as a publisher of a major newspaper, of a major website, to have the tools and the outlook to help people communicate with each other to give their stories out to the rest of the world, to help people inform one another," said an editor at *USA Today*. "I think we're well-positioned to help online conversation and online information exchange evolve."

The same editor added that the earlier detachment of journalists from their audiences has made the inclusion of users in the online product even more necessary. "There really isn't a friendship underlying the media-public relationship from the beginning," he said. "So we have a lot of work to do there to repair the relationship because it is good for everyone to have this."

Other journalists, however, said they did not expect the integration of user-generated content to have a positive impact on societal communication.

"I don't believe in that 'voice of democracy' kind of argument," said a Croatian journalist at *Vecernji List*. A journalist at The Marker Café (Israel) also pointed out that many colleagues fear online communication in general might replace journalism, destroying the profession and not offering anything adequate in its place.

"The thing that really scares them [*the print journalists*] the most is that one day there will be no newspapers, no press," he said. "That is it, no more press – just the Internet. This is a great fear that journalists have."

9.4.5 Sense-making Strategies

As these examples from the vast set of interview data show, journalists have adopted several strategies to make sense of participatory journalism – and they correlate closely with the different levels of analysis described above. They reflect attempts to deal with change in the communication process at the micro, meso and macro levels, as shown in Table 9.1.

Our interviewees also mentioned the secondary effects of these changes – the reaction by their professional peers. Their statements expressed concern about changes brought about by technology, particularly the integrated social network of the Internet, coming too fast for journalists or media institutions to adjust.

"People are having a hard time adapting," said a journalist at *24 Hours* (Croatia). "We feel like we are swimming in a sea of changes." An Israeli colleague at Ynet said the inclusion of user-generated content "demands open-mindedness on the journalist's part, more and more open-mindedness, and not feeling threatened, which is the keyword for lots of journalists, who feel that any moment the users are coming to take away their livelihood."

A community editor at *Süddeutsche Zeitung* (Germany) attributed the problem to journalists' general self-perception, saying editors were "much too vain" to allow a blending of journalists and users. Others pointed to differences among the kinds of journalists affected by user contributions. "Online journalists are adaptable, traditional journalists less so," said a journalist at *Vecernji List* (Croatia).

9.5 Conclusion

The factors we have considered in this chapter are many and varied – too many and too varied to paint a clear picture of how the changes considered here and throughout the book will ultimately affect the practice of journalism. There do not appear to be any universal perceptions about participatory journalism. Certainly, not everyone is enthusiastic about user input, but neither is there shared resistance to the forms of user contributions that were being explored at the time of our study.

The variations themselves cause some tension, as the speed of change is not consistent among countries, media companies, newsrooms within these companies, groups within these newsrooms or individual journalists within these groups.

Contradictory orientations can be challenging to resolve. For example, some journalists expressed a personal openness to participatory journalism that did not fit the organization's traditional orientation at the structural level – which in turn was contrary to the generally positive orientation encountered elsewhere in the same country.

What then can we say about the significance of the phenomenon of participatory journalism and its relevance for the future of journalism?

From a theoretical standpoint, the integration of user input in the professional process of producing journalism can be correlated to the growing communicative complexity in society. But did the technological changes allow for more complexity, or did the complexity lead to a need for technological and professional solutions? It is not unlikely that these were synchronous or even circular developments, feeding and continually influencing one another.

In any case, our interview data show that this process is accompanied by a fair amount of occupational stress, as practitioners of something traditionally called "journalism" try to retain its structure and integrity, its rules and roles, its organizations and its traditions.

Neither the effort, nor its outcome is decided by one person or one organization, or at a single level. Some journalists, some organizations and even some countries seem to be more traditional than others, as we saw back in Chapter 3. They seem more likely to try to cling to what has worked in the past, trusting the tried and true more than the as-yet-unfulfilled promises of a new media future.

On the other hand, the risk-takers, some of whom even are participatory journalism evangelists as described in Chapters 4 and 5, see change as beneficial. Here too, responses vary not only among individuals but also among broader groups, as tentatively suggested by preliminary indications of a central European tendency toward structural preservation or an Anglo-American one toward a faith in change.

These multi-level struggles lead to development that proceeds at an uneven pace. The future of journalism will be decided in this dynamic process of synchronous change and structural preservation.

The future is always uncertain, but our research makes us inclined to believe that change is inevitable. The technological developments that enabled participatory journalism are irreversible, and so are the social and communicative restructuring processes that are well under way.

However, traditional journalism may succeed at preserving some or all of its integrity in a changed environment – if it finds a way to adapt to a new situation without destabilizing the core of its existence and without jeopardizing its function in society.

Participate!

1. What are the differences between earlier and simpler societies and modern media societies? What is meant by the term "hyper-complex societies"? Do you think we are living in such a society? What might the next stage be?
2. In this chapter, we mentioned three sociological "levels" of understanding the ongoing changes in journalism. What are these levels, and how do they apply to journalists' reactions to user-generated content? Can you also apply them to other changes in communication, such as the spread of mobile delivery?
3. Why is the pace of change related to participatory journalism uneven? In what ways do the variations create tension and conflict in media organizations and newsrooms?

References

Anderson, Chris (2006) *The long tail: Why the future of business is selling less of more*, New York: Hyperion.

Andsager, Julie, and H. Allen White (2007) *Self versus others: Media, messages and the third-person effect*, Mahwah, New Jersey: Lawrence Erlbaum Associates.

Carey, James W. (1998) The Internet and the end of the national communication system: Uncertain predictions of an uncertain future, *Journalism & Mass Communication Quarterly* 75 (1): 28–34.

Carey, James W. (1989) *Communication as culture: Essays on media and society*, Boston: Unwin Hyman.

Christians, Clifford G., Theodore L. Glasser, Dennis McQuail, Kaarle Nordenstreng and Robert A. White (2009) *Normative theories of the media: Journalism in democratic societies*, Urbana: University of Illinois Press.

Domingo, David, Thorsten Quandt, Ari Heinonen, Steve Paulussen, Jane B. Singer and Marina Vujnovic (2008) Participatory journalism practices in the media and beyond: An international comparative study of initiatives in online newspapers, *Journalism Practice* 2 (3): 326–342.

Görke, Alexander, and Armin Scholl (2006) Niklas Luhmann's theory of social systems and journalism research, *Journalism Studies* 7 (4): 644–655.

Granovetter, Mark S. (1973) The strength of weak ties, *American Journal of Sociology* 78: 1360–1380.

Haas, Tanni (2005) From "public journalism" to the "public's journalism"? Rhetoric and reality in the discourse on weblogs, *Journalism Studies* 6 (3): 387–396.

Innis, Harold (1951) *The bias of communication*, Toronto: University of Toronto Press.

Innis, Harold (1950) *Empire and communications*, Oxford: Clarendon Press.

Larson, Margali Sarfetti (1977) *The rise of professionalism: A sociological analysis*, Berkeley: University of California Press.

Lowrey, Wilson (2006) Mapping the journalism-blogging relationship, *Journalism* 7 (4): 477–500.

Paterson, Chris A., and David Domingo (2008) *Making online news: The ethnography of new media production*, New York: Peter Lang Publishing.

Prensky, Marc (2001) Digital natives, digital immigrants, *On the Horizon* 9 (5). Accessed 15 January 2010 from: http://www.marcprensky.com/writing/Prensky – Digital Natives, Digital Immigrants – Part1.pdf

Quandt, Thorsten (2005) *Journalisten im Netz (Journalists in the Net)*, Wiesbaden: Verlag für Sozialwissenschaften.

Quandt, Thorsten, Martin Löffelholz, David Weaver, Thomas Hanitzsch and Klaus-Dieter Altmeppen (2006) American and German online journalists at the beginning of the 21st century: A bi-national survey, *Journalism Studies* 7 (2): 171–186.

Shoemaker, Pamela J., and Stephen D. Reese (1996) *Mediating the message: Theories of influences on mass media content*, Reading, Massachusetts: Addison Wesley Longman.

10

Fluid Spaces, Fluid Journalism
The role of the "active recipient" in participatory journalism
Alfred Hermida

It has become virtually impossible to visit a news website without stumbling across a call for participation. Exhortations to **users** to speak their minds, express their opinions, upload a photo, take a **poll** or share a story with their friends, among other participatory options, have all become common features of the online news landscape.

This concluding chapter summarizes how leading national newspapers have sought to include **audience** members in the process and practice of online journalism in the late 2000s. It highlights key trends identified in our international comparative study, and it offers a final look at the emerging relationships between journalists and users that our interviewees described.

10.1 A Participatory Culture

As established media institutions have expanded into digital environments, they have adopted the discourse of active audiences, talking about users rather than readers. Scholars such as Henry Jenkins (2006) have written about the emergence of a participatory culture, spurred by the rise of networked and interactive digital technologies that empower citizens to express themselves.

Participatory Journalism: Guarding Open Gates at Online Newspapers, First Edition.
Jane B. Singer, Alfred Hermida, David Domingo, Ari Heinonen, Steve Paulussen, Thorsten Quandt, Zvi Reich, and Marina Vujnovic.

Media technologies of creation, publication and dissemination that were once the privilege of capital-intensive industries are now widely available, often at little or no cost. *Time* magazine recognized this trend when it named "You" as Person of the Year 2006, paying tribute to the millions of web users who contribute to sites such as Wikipedia, YouTube and Flickr, and highlighting "community and collaboration on a scale never seen before" (Grossman 2006).

There is a degree of hyperbole in such statements. Alternative or do-it-yourself media are scarcely a new phenomenon (Phillips 2003; Duncombe 1997), and news consumers have long been able to talk back to mainstream media through options such as letters to the editor or radio call-in programs, as we outlined in Chapter 6.

However, the "self-produced media" (Croteau 2006) made possible by today's digital technologies are creating opportunities for new forms of media participation, production and distribution on an unprecedented scale, and continued expansion seems inevitable. Citizens of the twenty-first century are taking advantage of these opportunities in spaces both outside and inside those provided by traditional news organizations.

News, then, has become a personal, social and participatory experience for growing numbers of citizens (Purcell *et al.* 2010), and the newspaper websites described in this book were already very much a part of this trend at the time of our study in 2007 and 2008. They were letting the public into the previously closed world of journalism, offering areas for audience members to participate in the news despite the concerns of individual journalists and news managers about the quality of the contributions, potential legal risks or perceived threats to the profession.

Throughout the study, we found mixed feelings among the editors we interviewed, who often expressed both apprehension and support for involving audiences in the process of journalism.

Such contradictory views are understandable at a time when journalism is in a state of flux and, arguably, even crisis. Our book has described not only these conflicted attitudes but also the tools and strategies that journalists at major news outlets were adopting to motivate, engage and connect with users in online spaces.

We suggest that at the moment, journalists see audiences as what we call "active recipients" of information – somewhere between passive receivers and active creators of content.

Journalists expect readers to act when an event happens – for instance by contributing eyewitness reports, photos and video – and then react once a professional has shepherded the information through the **news production stages** of **filtering**, **processing** and **distributing** the news. In other words, as we discuss further below, the user has a generally appreciated but mostly serendipitous role at the initial **access/observation stage**, an increasingly commonplace role at the post-publication **interpretation** stage – but relatively little impact on the crucial stages in between.

This concluding chapter summarizes the evidence our study suggests for that view.

10.2 "Active Recipients"

As this book has illustrated, numerous questions remain about how users can, should and do participate in the news process; the impact on the ways that journalists work; and ultimately, the shape of journalism in the twenty-first century.

We strongly believe that the old media will not "shrivel up and die" (Croteau 2006: 343). Instead, we anticipate that they will continue the tentative explorations discussed throughout this book, shifting away from the "'we write, you read' dogma of modern journalism" (Deuze 2003: 220) and learning how to adapt to a more collaborative media environment in which journalists share the creation and dissemination of the news with users.

10.2.1 Tools for Debate

As we saw beginning in Chapter 2 and detailed throughout the chapters that followed, news organizations today are using a range of options to draw the reader into their journalism. These options range from appeals for video of a breaking news event to solicitation of a user's take on the issue of the day and more.

The technical tools that facilitate participation, as well as the way those tools are implemented, are constantly evolving to offer new ways for users to contribute to online news sites (Thurman and Hermida 2010; Hermida and Thurman 2008). Indeed, they have kept on changing, in many cases significantly, since we interviewed the journalists whom you have encountered here.

This constant adaptation is to be expected. Newspapers and other news organizations are operating in a relatively new media environment, one in which technological innovation is both central and exalted.

To take just one example from among the papers in our study, the *Guardian* (UK) first implemented user **forums** or discussion boards in 1999. When we talked with *Guardian* journalists in early 2008, they were wrestling with the management of user **comments** in selected areas of their website. Today, the paper uses social networks and a myriad of other tools to enable users to contribute to the website in many more ways, as well as to share the news with friends and other online users all over the world.

10.2.2 The Rest of the Story

However, the growth in the number of participatory spaces and technologies paints only part of the picture, and a potentially misleading one at that. It suggests that journalists are wholeheartedly embracing opportunities to open up the news to the public and share jurisdiction over a space that traditionally belonged to them.

That would be a highly oversimplified view. As this book has shown, available tools are being used to channel user involvement differently – and to different degrees – in each of the five stages of news production we outlined at the start.

The approaches taken by the online newspapers in our study varied, though considerably less than might be expected, given that they represented ten different nations and ten different news environments. Although we only interviewed journalists working for newspaper companies, we believe their views are broadly indicative of a profession that has well-established and commonly shared norms and practices (Weaver 1998).

As we have seen repeatedly, the interpretation stage – which enables users to offer their input only after an item has been published – was the most open to active user participation in every country. Comments on stories, in particular, were by far the most popular tool used by these newspapers at the time of our study. Since then, users have been given more opportunities to distribute the news, for instance through the use of **social media** and **social networking** sites, but comments remain a dominant participatory format.

However, journalists expressed little inclination to relinquish control over the process of making decisions about what news is and how that news should be reported, issues that arise at earlier stages of story production. Nor have they taken significant steps in that direction more recently. Audience participation was, and largely remains, framed as the user's ability to debate what the journalists have produced rather than as input into how the news is produced in the first place, including how it is selected, gathered, filtered or edited.

We should not underestimate the significance of user comments. The spaces for comments are far more open and unfettered than, for example, letters to the editor. As we explored in Chapter 6, comments provide an accessible, instant means for citizens to share their thoughts on a story, creating an immediate feedback loop for journalists and news managers. While this participatory format only takes the temperature of those readers who actively engage with the content, the ability to gauge virtually instant reaction to a published story offers a relatively recent, and often new, experience for journalists (Hermida 2009).

That said, the relationship between journalists and audience members remains rooted in long-established power dynamics, as we explore in the next section.

10.2.3 The Battle Over Fortress Journalism

Journalists are used to owning the news, in the most basic sense that they decide what and how to report. Yet at the same time, journalism has always been expected to provide a way for voices from outside the media to be heard (Christians *et al.* 2009).

As we explained in Chapter 9, **participatory journalism** would appear to be a logical extension of this function. In theory, user input would contribute to a more democratic and representative media and be welcomed as such by journalists.

To some extent, the journalists we interviewed did appreciate having tools that let them hear from the public. For example, we encountered a general interest in developing users as sources for news tips or audio-visual information, especially about breaking news.

But in most cases, the journalist remained the **gatekeeper**, deciding whether this material was worthy of inclusion on the website or newspaper.

Participatory tools have been adopted more widely as listening devices than as devices for a dialogue between journalists and audiences. We found that the notion of entering into a substantive exchange of ideas and views with users had not become part of the journalist's job or mind set. Audiences still were kept well outside the news production process.

Senior BBC editor Peter Horrocks has dubbed this attitude "fortress journalism," with journalists in the role of professionals who work in powerful institutions with thick walls. But, he added, "the fortresses are crumbling, and courtly jousts with fellow journalists are no longer impressing the crowds" (Horrocks 2009: 6).

The online newspaper journalists we interviewed were well aware of the forces gnawing at the foundations of fortress journalism, as we saw beginning in Chapter 3. They are caught between two worlds, one involving participatory forms of media production and the other relying on longstanding norms of professional control.

As a result, newsrooms are torn between encouraging users to engage in the new process through multiple tools while at the same time defending the core of news production as the preserve of professionals. This struggle is taking place not only on an individual level but also at organizational and societal levels, as we described in the previous chapter.

Overall, our interviews suggested two camps. One group of journalists clung to tradition and tended to fall back on proven and trusted methods. The other group, whom we dubbed **Web 2.0** "evangelists" in Chapters 4 and 5 and "integrationists" in Chapter 9, were more open to change and put their faith in the promise of new media.

These categorizations are broad generalizations, but they serve to highlight the tensions playing out in the established media. The attitudes tended to color each journalist's outlook on **user-generated content**. Defenders of tradition were likely to view user material as something of a threat to journalism that needed to be contained. Evangelists saw it as a way to reinvigorate journalism and transform relationships with audiences.

It is much harder to determine *why* a journalist or newspaper fell into either camp. Our interviews indicated that some of the difference seemed related to age, the nature of the publication or the culture of the country, but none of those factors provides a wholly satisfactory answer. As we saw in Chapter 9, these issues play out on multiple levels and are subject to many other influences, which helps explain the uneven pace of media adoption of participatory tools.

Despite the variations, however, participation has become a fixture for online newspapers. The next section reviews our findings about changes in newsroom duties, roles and structures.

10.3 New Relationships, New Roles

At the same time as journalists are navigating new relationships with audiences, they are also negotiating new working practices and newsroom structures.

Traditional newsrooms tend to have fixed hierarchies, with a top-down organizational structure and clearly delineated roles and responsibilities. By comparison, online newsrooms tend to have a flatter structure.

The organizational structure of the newsroom contributes to the degree of interactivity on the website it produces (Boczkowski 2004). As discussed in Chapter 4, our interviews indicated that a flat, integrated print and online newsroom structure seemed more conducive to encouraging interactions between journalists and users than the more hierarchical structure.

But our research indicated a discrepancy between editors' beliefs and newsroom practices. Journalists who worked in separate online newsrooms felt they had more freedom to experiment with new forms of user engagement, while **integrated newsrooms** that brought together print and online teams tended to be more conservative.

Other studies have indicated that journalistic culture strongly influences the adoption of new technologies and trends (Paterson and Domingo 2008; Silcock and Keith 2006; Singer 2004). In the case of integrated newsrooms, the print culture has seemed to outweigh the online culture, reflecting its long-standing position as the dominant media format for news organizations such as the ones we studied.

Another factor shaping how newsrooms handled participation was the size of the national media market. Newspapers in the larger markets, including France, Germany, Spain, the United Kingdom and the United States, generally maintained distinct audience **participation teams**. Most newspapers in the smaller media markets tended to share responsibilities for managing user input among the online journalists. Economics, rather than just culture, is evidently one of the ingredients in molding how newspaper organizations are reorganizing news production processes, as discussed in Chapter 8.

10.3.1 Conversation Facilitators

Participatory journalism also was having an impact on the work of the journalist at an individual level. Traditionally, the journalist's job has been to gather, filter, edit and publish the news – the components of a gatekeeping role. This role remained identifiable in newsrooms where journalists were responsible for monitoring and filtering user feedback. For instance, as described in Chapters 4, 6 and 7, journalists took on the role of comment **moderators**, making decisions about what is published and what is deleted.

But our study found that a new role was emerging, one that focused journalists' attention more on facilitating the conversation than on controlling it.

Our interviewees used a variety of labels for this new role, including "**community managers**," "coaches" and "coordinators." Newsrooms had different job descriptions for this new position, as well. But across the newspapers instituting this facilitator function, the focus was on working with the community of users.

In some cases, the community manager or editor served as a bridge between readers and the newsroom, such as at the *Telegraph* (UK). At other publications, such as the *Guardian* (UK), the position was seen as more strategic, with responsibility for developing plans to foster greater reader engagement.

The shift away from the basic gatekeeping role was evident in the trend toward **post-moderation** of user comments, as well. Earlier studies, such as the research conducted by Hermida and Thurman (2008), found that editors preferred retaining editorial control over user submissions. But our research suggested that the concept of curation as an alternative to moderation has gained ground in newsrooms, as outlined in Chapter 5.

Rather than having journalists spend hours identifying and removing the worst user submissions, a curation strategy devotes resources to highlighting the best content. Some of our newsrooms already had taken this a step further, such as LePost.fr (France) and *Het Nieuwsblad* (Belgium), with journalists actively mentoring contributors to improve the quality of submissions.

Newspapers also were recruiting audience members to help with this curation. For example, some editors talked about the need to involve users in policing content.

In part, this interest in engaging users in site oversight can be seen as a way to reduce the economic burden of managing the growing volume of public contributions. After all, these users are offering their time and services for free, as we discussed in Chapter 8.

However, it also suggests that journalists may be starting to see participatory journalism as a collaborative process, in which both professionals and amateurs have a role to play. The next section explores how this partnership is playing out in newsrooms.

10.4 Working with the Audience

Singer (2008: 75) has argued that "in a networked world, there no longer is the 'journalist,' 'audience' and 'source.' There is only 'us'." While journalists are, arguably, more aware of the "us" in the contemporary media environment, our interviewees indicated a great deal of ambivalence toward the notion of more collaborative forms of journalism, as described in Chapter 3 and elsewhere throughout this book. Traditionally, journalists have not been expected to engage in a dialogue with users. Yet increasingly, that is exactly what they are being asked to do.

The tension between the benefits of opening up the journalistic process and the need to defend the profession of journalism permeated our interviews. As Deuze and his colleagues pointed out several years ago, participatory ideals clash with notions of professional distance in journalism, "notions which tend to exclude rather than to include" (2007: 335).

Journalism has developed as a profession in which designated individuals use their expertise and intelligence to create finished products, such as the news story or the printed newspaper. The Internet, on the other hand, offers participatory mechanisms that facilitate distributed and collective expertise.

Journalists are seeking to balance conflicting pressures as they incorporate the audience into the work of the newsroom. Again, some newspapers have encouraged and even solicited dedicated readers to help co-police user material. And at least among the leading national newspapers in our study, nearly all invite their audience to have their say on the news of the day.

10.4.1 Open and Shut

However, certain bastions of journalism are more fiercely protected than others. As described above, journalists are reluctant to allow users to become co-producers of editorial material, instead seeing audience members as a source of content – particularly eyewitness information, such as photos or descriptions of a breaking news event – that can be fed into professionally produced news reports. The proliferation of digital technologies such as smart phones has made it easy for the public to capture and send content to newsrooms eager for such raw material.

In this relationship, the user is seen as a "public sensor," becoming the eyes and ears of the newsroom, as described in Chapter 3. Clearly, a journalist cannot be everywhere, so it is hardly surprising that editors appreciated how a large number of sensors can expand the reach of journalism, particularly at a time of when the number of journalists in the newsroom is falling.

The potential here goes beyond news tips and audio/visual material sent in by the public. Some of our interviewees also spoke of additional ideas and directions for a story generated through user comments, though the value of this perceived benefit was tempered with concerns about the quality of the information received.

These are examples of how journalism is becoming a more collaborative practice, albeit one in which the journalist retains oversight of the process. Several of the newspapers were already going further at the time of our study, exploring more collective ways of producing the news. We found examples of partnerships between professional journalists and amateur contributors both on specific stories and on new web initiatives, for instance the use of **crowdsourcing** by the *National Post* (Canada) to report a major fire in Toronto.

The prospect of a legion of amateur volunteers doing the work that professionals have been trained and paid to do is a chilling notion for many journalists. While these fears are understandable, it is misguided to expect amateurs to produce work that meets the standards of a professional culture or class.

Rather, we found that the initiatives that appeared to hold the most promise involved "**pro-am journalism**," or collaboration between professionals and amateurs, such as the Belgian **hyperlocal** news site *HasseltLokaal* mentioned in Chapter 2. In these experiments, the journalist's task was to coordinate and motivate contributors, playing the role of community leader discussed earlier. Howe (2009) suggests that we are all better served when the crowd complements what journalists do, rather than trying to replace it.

Alan Rusbridger, the editor in chief of the *Guardian* (UK), has described the trend towards greater public participation as the "mutualisation" of the newspaper (2009). As Singer (2008) suggested, this mutualized future is based on a shift away from an "us" and "them" approach to journalism and toward an emphasis on the "we."

While we found some signs that journalism is heading in this direction, the newspapers we studied were still far from such a mutualized state, at least at the time of our interviews in late 2007 and early 2008. Journalists sought to find ways to maintain their professional status, not to redefine the professional practice of journalism.

In other words, news organizations are trying to marry a more collaborative approach with a system of editorial control.

10.4.2 Spaces for the Public

The proliferation of places for audience members to inject their presence into online newspapers could give the impression that the media have adopted a more open and participatory approach to the news. For example, comments on stories, as discussed in Chapter 6, do represent a dramatic expansion in citizens' ability to make their voices heard, offering immediate and often unfiltered reaction to a news event.

But although journalists are making this form of participation available, they are not necessarily enthusiastic about it. Nor do they see it as "journalism."

On the contrary, we found that most editors viewed comments as separate and distinct from professionally produced content, even if they both appear on the same website. While journalists may appreciate the feedback provided by comments, most did not consider responding to comments or otherwise interacting with the users who provided them as part of their professional duties.

Comments are posted once the journalist has completed his or her work. Again, few interviewees considered the debate generated by a story as part of the journalistic process; instead, they viewed the user discussion as something that occurs after the journalism is finished.

Particularly in larger media markets, comment moderation was not seen as part of the journalist's role or job duties at all. Some newspapers divorced moderation from the newsroom completely, instead **outsourcing** it to an external company.

In general, then, content from the public is not only considered separate from the journalistic process but it also is structurally conceptualized as an "other" space. The technological construction of distinct spaces for user content is one of the ways that journalists are seeking to maintain jurisdiction over the news.

One of the trends we tentatively identified was a difference in approach between highbrow and populist newspapers, as outlined in Chapter 5. The outlets that considered themselves "newspapers of record," such as *El País* (Spain) or *Haaretz* (Israel), tended to favor creating separate sections or even separate websites for contributions from the public. The effect was to marginalize public input by setting up playgrounds for users, while protecting the overall reputation of the newspaper as the trustworthy chronicler of events.

In fact, the perceived need to protect the reputation of the brand by separating amateur and professional content has emerged as a central concern in participatory journalism among elite news outlets (Singer and Ashman 2009; Hermida and Thurman 2008).

In contrast, relatively populist titles were more likely to involve user input in their news production process. Editors at *24 Hours* (Croatia), Ynet and NRG (Israel), *20 Minutos* (Spain) and *USA Today* were among those more likely to view the audience as potential sources for ideas and stories. The difference in approach to user content indicated that the more populist publications in our study placed a higher priority on reflecting the interests of their readers.

10.5 Guarding Open Gates

Even at these newspapers, however, journalists were not surrendering their traditional position as the gatekeeper. They were still making decisions about what made or did not make the news, and they also were passing judgment on the quality of material received from the public.

In doing so, journalists were guided by a set of ethical principles that are being tested by an open, networked media space, as discussed in Chapter 7. They saw themselves as information guardians with a commitment to truth and fairness that can be strained by the incorporation of contributions from outside the newsroom. Questions surrounding the veracity of user input or the abusive nature of some contributions continue to vex journalists seeking to maintain the newspaper's credibility and reputation (Singer and Ashman 2009; Hermida and Thurman 2008).

The newspapers in our study generally adopted two initiatives to tackle these and related issues. Some took a hands-on approach, aiming to filter out poor-quality, abusive or potentially illegal material. But others took the opposite stand, fearing that they would become legally responsible if they started policing user content. These journalists worried that they could be held liable not just for what they wrote online but also for what audience members wrote.

In response, one strategy that emerged in our study involved promoting the good material rather than trying to eliminate the bad. This approach represented an interesting way of rethinking the function of the gatekeeper, with the role of the journalist being to identify and highlight the "good stuff" rather than prevent the "bad stuff" from being published in the first place.

10.5.1 The Evolution of Community Online

For our study, we focused on newspapers in Western democracies, as one of the functions of journalism in these societies is to promote democratic deliberation. Such a role, in fact, is at the core of a broadly shared journalistic culture.

In theory, the ability of citizens to play a greater part in the news should invigorate the public sphere. For some, the Internet itself is a force for democracy, a medium that "will give voice to people who've felt voiceless" (Gillmor 2006: xviii).

Some of the journalists we interviewed mentioned this potential of participatory journalism to democratize the media conversation. However, they generally framed this capability in the context of providing space for a greater diversity of voices rather than democratizing the journalistic process itself. And the notion of participatory journalism as a force for democracy was far from the main reason for undertaking any such initiatives.

Far more pressing in the minds of journalists were the financial straits in which the news industry found itself at the time of our study. Giving voice to the voiceless was all well and good, but the imperative of ensuring the survival of the newspaper was a more urgent preoccupation among the editors we interviewed, as indicated in Chapter 8. Online, newspapers compete against traditional rivals internationally as well as nationally, along with bloggers, social networking sites, and a rapidly and steadily expanding number of other information providers.

Our interviewees saw offering a variety of ways for users to engage with the website as a vital way to create and strengthen audience loyalty. In their view, participatory journalism emerged as a key instrument in the battle to gain and retain audiences in a fragmented online media environment. The pressure on news outlets is not just to attract visitors to the website but also, and more importantly, to keep them engaged with the content for some length of time.

In the print era, a newspaper could count on a community of readers, often defined by geography or political outlook. News typically related to a geographic community, one as small as a town or, in the case of the papers in our study, as large as a nation. The residents of that community, whether large or small, were both sources of and audiences for the news it provided.

In countries with a strong national press, such as Britain, readers also might self-identify with the political slant of a publication. For example, liberal Britons would tend to be *Guardian* readers while conservatives would more likely favor the *Telegraph*.

Generating that same sense of personal connection online has proved significantly more challenging given the wealth of choices available. People are mixing and matching news from old and new media. In the United States, for instance, an overwhelming majority of Americans now get their news from multiple platforms, including television, newspapers, radio and the Internet – and online, they may visit half a dozen different news sites on a typical day (Purcell *et al.* 2010).

In this fragmented environment, journalists see the provision of participatory spaces in which users can share content and connect with one another as a way to restore the sense of a personal bond to their publication. Users thus are able to define and choose the peer communities they want to be involved with by seeking, finding and connecting with like-minded individuals on a newspaper website, as discussed in Chapter 3. Journalists in our study saw both social and economic benefits from providing spaces for this horizontal communication among users.

10.6 Conclusion

We started this book by talking about journalism's journey – the evolution of the newspaper from a printed physical record of the day's events to a fluid online product that is continually a work in progress.

Clear understandings of what journalism is and who journalists are have been eroded by the affordances of networked digital technologies. Throughout the book, we have explored how online newspaper professionals in ten Western democracies have sought to involve "the people formerly known as the audience" (Rosen 2006) in the day-to-day work of journalism, balancing long-established and strongly rooted routines, practices and norms with the demands of a twenty-first century media environment.

We found broadly consistent views of what journalism is and how it should be practiced across the two dozen publications in our study, indicating that journalists share a governing occupational ideology across borders regardless of nationality or the nature of the newspaper for which they work. Earlier studies (Deuze 2002; Weaver 1998) also have found a high degree of homogeneity among journalists in different countries. This ideology permeates everything journalists do, including the way they see their relationship to the audience, and helps justify the status of journalism as a professional culture.

However, the notion of "fortress journalism" (Horrocks 2009) is ill-suited to an open, participatory and collaborative network. As Deuze has suggested, "instead of having some kind of control over the flow of (meaningful, selected, fact-checked) information in the public sphere, journalists today are just some of the many voices in public communication" (2008: 12).

Our interviewees were keenly aware that the media world has changed and will continue to change. And they recognized the imperative to be more open to the contributions of users.

But the dilemma for newspapers is how to open up a closed profession to people who have traditionally been kept outside of the journalistic process – taking advantage of the new opportunities without undermining traditional values and practices. What emerged in our study is a view of news organizations that are seeking to provide more avenues for audience involvement but simultaneously to protect the professional status of the journalist.

Our interviewees realized that the people formerly known as the audience have transformed into something else. We don't quite have a word for it. In this book, we have referred to the people contributing to media websites as "users," as the word suggests a more active public than terms such as "readers" or "viewers." And we have used the term "participatory journalism" to describe how mainstream media organizations have sought to integrate the public in online versions of their print publications.

But our research suggests that deep down, most journalists do not view the user as an active participant in the news. Participating in the news would require newsrooms to open to the public all the stages of the journalistic process outlined in Chapter 2. This was simply not happening. Online newspapers have accommodated participation within the limitations of long-held and relatively static principles. The audience is primarily viewed as a source for selected information and for editorial argumentation.

As we have seen, users are involved at the start of the journalism and again once that journalism is finished. But the crucial and central processes – deciding what news is and how to cover and present it – remain almost entirely under the journalist's control.

Journalists, then, tend to view the user as an active recipient of the news rather than as an active participant in the news.

Practitioners today expect the public to do more than consume the news. Users are urged to send news tips, photos or videos, to add their interpretation of a story, or to share a link with friends. In other words, the public is expected to do something with the news – to act and react – and newsrooms have adopted tools to foster and facilitate such activities.

Overall, though, users are being kept outside of the news process itself. They are still, overall, receivers of information created and controlled by the journalist.

This is not to say that journalism has not changed. It has, considerably, and it will continue to do so. Throughout this book, we have documented examples of a more open approach to journalism, either through collaborations between professionals and users or through spaces populated and managed by users themselves.

In the future, expanding participation may drive the profession toward an even more mutualized and reciprocal, fluid form of journalism, with journalists finding their place in a collaborative media culture. At least, that is our hope.

Participate!

1. What is involved in being an "active recipient" of the news? Do you agree that it is the primary role of newspaper website users today? Should it be?
2. Why are journalists hesitant to involve audiences in their work? What are the risks and opportunities in giving the public a greater say in how the news is gathered, reported and distributed?
3. How might a news publication provide more opportunities for audience members to become active participants throughout all stages of the journalism process?

References

Boczkowski, Pablo J. (2004) The processes of adopting multimedia and interactivity in three online newsrooms, *Journal of Communication* 54 (2): 197–213.

Christians, Clifford G., Theodore L. Glasser, Denis McQuail, Kaarle Nordenstreng and Robert A. White (2009) *Normative theories of the media: Journalism in democratic societies*, Urbana: University of Illinois Press.

Croteau, David (2006) The growth of self-produced media content and the challenge to media studies, *Critical Studies in Media Communication* 23 (4): 340–344.

Deuze, Mark (2008) Understanding journalism as newswork: How it changes, and how it remains the same, *Westminster Papers in Communication and Culture* (2): 4–23.

Deuze, Mark (2003) The web and its journalisms: Considering the consequences of different types of news media online, *New Media & Society* 5 (2): 203–230.

Deuze, Mark (2002) *Journalists in the Netherlands: An analysis of the people, the issues and the (inter-) national environment*, Amsterdam: Het Spinhuis.

Deuze, Mark, Axel Bruns and Christoph Neuberger (2007) Preparing for an age of participatory news, *Journalism Practice* 1 (3): 322–338.

Duncombe, Stephen (1997) *Notes from the underground: Zines and the politics of alternative culture*, London: Verso.

Gillmor, Dan (2006) *We the media: Grassroots journalism by the people, for the people*, Sebastopol, California: O'Reilly.

Grossman, Lev (2006, 13 December) *Time*'s Person of the Year, *Time*. Accessed 21 January 2010 from: http://www.time.com/time/magazine/article/0,9171,1569514,00.html

Hermida, Alfred 2009 The blogging BBC, *Journalism Practice* 3 (3): 1–17.

Hermida, Alfred, and Neil Thurman (2008) A clash of cultures: The integration of user-generated content within professional journalistic frameworks at British newspaper websites, *Journalism Practice* 2 (3): 343–356.

Horrocks, Peter (2009) "The end of fortress journalism." In: Miller, Charles (ed) *The future of journalism*, London: BBC College of Journalism: 6–17.

Howe, Jeff (2009) *Crowdsourcing: Why the power of the crowd is driving the future of business*, New York: Three Rivers.

Jenkins, Henry (2006) *Convergence culture*, New York: New York University Press.

Paterson, Chris, and David Domingo (2008) *Making online news: The ethnography of new media production*, New York: Peter Lang.

Phillips, Peter (2003) *The Project Censored guide to independent media and activism*, New York: Seven Stories Press.

Purcell, Kristen, Lee Rainie, Amy Mitchell, Tom Rosenstiel and Kenny Olmstead (2010) Understanding the participatory news consumer, Pew Internet and American Life Project. Accessed 9 April 2010 from: http://www.pewinternet.org/Reports/2010/Online-News.aspx

Rosen, Jay (2006) The people formerly known as the audience, PressThink. Accessed 25 March 2010 from: http://journalism.nyu.edu/pubzone/weblogs/pressthink/2006/06/27/ppl_frmr.html

Rusbridger, Alan (2009, 19 October) First read: The mutualised future is bright, *Columbia Journalism Review*. Accessed 14 March 2010 from: http://www.cjr.org/reconstruction/the_mutualized_future_is_brigh.php

Silcock, B. William, and Susan Keith (2006) Translating the Tower of Babel? Issues of definition, language and culture in converged newsrooms, *Journalism Studies* 7 (4): 610–627.

Singer, Jane B. (2008) The journalist in the network: A shifting rationale for the gatekeeping role and the objectivity norm, *Tri'podos* 23: 61–76.

Singer, Jane B. (2004) More than ink-stained wretches: The resocialization of print journalists in converged newsrooms, *Journalism & Mass Communication Quarterly* 81 (4): 838–856.

Singer, Jane B., and Ian Ashman (2009) "Comment is free, but facts are sacred:" User-generated content and ethical constructs at the *Guardian*, *Journal of Mass Media Ethics* 24: 3–21.

Thurman, Neil, and Alfred Hermida (2010) "Gotcha: How newsroom norms are shaping participatory journalism online." In: Monaghan, Garrett, and Sean Tunney (eds.) *Web journalism: A new form of citizenship*, Eastbourne: Sussex Academic Press: 46–62.

Weaver, David (1998) *The global journalist: News people around the world*, Cresskill, New Jersey: Hampton Press.

Appendix
About Our Study

The study that forms the basis for this book rests on 67 in-depth interviews at leading national newspapers and their affiliated websites in ten Western democracies large and small, new and well-established: Belgium, Canada, Croatia, Finland, France, Germany, Israel, Spain, the United Kingdom and the United States. All of the included websites are affiliated with mainstream general-interest publications, and all attracted large numbers of unique users at the time of our study. This appendix contains a brief description of each paper.

As the accompanying list of interviewees shows, they included high-ranking editors and online staff, as well as journalists responsible for the development and maintenance of "online communities" wherever possible. Working individually, our team of eight researchers arranged and conducted the interviews in newsrooms in late 2007 and 2008, and each of us has written at least one chapter of this book based on what we collectively learned.

We structured each interview around a common set of questions and a shared framework stemming from our earlier explorations of user input into the news-production process (Domingo *et al.* 2008). In particular, we were interested in:

- Channels available for user participation and the rationale for choosing them.
- New newsroom practices stemming from interactions with audience members.
- Strategies for managing and making use of user contributions.
- Feedback or other indications of what users think about their own increasing presence on newspaper websites.

Participatory Journalism: Guarding Open Gates at Online Newspapers, First Edition.
Jane B. Singer, Alfred Hermida, David Domingo, Ari Heinonen, Steve Paulussen, Thorsten Quandt, Zvi Reich, and Marina Vujnovic.

- Journalists' views of the implications of the trend toward increased integration of user contributions, including its effect on the role of the journalists now and in the future. We explicitly encouraged interviewees to talk about specific implications within their own nation's media and civic culture.

After the interviews were taped and transcribed, textual analysis of the transcriptions was used to identify themes and key ideas. The categories or themes that we collectively identified across our interviews included journalistic work and routines; journalists' motives or rationales for opening up their websites to user input; user roles as perceived by our interviewees; and journalists' own self-perceptions and ideologies.

All relevant information from each interview was translated into English if the interview was conducted in another language. A document for each country was then created and shared among all eight researchers, highlighting relevant data related to each theme as well as other material the interviewer deemed of interest or importance.

Although we live and work in different countries, we remained in close contact through email and joint access to an online document-sharing platform throughout the process of conducting our interviews, analyzing our data and writing up our findings. Various members of the team also met face-to-face a number of times, forming a series of checkpoints that we found invaluable for coordinating our efforts.

The websites and their associated newspapers, along with the interviewees at each news outlet, are listed alphabetically by country and described below. Interviewees are indicated by job title in order to preserve the confidentiality that some requested. The descriptions focus on the offerings of the newspaper website at the time of our study – but all have continued to evolve since, particularly in their use of social media and other participatory journalism features.

Most interviewees worked primarily with the website, and a few with the print paper; some, for instance editors-in-chief, oversaw both products. All interviewees were able to speak knowledgeably about the newspaper's website and its participatory journalism efforts. Usage and circulation figures are provided by national auditing agencies in each country, where available, and unless otherwise noted are from early 2010, at the end of the decade in which these enormous changes have taken place.

BELGIUM

Standaard.be

Established in 1914 and currently owned by the Belgian media group Corelio, *De Standaard* is the top-quality Flemish newspaper. It had a print circulation of 103,000 in 2008. In 1995, the paper was among the first in Belgium to launch a website, and at the start of the twenty-first century, De Standaard Online was the most popular online newspaper in Flanders. However, since 2003, the site has lost market share because of new competitors, including the websites of the Flemish public broadcaster VRT and the popular dailies *Het Laatste Nieuws* and *Het Nieuwsblad*. In February 2010, the website of *De Standaard* received about 205,000 unique visitors daily.

Standaard.be interviewees:

- Editor-in-Chief
- Online Editorial Team Leader
- Online Editor / Webmaster

Nieuwsblad.be

Het Nieuwsblad, which also is owned by Corelio, has a print circulation of around 300,000, making it the second-largest newspaper in Flanders (behind *Het Laatste Nieuws*). Only in the late 2000s did the newspaper begin to invest in its website, which today is the most popular among online Flemish newspapers, generating an average of 332,000 unique visitors per day as of February 2010. *De Standaard* and *Het Nieuwsblad* have their own editorial teams, but the same editor-in-chief is responsible for the overall print and online strategy and operations of both Corelio newspapers. *Het Nieuwsblad* tries to use voluntary citizen reporters for online content on its local news pages.

Nieuwsblad.be interviewees:

- Editor-in-Chief (who also is Editor-in-Chief of *De Standaard*)
- Online News Manager
- Online Editor / Regional Coordinator / Community Manager

GVA.be / HBVL.be

Gazet van Antwerpen, a Flemish newspaper established in 1891, was bought by Concentra media group, the publisher of *Het Belang van Limburg*, in 1996. Although the Concentra newspapers are distributed nationally, both have strong links to their local communities: *Gazet van Antwerpen* is the most-read newspaper in the province of Antwerp, and Het *Belang van Limburg* generates more than 80 percent of the newspaper readership in the province of Limburg. The newspapers have print circulations of 125,000 and 112,000, respectively. There is strong synergy between their websites. A single online staff produces most of the editorial content, with the exception of local news pages. Both websites have invested heavily in local news, with online pages corresponding to every town in Antwerp and Limburg. In February 2010, GVA.be received about 112,000 unique visitors per day, while HBVL.be attracted around 92,000 unique daily visitors. The Concentra media group was the first in Belgium to explore the potential of citizen journalism for hyperlocal news reporting.

GVA.be and HBVL.be interviewees:

- Online Content Manager
- Editor / Community Coordinator

CANADA

TheGlobeAndMail.com

The Globe and Mail is one of two national Canadian newspapers. Based in Toronto, Ontario, it has been in print since 1844 under a variety of names and describes itself as a daily must-read for Canadians. It is published six days a week, with a combined weekly readership total of 2.8 million. Although it also serves as a Toronto metropolitan paper, *The Globe and Mail* publishes several regional editions that feature content tailored to various Canadian provinces. TheGlobeandMail.com was launched in 1995 and reaches 1.6 million users a month. Comments on stories, which generally are post-moderated, are the most prominent form of audience participation on the website. Users must register and provide a valid email address in order to post a comment.

TheGlobeandMail.com interviewees:

- Executive Editor
- Managing Editor for News
- Online News Editor

NationalPost.com

The *National Post* is a relative newcomer to the Canadian media scene, founded in 1998 by media baron Conrad Black as a newspaper with a national focus. It is known for its politically conservative, pro-business viewpoint. The *National Post* publishes Monday to Saturday and has a cumulative weekly readership of 1.1 million for its national edition, with more than half its readers in Toronto. Although it has had a web presence almost since its inception, editorial control over much of the content and layout of the site was limited until 2008, when parent corporation Canwest Global relaxed its corporate web standards and the paper was able to develop a look and feel to match its print product design. Audience participation options are limited. Because of technical limitations of the news-production system, users can comment on journalists' blogs but not on stories. Users are required to register with a valid email address to post comments, which are post-moderated by journalists.

NationalPost.com interviewees:

- Online Associate Editor
- Online Executive Producer
- Web Editor

CROATIA

Vecernji.hr

The conservative newspaper *Večernji List* was founded in 1959 and is owned by Austrian media company Styria. The newspaper's headquarters are in Zagreb, but the paper has ten regional editions. The online operation debuted in 1999 and was re-launched in 2005 with a stronger commitment to online news. The first audience participation features of Vecernji.hr were developed two years later. The print newspaper has a circulation of around 100,000, and the website attracts about 500,000 unique users each month.

Vecernji.hr interviewees:

- Online Executive Editor
- Editor of Multimedia
- Online Sports Editor

24Sata.hr

24 Sata ("24 Hours") is the youngest daily newspaper in Croatia, launched by Styria in 2005. Tabloid in format and content, it is published in Zagreb and has a circulation of about 150,000. The newspaper is aimed at a young urban audience, with a morning edition that is cheaper than its newsstand competitors, along with a free evening edition. The website, which attracts around 600,000 unique users monthly, was launched at the same time as the print edition and is produced by the same staff in an integrated newsroom. 24Sata.hr been more active than other Croatian newspaper websites in developing audience participation features, inviting its users to become "citizen journalists."

24Sata.hr interviewees:

- Online Desk Co-Editor
- Community / UGC Editor

FINLAND

HS.fi

Based in the capital of Helsinki, *Helsingin Sanomat* is the leading newspaper in Finland as a whole, as well as the dominant newspaper in the metropolitan area of Southern Finland. Its circulation in 2008 was 412,000, making it the biggest newspaper in the Nordic countries; circulation dipped to 398,000 in 2009. HS.fi had between 1.3 million and 1.4 million unique browsers in early 2010. There were 320 editorial employees at *Helsingin Sanomat* in 2009. The separate online newsdesk of HS.fi works closely with the main newsroom.

HS.fi inteviewees:

- Editor-in-Chief
- Online Editor
- Online Journalist

Kaleva.fi

Privately owned *Kaleva*, one of the few newspapers in Finland that is not part of a chain, is based in the northern city of Oulu but is the leading regional daily in a very large area in the northern part of the country. Its print circulation was 82,000 in 2008 and 21,000 in 2009; its affiliated website had between 150,000 and 195,000 unique visitors in the first ten weeks in 2010. *Kaleva* had 130 editorial employees in 2009, and as at the *Helsingin Sanomat* website, online journalists work closely with the main newsroom.

Kaleva.fi interviewees:

- Managing Editor
- Online Editor
- Online Journalist

FRANCE

LeFigaro.fr

The oldest of France's daily newspapers, this politically conservative/center-right daily was founded as a satirical weekly in 1826. Its audience is generally well-educated and relatively well-off. In the 1940s, it was the nation's leading daily, but by the mid-2000s its circulation had fallen to the point that it needed to be bailed out in order to survive. *Le Figaro* launched its website in the mid-1990s, with a re-launch in 2005. LeFigaro.fr is separate from the print operation. All articles are open to comments, which are moderated, and the site also offers social networking features.

LeFigaro.fr interviewees:

- Online Editor-in-Chief
- New Media Director
- Interactive Marketing Director

LeMonde.fr / LePost.fr

France's "newspaper of record," founded in 1944 at the behest of Charles de Gaulle, *Le Monde* is the preferred daily of French intellectuals, civil servants and academics. Among French newspapers, it gives the most detailed coverage of politics and world events, serving as a forum for highbrow debate and discussion. *Le Monde* is politically moderate or center-left. In recent years, the paper has struggled economically. LeMonde.fr, launched in 1995, is part of Le Monde Interactif, an autonomous affiliate of *Le Monde*. The site offers chats, blogs and comments to paying subscribers. In September 2007, Le Monde Interactif launched LePost.fr, a web-only publication offering news provided by users, supplemented by staff journalists who act as "coaches" for those users. The site was attracting more than two million unique visitors a month in mid-2009.

LeMonde.fr and LePost.fr interviewees:

- Online Editor-in-Chief (LeMonde.fr)
- Editor-in-Chief (LePost.fr)
- Online Community Journalist / Editor (LeMonde.fr)

GERMANY

FAZ.net

Frankfurter Allgemeine Zeitung (FAZ), one of five national quality newspapers in Germany, began publishing in 1949. An independent newspaper published six days a week, it defines itself as a "newspaper for Germany" and reports on the whole country, amassing a circulation of more than 370,000. *FAZ* is led by a committee of five editors who work collaboratively. The paper has been online since 2001, reaching around 1.7 million unique users a month. Although the website is independent from *FAZ*, print and online journalists cooperate closely in their daily work. Journalists moderate and oversee comments, which are the primary form of user participation. Users must register with a valid email address to comment on FAZ.net.

FAZ.net interviewees:

- Editor-in-Chief
- Sub-Editor-in-Chief
- Community Editor

Focus.de

Established in 1993 and produced by Burda Press, *Focus* is the third-largest news magazine in Germany, with a print circulation of around 590,000. It is published every Monday and is known for its politically conservative viewpoint. Focus.de, separately produced by Tomorrow Focus AG, attracts around 3.5 million unique visitors monthly. In 2007, the website was revamped and most of its participation features developed. The most prominent forms of audience participation are comments on stories and an online community service that hosts user photos and videos.

Focus.de interviewees:

- Editor-in-Chief
- Community Manager

Spiegel.de

Founded in 1947, *Der Spiegel* is the news magazine with the largest print circulation in Germany, more than one million copies as of 2009. It is known for its liberal viewpoint and investigative journalism, with exclusive news and analysis of current affairs. In 1994, *Der Spiegel* became the first news magazine worldwide with a website, which it has continued to develop as a focus of its publishing activities. Although print and online management are separate, staffs share know-how and ideas. The website's main participation channel is the Spiegel Online Forum, where user can comment on selected news stories that promise "controversial debate." Spiegel.de received 5.61 million unique visitors per month in 2009, making it the nation's most popular news website.

Spiegel.de interviewees:

* Co-Editor-in-Chief
* Community Project Leader and Einestages Editor

Sueddeutsche.de

Süddeutsche Zeitung, with a print circulation of 442,000, is the print market leader among the five national quality papers in Germany. Established in 1945 and published by Süddeutsche Press, the newspaper is known for its liberal viewpoint. Süddeutsche.de, which launched in 1995, has developed into a leading news and information portal with an independent editorial department. In 2006, the website unveiled a new design and concept, including new participation channels such as comments. Süddeutsche.de had around three million monthly unique users in 2009.

Sueddeutsche.de interviewees:

* Editor-in-Chief
* Community Editor
* Community Moderator

ISRAEL

Ynet.co.il

Ynet is the leading Israeli online news organization, launched in spring 2000 by *Yedioth Aharonoth*. The newspaper was founded in 1940 and currently is the most popular Israeli daily paper. Ynet functions independently of the newspaper, with original content and a dedicated staff that rarely cooperates editorially with the print organization. The website has developed its own social network and also offers portal services, including email accounts. Ynet is part of the early wave of websites that introduced user comments under each news item as far back as 2000.

Ynet.co.il interviewees:

* Vice-Editor, News Department
* Editor, Technology and Computers Section

NRG.co.il

NRG was launched in 2004 by Maariv group, the owner of *Maariv*, a daily tabloid created in 1948 by a group of journalists who deserted *Yedioth Aharonoth*, its bitter rival ever since. The newspaper's former website was Maariv Online, which mainly repurposed print content. NRG faces three main challenges: the financial difficulties of its parent company, the greater online success of competitor Ynet, and inconsistencies in its strategy and resource allocation. Although marketed as an independent enterprise, NRG has no reporting staff and relies on the print newspaper's reporters for content.

NRG.co.il interviewees:

- News Desk Chief
- User-generated Content Manager

Haaretz.co.il

Haaretz is Israel's elite newspaper, founded in 1918 as a British army news bulletin and becoming an independent daily under its current name a year later. The news website has evolved from its debut as a portal in 2000 to an independent news site. However, it continues to rely primarily on "shovelware" from the print paper, supplemented by updates from newspaper staff during the day. Haaretz Online has a limited readership but has sought to develop a social network of elite users who wish to communicate with other elite users. This network congregates around its subsidiary website, The Marker Café, a social network launched in 2007. It has 120,000 registered users, although not all are actively providing comments.

Haaretz.co.il and The Marker Café interviewees:

- Chief Online News Editor
- Social Networks Editor (for the group)

SPAIN

ElPaís.com

El País was founded in 1976, a few months after the death of dictator Francisco Franco. The daily soon became the newspaper of record in Spain and the nation's best-selling general-interest publication, with an average of 400,000 daily copies in 2009. The website was launched in 1996 as elpaís.es. Its evolution has included a controversial decision to put the entire website behind a paywall from 2002 to 2006. Access was opened again in 2007, and the website was renamed elpaís.com in 2007, an effort to position it as the global site for Spanish-language news. The new version also highlighted audience participation options.

ElPaís.com interviewees:

- Online Managing Editor
- Online Editor

- Senior Online Reporter and User Participation Coordinator
- Weblog Participation Manager.

20Minutos.es

20 Minutos is the Spanish franchise of 20 Min Holding, a European publisher of free newspapers. It is distributed in more than 50 cities throughout Spain and is the largest-circulation newspaper, with around 750,000 daily copies. The online edition, 20minutos.es, was launched in 2005. In January 2010, the news website had 9.8 million monthly unique users. Both the print and online versions include audience participation spaces.

20Minutos.es interviewees:

- Editor-in-Chief
- Online Managing Editor
- User Participation Manager

UNITED KINGDOM

Guardian.co.uk

The *Guardian* was founded as a weekly in 1821 and became a daily in the 1850s, espousing politically liberal editorial views. The newspaper is owned by the Scott Trust, which emphasizes quality journalism and plurality of expression. The *Guardian* has been online since 1999. Guardian.co.uk is the traffic leader among UK newspaper sites and has been a frequent winner of the Webby award for the world's best newspaper site. Its primary outlet for participatory journalism is Comment Is Free, which hosts blogs by staffers and outside contributors and attracts hundreds of thousands of comments each month. The website also allows user contributions in limited other areas and on its forums, which predate Comment is Free.

Guardian.co.uk interviewees:

- Head of Online Editorial Development
- Deputy Online Editor

Telegraph.co.uk

The *Daily Telegraph* was founded in 1855, and the print version of the daily paper is the top-selling quality paper in Britain. The politically conservative *Telegraph*, owned by the Barclay brothers, was the first British national newspaper and the first European daily to go online, launching its website in 1994. More recently, Telegraph.co.uk has been a leader in creating a converged news product from a newly reconfigured "hub and spoke" newsroom. The *Telegraph* has been innovative in creating online space for user contributions that go well beyond the comment function. Launched in May 2007, the My.Telegraph.co.uk section has developed as a user-generated blogging and personalization community, hosting tens of thousands of user blogs.

Telegraph.co.uk interviewees:

- Chief Information Officer, Telegraph Media Group
- Online Editor
- Print Executive Editor
- Online Community Manager
- Social Networks Content Editor (Community Editor)

UNITED STATES of AMERICA

USAToday.com

Founded in 1982 and owned by the Gannett Company, *USA Today* is the U.S. print national market leader, with more than 1.9 million daily copies sold on average in 2009. USAToday.com is the second-most popular newspaper website in the United States, with almost ten million unique monthly users. In December 2005, *USA Today* began the process of integrating the print and online newsrooms into one structure, with journalists in every section involved in updating the website and interacting with the audience. They developed most of the participation features between 2006 and 2007, when the website was revamped and a community manager appointed.

USAToday.com interviewees:

- Executive Editor
- Network Managing Editor
- Community Manager and Network Editor

WashingtonPost.com

Founded in 1877, the *Washington Post* is regarded as one of the U.S. newspapers of record, with a weekday circulation of nearly 600,000 and an elite audience interested in its national political coverage. WashingtonPost.com, launched in 1996, has an online audience of around nine million. Until 2009, the online newsroom was physically and culturally distinct from the print newsroom, but the paper has since pursued a strategy of newsroom integration. Audience participation options were available in the 1990s, but most of its current participatory features were developed between 2005 and 2007, overseen by a dedicated participation team.

WashingtonPost.com interviewees:

- Online Deputy Editor-in-Chief
- Online Assistant Managing Editor for News
- Interactivity and Community Editor

Glossary

All definitions apply to the way the term is used in the context of this book. Some terms have additional meanings in other fields.

access / observation stage of news production   This initial information-gathering stage is the one at which source material for a story is generated. Many of the journalists in our study saw a value in enabling users to provide news tips and on-the-scene updates.

agenda-setting   The ability to determine what media audience members will think about, and how they will think about it, through story selection and presentation – typically by a journalist. Broadly, news judgment involves decisions about what items belong on the public agenda. Journalists in our study also were concerned about users' potential ability to set the news agenda by influencing journalists' decisions about what they should cover.

audience   A collective term for the people who receive a media offering but are not involved in creating its contents. The term "audience member" has a passive connotation: An audience has no independent existence as a social entity but rather is defined only through its exposure to the media. Audiences can be identified according to various criteria, including content (for example, an audience for sports information), location, time or media outlet.

blog   Short for "weblog." A website with regular entries, commonly displayed in reverse-chronological order, that may include news, commentary or other topical information. A growing number of media websites "host" user blogs, meaning they

Participatory Journalism: Guarding Open Gates at Online Newspapers, First Edition.
Jane B. Singer, Alfred Hermida, David Domingo, Ari Heinonen, Steve Paulussen, Thorsten Quandt, Zvi Reich, and Marina Vujnovic.

provide a dedicated space on their websites for these blogs. In addition, most media websites now provide blogs created by the organization's journalists (sometimes called "**j-blogs**"), which commonly are open to user comments.

chats   Also called **collective interviews** or Q&As. The terms typically are used to identify online interviews with a newsmaker or journalist, with users submitting questions that the interviewee then answers. A journalist generally selects appropriate questions from those received.

citizen journalism   Content produced by citizens who play a role in collecting, reporting, analyzing and disseminating news and information, typically enabled by digital technologies. The term generally implies people without professional training or experience who take on at least some aspects of the professional journalists' role in one or more of the earlier **news production stages**. See "**participatory journalism**" and "**user-generated content**."

collective interviews   See "**chats**."

comments   User-generated posts attached to a published item, typically an article or blog entry, on a media website. Most news organizations moderate or screen user comments, either before or after publication; see "**moderator**."

community manager   The person, usually but not necessarily a journalist, in charge of user contributions to the media organization website. The community manager's tasks typically include encouraging user contributions, moderating or otherwise managing those contributions, resolving contributors' problems, and engaging other journalists in appreciating and interacting with users. At some newspapers, this person is referred to as a community editor.

content management system (CMS)   Software used in newsrooms to enable journalists to edit and publish various forms of content. Such tools are increasingly likely to handle publication to multiple platforms, including print and online; many also can accommodate input from outside as well as inside the newsroom.

convergence   The global trend in the media industry of bringing together technologies, products, personnel and geography drawn from previously distinct media areas, such as print and online. The term "convergence" is commonly (and confusingly) used to refer to media audiences, technologies, content, newsrooms and industries.

crowdsourcing   A system of constructing a story in which journalists request data, analysis or other assistance from audience members. The rationale for crowdsourcing is that there will be people, including experts, with the time and the willingness to contribute ideas to make a news story richer and more complete than it would have been if created solely by the journalist based on traditional news sources.

curation   A moderation strategy consisting of selecting and organizing (for instance, labeling or arranging) the best content contributed by users instead of simply deleting the worst items or those deemed inappropriate. Commonly, a curation model involves collaboration with users, who help identify valuable material.

distribution stage of news production   This is the stage at which a story is disseminated or made available for reading and, potentially, discussion. It essentially is the publication stage. Users are gaining input into this stage, primarily through **reputation systems** and the growing use of **social bookmarking** tools.

forums   There are two kinds of forums. One kind involves a discussion typically led by journalists and open only for a limited time, with topical questions posed by the newsroom and moderated submissions. In a different kind of forum, readers can initiate and engage in threaded online conversations or debates on topics of their choosing, with discussions typically remaining open for weeks or months, or even indefinitely.

gatekeeping   In journalism, the ability to determine what should be reported and published. Journalists have traditionally been the gatekeepers over news, deciding what goes into the news product that is delivered to readers, viewers or listeners. However, the wide-open online environment throws this role into question, as people outside the newsroom can and do publish all sorts of information.

hyperlocal   A term used to refer to coverage of news and events located within a narrow geographic area, such as a relatively small community or neighborhood. Hyperlocal content is intended to be consumed primarily by residents of the area, who also may take part in producing the content themselves.

integrated newsroom   As their websites have become increasingly dominant information products, many newspapers have opted for this organizational model, with the previously separated print and online operations merged into one multimedia newsroom. In principle, all journalists and editors in integrated newsrooms are expected to produce news content for multiple publishing platforms, such as print, online and **mobile**. Also sometimes referred to as "converged newsrooms"; see **"convergence."**

interpretation stage of news production   In this final stage, a story that already has been produced – typically though not necessarily by a journalist – is opened up to comment and discussion. In our study, this stage was the most likely to be open to user participation.

journalist blog ("j-blog")   A **blog** created by a journalist, published on a media website and typically open to user comments. J-bloggers may be explicitly encouraged to engage with people who write comments on their stories or columns.

micro-blog   A **blog** with very short entries, typically designed to allow users to generate rapid updates. As of 2010, Twitter was perhaps the best-known example.

mobile   A hand-held digital device, such as a cellular or mobile phone, a smart phone (for instance, an Android or an iPhone), or a personal digital assistant such as a Blackberry. Tablets such as the iPad also are small and lightweight enough to be considered mobile platforms; however, they were not yet a major factor at the time of the interviews described in this book.

moderator   The person, usually but not necessarily a journalist, responsible for filtering user comments and other contributions. The moderator's main task typically is to read comments posted by users on the media website, either before (**pre-moderation**) or after (**post-moderation**) they become visible to other users, and to remove inappropriate contributions.

news-production stages   In this book, we break the process of creating a news item into five stages, described in Chapter 2. They are the **access/observation stage**, the **selection/filtering stage**, the **processing/editing stage**, the **distribution stage** and the **interpretation stage**. The extent of user input allowed at each stage varied considerably among the newspapers in our study. However, in general, the interpretation stage – which included comments – was the most open to participation, and the selection/filtering stage was the most closed.

newsroom culture   The set of unwritten rules, tacit norms and shared values that define how work is done in the newsroom. Because professional journalists inherit and internalize these rules, norms and values through a process of socialization, changing newsroom culture is a difficult process that tends to happen only slowly if at all.

ombudsman   The person who handles complaints from the public. At newspapers, the ombudsman's role is to represent the readers and, if necessary, to mediate between journalists and the public. The newspaper ombudsman is sometimes called the "public editor" or the "reader's editor." At some newspapers, his or her function is becoming intertwined with the role of **community manager**.

outsourcing   The process of assigning work that could be undertaken by company employees to a third party or external provider. The move to outsourcing often is motivated by a desire to save costs. Some news organizations are outsourcing the task of comment moderation, though journalists typically set the moderation rules and retain final authority over difficult decisions.

participation team   A group of journalists or other professionals in the newsroom who are in charge of managing user participation.

participatory journalism   This is the term we use throughout this book to describe user contributions to the newspaper website. The participation can occur at various stages of the news-production process, and it can make use of a variety of tools. Participatory journalism includes comments as well as other more labor-intensive forms of what also is referred to as "**user-generated content**" and "**citizen journalism**."

paywall   A device for blocking access to all or part of a website unless the user pays for that access. Although not in use by the newspapers included in our study at the time we conducted our interviews, a growing number of news organization were beginning to consider paywalls.

polls   Topical questions posed by journalists, with users typically asked to make a multiple choice or binary response. Such polls provide instant and quantifiable feedback, and they generally are popular among users.

post-moderation   A strategy for managing user comments or other contributions in which items are published as soon as a user submits them. A moderator may subsequently review and/or remove such items if they are deemed to be problematic. Typically, responsibility for identifying problematic items is shared with other users. See "**moderator**."

pre-moderation   A strategy for managing user comments or other contributions in which every item submitted by a user is moderated and approved before publication. See "**moderator**."

pro-am journalism   A term used to describe the collaboration between professional journalists and users – or "amateurs" – in the production of journalism. This collaboration is most common on stories or topics that would be difficult for a professional journalist to effectively report without such assistance.

processing / editing stage of news production   This is the stage at which a story is created. It involves writing and editing an item for publication. In our study, journalists generally expressed at least some reluctance to giving users this capability, although a growing number of websites were hosting user **blogs** or soliciting **hyperlocal** contributions.

public interest   The notion that the mass media contribute to the good of democratic society by providing accurate and reliable news and information, enabling citizens to make informed choices. The idea that journalists serve the public interest also influences practitioner codes of ethics and performance standards.

registration   A requirement that users provide identifying information to the publisher of a website before they are allowed to do more than read the information it contains – for instance, to leave a comment or make some other contribution. Registration is a common strategy for managing user comments among organizations that rely on **post-moderation**.

report abuse button   An icon attached to each comment in some websites, enabling users to easily flag an item they find problematic for review by a **moderator**.

reputation systems   Tools that allow users to assign ratings, recommendations or other evaluative indicators to online content or its producers. Examples on newspaper websites include giving thumbs up (or down) to another user's comments and assigning stars to a journalist's story. Websites also commonly display content hierarchies, typically in a box showing which articles have been most read, most e-mailed or most commented on, among other criteria.

selection / filtering stage of news production   This is essentially the "**gate-keeping**" stage, at which decisions are made about what should be reported or published. In our study, it was the least likely of the five news production stages to be open to input from outside the newsroom; journalists were generally reluctant to cede this decision-making role to users.

social bookmarking   A method for users to share, organize, find and manage references to material they come across online. Widely used examples of social bookmarking tools – also called "widgets" – at the time of our study included Digg, Delicious and Stumbleupon.

social media   A term commonly used to refer to the "second generation" of interactive web applications such as **blogs**, wikis and **social networking sites**. A common characteristic of social media is that they facilitate and encourage user participation throughout the communication process, from content creation to publication to discussion. The term "**Web 2.0**" also is used to characterize these media forms and tools.

social networking site   An online service enabling people to create profiles, post information and identify friends, with whom they can easily share content and links. In the late 2000s, news organizations were actively developing their presence on social networking sites such as Facebook.

talkback   A term used by some media websites, primarily those in Israel, to refer to features that enable users to post **comments**, particularly on news stories.

users   We use this term throughout the book to describe members of the media audience who are taking an active role in engaging with and/or producing online content.

user-generated content (UGC)   Information or opinion in any format (for instance, text, photograph or video) provided by active audience members and typically published in a designated area on a media website. The term "UGC" is often used synonymously with "**participatory journalism**."

Web 2.0   See "**social media**."

References

This is a consolidated list of all the end-of-chapter references.

Abdul–Mageed, Muhammad M. (2008) Online news sites and journalism 2.0: Reader comments on Al Jazeera Arabic, *tripleC-Cognition, Communication, Co-operation* 6 (2): 59–76.

Albarran, Alan B., Sylvia M. Chan–Olmsted and Michael O. Wirth (2006) *Handbook of media management and economics*, Mahwah, New Jersey: Lawrence Erlbaum Associates.

Allan, Stuart (2006) *Online news*, Maidenhead, UK: Open University Press.

Amichai–Hamburger, Yair, Katelyn Y.A. McKenna and Tal Samuel–Azran (2008) E-empowerment: Empowerment by the Internet, *Computers in Human Behavior* 24 (5): 1776–1789.

Anderson, Benedict (1983) *Imagined communities: Reflections on the origin and spread of nationalism*, London: Verso.

Anderson, Chris (2006) *The long tail: Why the future of business is selling less of more*, New York: Hyperion.

Andrews, Paul (2003) Is blogging journalism? *Nieman Reports* 57 (3): 63–64.

Andsager, Julie, and H. Allen White (2007) *Self versus others: Media, messages and the third-person effect*, Mahwah, New Jersey: Lawrence Erlbaum Associates.

Associated Press (2010) Papers in Europe weather crisis better than US. ABC News/Money. Accessed 29 August 2010: http://abcnews.go.com/Business/wirestory?id=10909470&page=1

Aucoin, James (1997) Does newspaper call-in line expand public conversation? *Newspaper Research Journal* 18 (3): 122–140.

Avilés, José Alberto, and Miguel Carvajal (2008) Integrated and cross-media newsroom convergence: Two models of multimedia news production – the cases of Novotécnica and La Verdad Multimedia in Spain, *Convergence* 14 (2): 221–239.

Participatory Journalism: Guarding Open Gates at Online Newspapers, First Edition.
Jane B. Singer, Alfred Hermida, David Domingo, Ari Heinonen, Steve Paulussen, Thorsten Quandt, Zvi Reich, and Marina Vujnovic.
© 2011 Jane B. Singer, Alfred Hermida, David Domingo, Ari Heinonen, Steve Paulussen, Thorsten Quandt, Zvi Reich, and Marina Vujnovic. Published 2011 by Blackwell Publishing Ltd.

Bagdikian, Ben H. (2004) *The new media monopoly*, Boston: Beacon Press.

Bakker, Piet, and Mervi Pantti (2009) Beyond news: User-generated content on Dutch media websites. Paper presented at the Future of Journalism conference, Cardiff, Wales, September.

BBC News (2010, 9 July) Government announces review of libel laws. Accessed 12 September 2010: http://www.bbc.co.uk/news/10580758

Bergström, Annika (2009) The scope of user-generated content: User-contributions within the journalistic online context. Paper presented at the Future of Journalism conference, Cardiff, Wales, September.

Boczkowski, Pablo J. (2009) "Materiality and mimicry in the journalism field." In: Zelizer, Barbie (ed.) *The Changing Faces of Journalism: Tabloidization, Technology and Truthiness*, London and New York: Routledge.

Boczkowski, Pablo J. (2004a) *Digitizing the news: Innovation in online newspapers*, Cambridge, Massachusetts: MIT Press.

Boczkowski, Pablo J. (2004b) Books to think with, *New Media and Society* 6 (1): 144–150.

Boczkowski, Pablo J. (2004c) The processes of adopting multimedia and interactivity in three online newsrooms, *Journal of Communication* 54 (2): 197–213.

Bogart, Leo (1991) *Preserving the press: How daily newspapers mobilize to keep their readers*, New York: Columbia University Press.

Bowman, Shayne and Chris Willis (2003) *We media: How audiences are shaping the future of news and information*, The Media Center at the American Press Institute. Accessed 23 December 2010: http://www.hypergene.net/wemedia/weblog.php

Briggs, Mark (2009) *Journalism next: A practical guide to digital reporting and publishing*, Washington, DC: CQ Press.

Bruns, Axel (2008) *Blogs, Wikipedia, Second Life and beyond: From production to produsage*, New York: Peter Lang.

Bruns, Axel (2005) *Gatewatching: Collaborative online news production*, New York: Peter Lang.

Carey, James W. (2007) A short history of journalism for journalists: A proposal and essay, *The Harvard International Journal of Press/Politics* 12 (1): 3–16.

Carey, James W. (1998) The Internet and the end of the national communication system: Uncertain predictions of an uncertain future, *Journalism & Mass Communication Quarterly* 75 (1): 28–34.

Carey, James W. (1989) *Communication as culture: Essays on media and society*, Boston: Unwin Hyman.

Charity, Arthur (1995) *Doing public journalism*, New York: Guilford Press.

Chittum, Ryan (2009, 19 August) Newspaper industry ad revenue at 1965 levels, *Columbia Journalism Review*. Accessed 15 March 2010: http://www.cjr.org/the_audit/newspaper_industry_ad_revenue.php

Christians, Clifford G., Theodore L. Glasser, Denis McQuail, Kaarle Nordenstreng and Robert A. White (2009) *Normative theories of the media: Journalism in democratic societies*, Urbana: University of Illinois Press.

Chyi, Hsiang Iris (2005) Willingness to pay for online news: An empirical study on the viability of the subscription model, *Journal of Media Economics* 18 (2): 131–142.

Chyi, Hsiang Iris, and George Sylvie (2001) The medium is global, the content is not: The role of geography in online newspaper markets, *Journal of Media Economics* 14 (4): 231–248.

Cooper, Tom (1990) Comparative international media ethics, *Journal of Mass Media Ethics* 5 (1): 3–14.

Coté, Mark, and Jennifer Pybus (2007) Learning to immaterial labour 2.0: MySpace and social networks, *Ephemera: Theory and politics in organization* 7 (1): 88–106.

Croteau, David (2006) The growth of self-produced media content and the challenge to media studies, *Critical Studies in Media Communication* 23 (4): 340–44.

Curran, James (1997) "Rethinking the media as a public sphere." In: Dahlgren, Peter, and Colin Sparks (eds.) *Communication and citizenship: Journalism and the public sphere*, London: Routledge: 27–58.

Darnton, Robert (1975) Writing news and telling stories, *Daedalus* 104 (2): 175–194.

Dean, Jodi (2008) "Communicative capitalism: Circulation and the foreclosure of politics." In: Boler, Megan (ed.) *Digital media and democracy*, Cambridge, Massachusetts: MIT Press: 101–123.

Deuze, Mark (2010) *Managing media work*, Thousand Oaks, CA: Sage.

Deuze, Mark (2008) "Professional identity in a participatory media culture." In: Quandt, Thorsten, and Wolfgang Schweiger (eds.) *Journalismus online – Partizipation oder Profession?* Wiesbaden: VS Verlag für Sozialwissenschaften: 251–261.

Deuze, Mark (2008) Understanding journalism as newswork: How it changes, and how it remains the same, *Westminster Papers in Communication and Culture* (2): 4–23.

Deuze, Mark (2007) *Media work*, Cambridge, Massachusetts: Polity Press.

Deuze, Mark (2006) Participation, remediation, bricolage: Considering principal components of a digital culture, *The Information Society* 22: 63–75.

Deuze, Mark (2005) Towards professional participatory storytelling in journalism and advertising, *First Monday* 10 (7). Accessed 26 March 2010: http://firstmonday.org/htbin/cgiwrap/bin/ojs/index.php/fm/article/viewArticle/1257/1177

Deuze, Mark (2003) The Web and its journalisms: Considering consequences of different types of media online, *New Media and Society* 5 (2): 203–230.

Deuze, Mark (2002) *Journalists in The Netherlands: An analysis of the people, the issues and the (inter-) national environment*, Amsterdam: Het Spinhuis.

Deuze, Mark, Axel Bruns and Christoph Neuberger (2007) Preparing for an age of participatory news, *Journalism Practice* 1 (3): 322–338.

Dewey, John (1927) *The public and its problems*, New York: H. Holt and Company.

Dimitrova, Daniela V., and Jesper Strömbäck (2009) Look who's talking, *Journalism Practice* 3 (1): 75–91.

Domingo, David (2008) Interactivity in the daily routines of online newsrooms: Dealing with an uncomfortable myth, *Journal of Computer-Mediated Communication* 13 (3): 680–704.

Domingo, David, Thorsten Quandt, Ari Heinonen, Steve Paulussen, Jane B. Singer and Marina Vujnovic (2008) Participatory journalism practices in the media and beyond: An international comparative study of initiatives in online newspapers, *Journalism Practice* 2 (3): 326–342.

Drucker, Peter (1969) *The age of discontinuity: Guidelines to our changing society*, New York: Harper and Row.

Duncombe, Stephen (1997) *Notes from the underground: Zines and the politics of alternative culture*, London: Verso.

Emerson, Thomas I. (1970) *The system of freedom of expression*, New York: Random House.

Entman, Robert M. (2010) Improving newspapers' economic prospects by augmenting their contributions to democracy, *The International Journal of Press/Politics* 15 (1): 104–125.

Ericson, Richard V., Patricia M. Baranek and Janet B.L Chan (1989) *Negotiating control: A study of news sources*, Milton Keynes, UK: Open University Press.

Fortunati, Leopoldina, Mauro Sarrica, John O'Sullivan, Aukse Balcytiene, Halliki Harro-Loit, Phil Macgregor, Nayla Roussou, Ramón Salaverria and Federico De Luca (2009) The influence of the Internet on European journalism, *Journal of Computer-Mediated Communication* 14 (4): 928–963.

Gade, Peter J. (2008) Journalism guardians in a time of great change: Newspaper editors' perceived influence in integrated news organizations, *Journalism & Mass Communication Quarterly* 85 (2): 331–352.

Gade, Peter J. (2004) Newspapers and organizational development: Management and journalist perceptions of newsroom cultural change, *Journalism & Communication Monographs* 65: 3–55.

Gade, Peter J., and Earnest L. Perry (2003) Changing the newsroom culture: A four-year case study of organizational development at the *St. Louis Post-Dispatch*, *Journalism & Mass Communication Quarterly* 80 (2): 327–347.

Gans Herbert J. (2009) "Can popularization help the news media?" In: Zelizer, Barbie (ed.) *The Changing Faces of Journalism*, New York: Routledge: 17–28.

Gans, Herbert J. (2003) *Democracy and the news*, New York: Oxford University Press.

Gans, Herbert J. (1979) *Deciding what's news: A study of CBS Evening News, NBC Nightly News, Newsweek, and Time*, New York: Pantheon.

Gillmor, Dan (2006) *We the media: Grassroots journalism by the people, for the people*, Sebastopol, California: O'Reilly.

Goffman, Erving (1981) *Forms of talk*, Philadelphia: University of Pennsylvania Press.

Görke, Alexander, and Armin Scholl (2006) Niklas Luhmann's theory of social systems and journalism research, *Journalism Studies* 7 (4): 644–655.

Granovetter, Mark S. (1973) The strength of weak ties, *American Journal of Sociology* 78: 1360–1380.

Grossman, Lev (2006, 13 December) *Time*'s Person of the Year, *Time*. Accessed 21 January 2010: http://www.time.com/time/magazine/article/0,9171,1569514,00.html.

guardian.co.uk (2009, 7 May) Frequently asked questions about community on guardian.co.uk. Accessed 19 February 2010: http://www.guardian.co.uk/community-faqs

Haas, Tanni (2005) From "public journalism" to the "public's journalism"? Rhetoric and reality in the discourse on weblogs, *Journalism Studies* 6 (3): 387–396.

Habermas, Jürgen (1989) *The structural transformation of the public sphere* (Thomas Burger, trans.), Cambridge, Massachusetts: MIT Press.

Hafez, Kai (2002) Journalism ethics revisited: A comparison of ethics codes in Europe, North Africa, the Middle East and Muslim Asia, *Political Communication* 19 (2): 225–250.

Haner, Lior (2006, 4 December) Users will be required to register their name before posting comments for articles. The Marker Café. Accessed 23 January 2010: http://www.themarker.com/tmc/article.jhtml/tmc/article.jhtml?ElementId=skira 20061204_796519

Hapogian, Arthur (1993) Sound off turns readers into participants, *The Masthead* (spring): 16–17.

Hartley, John (2008) "Journalism as human right: The cultural approach to journalism." In: Löffelholz, Martin, and David Weaver (eds.) *Global journalism research. Theories, methods, findings, future*, Malden, Blackwell: 39–51.

Harrison, Jackie (2010) User-generated content and gatekeeping at the BBC hub, *Journalism Studies* 11 (2): 243–256.

Harris Poll (2006) Doctors and teachers most trusted among 22 occupations and professions, Harris Interactive. Accessed 28 February 2010: http://www.harris-interactive.com/harris_poll/index.asp?PID=688

Hayes, Alfred S., Jane B. Singer and Jerry Ceppos (2007) The credible journalist in a digital age, *Journal of Mass Media Ethics* 22 (4): 262–279.

Heinonen, Ari (1999) *Journalism in the age of the Net: Changing society, changing profession*, Tampere: Acta Universitatis Tamperensis 685.

Heinonen, Ari, and Heikki Luostarinen (2008) "Reconsidering 'journalism' for journalism research." In: Löffelholz, Martin, and David Weaver (eds.) *Global journalism research: Theories, methods, findings, future*, Malden, Massachusetts: Blackwell: 227–239.

Herbst, Susan (1995) On electronic public space: Talk shows in theoretical perspective, *Political Communication* 12 (3): 263–274.

Herbert, Jack, and Neil Thurman (2007) Paid content strategies for news websites: An empirical study of British newspapers' online business models, *Journalism Practice* 1 (2): 208–226.

Hermida, Alfred (2009) The blogging BBC, *Journalism Practice* 3 (3): 1–17.

Hermida, Alfred, and Neil Thurman (2008) A clash of cultures: The integration of user-generated content within professional journalistic frameworks at British newspaper websites, *Journalism Practice* 2 (3): 343–356.

Hollander, Barry A. (1996) Talk radio: Predictors of use and effects on attitudes about government, *Journalism & Mass Communication Quarterly* 73 (1): 102–13.

Horrocks, Peter (2009) "The end of fortress journalism." In: Miller, Charles (ed) *The future of journalism*, London: BBC College of Journalism: 6–17.

Howe, Jeff (2009) *Crowdsourcing: Why the power of the crowd is driving the future of business*, New York: Three Rivers.

Innis, Harold (1951) *The bias of communication*, Toronto: University of Toronto Press.

Innis, Harold (1950) *Empire and communications*, Oxford: Clarendon Press.

Isaacson, Walter (2009, 5 February) How to save your newspaper, *Time*. Accessed 15 March 2010: http://www.time.com/time/business/article/0,8599,1877191–1,00.html

Jarvis, Jeff (2006) Networked journalism, BuzzMachine, July 5. Accessed 18 September 2008: http://www.buzzmachine.com/2006/07/05/networked-journalism/

Jenkins, Henry (2006) *Convergence culture: Where old and new media collide*, New York: New York University Press.

Jenkins, Henry, and David Thorburn (2003) *Democracy and new media*, Cambridge, Massachusetts: MIT Press.

Kabalyon, G. (2009) "Ilan king of Israel." In: Shoham, Shlono Giora, and Uri Timor (eds.) *Penology issues in Israel*, Kiriyat Bialik, Israel: Ach Publishers.

Kilman, Larry (2010, 4 March) 20th World Newspaper Ad Conference: Where will the money come from? Shaping the Future of the Newspaper / World Association of Newspapers. Accessed 15 March 2010: http://www.sfnblog.com/advertising/2010/03/20th_world_newspaper_ad_conference_where.php

Kim, Jin Woo, and Eun Ja Her (2008) Inducing journalistic values from grass-root level discourse on journalism: An explorative analysis of user comment replies posted on online news articles. Paper presented at the International Association for Media and Communication Research, Stockholm, Sweden, July.

Kocher, Renate (1986) Bloodhounds or missionaries: Role definitions of German and British journalists, *European Journal of Communication* 1 (1): 43–64.

Kogen, R. (2005) The rules of discourse in Israeli news sites. Unpublished MA thesis, submitted to the Department of Communication Studies, the Hebrew University, Jerusalem.

Kohn, Ayelet, and Motti Neiger (2007) "To Talk and TalkBack: Analyzing the Rhetoric of Talkbacks in Online Journalism." In: Swartz Altshuler, Tehila (ed.) *Online newspapers in Israel*, Jerusalem: Israel Democracy Institute: 321–350.

Kovach, Bill, and Tom Rosenstiel (2007) *The elements of journalism: What newspeople should know and the public should expect*, New York: Three Rivers Press.

Laitila, Tiina (1995) Journalistic codes of ethics in Europe, *European Journal of Communication* 10 (4): 527–544.

Larson, Margali Sarfetti (1977) *The rise of professionalism: A sociological analysis*, Berkeley: University of California Press.

Lasica, J.D. (2003, 7 August) What is participatory journalism? *Online Journalism Review*. Accessed 21 March 2010: http://www.ojr.org/ojr/workplace/1060217106.php

Lemonnier, Pierre (1993) *Technological choice: Transformations in material culture since the Neolithic*, London and New York: Routledge.

Leonard, Thomas C. (1999) "Making readers into citizens – the old-fashioned way." In: Glasser, Theodore L. (ed.) *The idea of public journalism*, New York: Guilford Press.

Levinson, Stephen C. (1988) "Putting linguistics on a proper footing: Explorations in Goffman's concepts of participation." In: Drew, Paul, and Anthony J. Wootton (eds.) *Erving Goffman: Exploring the interaction order*, Cambridge, Massachusetts: Polity Press: 161–227.

Lewis, Justin, Andrew Williams and Bob Franklin (2008) Four rumours and an explanation: A political economic account of journalists' changing newsgathering and reporting practices, *Journalism Practice* 2 (1): 27–45.

Lowrey, Wilson (2006) Mapping the journalism-blogging relationship, *Journalism* 7 (4): 477–500.

Manning, Paul (2001) *News and news sources: A critical introduction*, London: Sage.

Mäntylä, Jorma, and Juha Karilainen (2008) Journalistietiikan kehitys Suomessa ja Euroopassa 1995–2007 (Development of journalism ethics in Finland and Europe 1995–2007), University of Tampere, Department of Journalism and Mass Communication. Publications B 49/2008. Accessed 11 February 2010: http://tampub.uta.fi/tiedotusoppi/978-951-44-7262-6.pdf

Martin, Shannon E., and Kathleen A. Hansen (1998) *Newspapers of record in a digital age: From hot type to hot link*, Westport, Connecticut: Praeger Publishers.

McAthy, Rachel (2010, 10 September) National newspaper ABCs show continued decline, Journalism.co.uk. Accessed 13 September 2010: http://www.journalism.co.uk/2/articles/540534.php

McKenna, Katelyn Y.A., and Amie S. Green (2002) Virtual group dynamics, *Group Dynamics* 6: 116–127.

McLellan, Michele, and Tim Porter (2007) *News, improved. How America's newsrooms are learning to change*, Washington D.C.: CQ Press.

McNair, Brian (2000) *Journalism and democracy: An evaluation of the political public sphere*, London, Routledge.

McQuail, Denis (2000) *McQuail's mass communication theory*, London: Sage.

Melamed, Orly (2006) The talkback in Israel: A reflecting and intensifying mirror or a pendulum that balances and corrects the journalistic discourse. Unpublished MA thesis, submitted to the Department of Communication Studies, the Hebrew University, Jerusalem.

Metykova, Monika (2009) "A key relation: Journalists and their publics." In: Preston, Paschal (ed.), *Making the news: Journalism and news cultures in Europe*, London, Routledge: 129–143.

Meyer, Philip (2009) *The vanishing newspaper: Saving journalism in the information age*, Columbia, MO: University of Missouri Press.

Meyer, Philip (2008, October/November) The elite newspaper of the future, *American Journalism Review*. Accessed 11 September 2010: http://www.ajr.org/article.asp?id=4605

Mitchell, Bill, and Steele, Bob (2005) Earn your own trust, roll your own ethics: Transparency and beyond. Paper presented to the Blogging, Journalism and Credibility Conference, Harvard University, Cambridge, Massachusetts, January. Accessed 28 December 2009: http://cyber.law.harvard.edu/sites/cyber.law.harvard.edu/files/webcredfinalpdf_01.pdf

Mitchelstein, Eugenia, and Pablo J. Boczkowski (2009) Between tradition and change: A review of recent research on online news production, *Journalism* 10 (5): 562–586.

Mosco, Vincent (1996) *The political economy of communication: Rethinking and renewal*, London: Sage.

Newspaper Association of America (2010) Total paid circulation. Accessed 16 March 2010: http://www.naa.org/TrendsandNumbers/Total-Paid-Circulation.aspx

Nichols, John, and Robert W. McChesney (2010, 7 January). How to save journalism, *The Nation*. Accessed 15 March 2010: http://www.thenation.com/doc/20100125/nichols_mcchesney

Örnebring, Henrik (2008) The consumer as producer – of what? *Journalism Studies* 9 (5): 771–785.

Paterson, Chris, and David Domingo (2008) *Making online news: The ethnography of new media production*, New York: Peter Lang.

Paulussen, Steve (2004) Online news production in Flanders: How Flemish online journalists perceive and explore the Internet's potential, *Journal of Computer-Mediated Communication* 9 (4).

Paulussen, Steve, Ari Heinonen, David Domingo and Thorsten Quandt (2007) Doing it together: Citizen participation in the professional news making process, *Observatorio Journal* 1 (3): 131–154.

Paulussen, Steve, and Pieter Ugille (2008) User generated content in the newsroom: Professional and organisational constraints on participatory journalism, *Westminster Papers in Communication and Culture* 5 (2): 24–41.

Pérez–Peña, Richard (2010, 20 January) *The Times* to charge for frequent access to its web site, *The New York Times*. Accessed 15 March 2010: http://www.nytimes.com/2010/01/21/business/media/21times.html

Pew Project for Excellence in Journalism (2010) Newspapers: Audience, The state of the news media: An annual report on American journalism. Accessed 11 September 2010: http://www.stateofthemedia.org/2010/newspapers_audience.php

Pew Project for Excellence in Journalism (2009a) Overview: Introduction, The state of the news media: An annual report on American journalism. Accessed 21 March 2010: http://www.stateofthemedia.org/2009/narrative_overview_intro.php?cat=0&media=1

Pew Project for Excellence in Journalism (2009b) Newspapers: News investment, The state of the news media: An annual report on American journalism. Accessed 15 March 2010: http://www.stateofthemedia.org/2009/narrative_newspapers_newsinvestment.php?cat=4&media=4

Pew Project for Excellence in Journalism and Rick Edmonds (2010) Newspapers: Summary essay, The state of the news media: An annual report on American journalism. Accessed 12 September 2010: http://www.stateofthemedia.org/2010/newspapers_summary_essay.php

Pew Project for Excellence in Journalism and Rick Edmonds (2009) Newspapers: introduction, The state of the news media: An annual report on American journalism. Accessed 21 March 2010: http://www.stateofthemedia.org/2009/narrative_newspapers_intro.php?media=4

Pew Research Center's Project for Excellence in Journalism (2010) Understanding the participatory news consumer: How Internet and cell phone users have turned news into a social experience. Accessed 21 March 2010: http://www.journalism.org/analysis_report/understanding_participatory_news_consumer

Pew Research Center's Project for Excellence in Journalism (2008) The changing newsroom. Accessed 16 January 2010: http://www.journalism.org/node/11961.

Phillips, Peter (2003) *The Project Censored guide to independent media and activism*, New York: Seven Stories Press.

Prensky, Marc (2001) Digital natives, digital immigrants, *On the Horizon* 9 (5). Accessed 15 January 2010: http://www.marcprensky.com/writing/Prensky Digital Natives, Digital Immigrants - Part1.pdf

Preston, Paschal (2009) *Making the news: Journalism and news cultures in Europe*, London: Routledge.

Purcell, Kristen, Lee Rainie, Amy Mitchell, Tom Rosenstiel and Kenny Olmstead (2010) Understanding the participatory news consumer, Pew Internet and American Life Project. Accessed 9 April 2010: http://www.pewinternet.org/Reports/2010/Online-News.aspx

Quandt, Thorsten (2005) *Journalisten im Netz (Journalists in the Net)*, Wiesbaden: Verlag für Sozialwissenschaften.

Quandt, Thorsten, Martin Löffelholz, David Weaver, Thomas Hanitzsch and Klaus–Dieter Altmeppen (2006) American and German online journalists at the beginning of the 21st century: A bi-national survey, *Journalism Studies* 7 (2): 171–186.

Quinn, Stephen (2005) Convergence's fundamental question, *Journalism Studies* 6 (1): 29–38.

Reader, Bill (2007) Air mail: NPR sees "community" in letters from listeners, *Journal of Broadcasting & Electronic Media* 51 (4): 651–669.

Regan, Tom (2003) Weblogs threaten and inform traditional journalism, *Nieman Reports* 57 (3): 68–70.

Reich, Zvi (2009) Weaving the thread: Gatekeeping and filtering strategies for user comments. Paper presented to the conference of the International Communication Association, Chicago, May.

Richardson, John E., and Bob Franklin (2004) Letters of intent: Election campaigning and orchestrated public debate in local newspapers' letters to the editor, *Political Communication* 21: 459–478.

Robinson, Sue (2007) "Someone's gotta be in control here": The institutionalization of online news and the creation of a shared journalistic authority, *Journalism Practice* 1 (3): 305–321.

Rosen, Jay (2006) The people formerly known as the audience, PressThink. Accessed 11 February 2010: http://journalism.nyu.edu/pubzone/weblogs/pressthink/2006/06/27/ppl_frmr.html

Rothenberg, Ignaz (1946) *The newspaper: A study in the workings of the daily press and its laws*, London: Staples Press.

Rusbridger, Alan (2009, 19 October) First read: The mutualised future is bright, *Columbia Journalism Review*. Accessed 14 March 2010: http://www.cjr.org/reconstruction/the_mutualized_future_is_brigh.php

Ryfe, David M. (2009) Broader and deeper: A study of newsroom culture in a time of change, *Journalism* 10 (2): 197–216.

Sayare, Scott (2009) As Web challenges French leaders, they push back, *The New York Times*. Accessed 20 February 2010: http://www.nytimes.com/2009/12/13/world/europe/13paris.html.

Schudson, Michael (2003) *The sociology of news*, New York: W. W. Norton.

Schudson, Michael (2000) "The sociology of news production revisited (again)." In: Curran, James, and Michael Gurevitch (eds.) *Mass media and society* (3rd edn.), London: Edward Arnold.

Scollon, Ronald (1998) *Mediated discourse as social interaction: A study of news discourse*, Reading, Massachusetts: Addison Wesley.

Shedden, David (2010, 18 August) Entrepreneurial journalism, PoynterOnline. Accessed 7 September 2010: http://www.poynter.org/column.asp?id=132&aid=176024

Shoemaker, Pamela J., Martin Eichholz, Eunyi Kim and Brenda Wrigley (2001) Individual and routine forces in gatekeeping, *Journalism & Mass Communication Quarterly* 78 (2): 233–246.

Shoemaker, Pamela J., and Stephen D. Reese (1996) *Mediating the message: Theories of influences on mass media content*, Reading, Massachusetts: Addison Wesley Longman.

Shoemaker, Pamela J., Tim P. Vos and Stephen D. Reese (2008) "Journalists as gatekeepers." In: Wahl-Jorgensen, Karin, and Thomas Hanitzsch (eds.) *Handbook of journalism studies*, New York: Routledge: 73–87.

Silcock, B. William, and Susan Keith (2006) Translating the Tower of Babel? Issues of definition, language and culture in converged newsrooms, *Journalism Studies* 7 (4): 610–627.

Singer, Jane B. (2010) Journalism ethics amid structural change, *Daedalus: The Journal of the American Academy of Arts and Sciences* 139 (2): 89–99.

Singer, Jane B. (2010) Quality control: Perceived effects of user-generated content on newsroom norms, values and routines, *Journalism Practice* 4 (2): 127–142.

Singer, Jane B. (2008) The journalist in the network: A shifting rationale for the gatekeeping role and the objectivity norm, *Trípodos* 23: 61–76.

Singer, Jane B. (2004) More than ink-stained wretches: The resocialization of print journalists in converged newsrooms, *Journalism & Mass Communication Quarterly* 81 (4): 838–856.

Singer, Jane B. (2004) Strange bedfellows? Diffusion of convergence in four news organizations, *Journalism Studies* 5 (1): 3–18.

Singer, Jane B., and Ian Ashman (2009) "Comment is free, but facts are sacred:" User-generated content and ethical constructs at the *Guardian, Journal of Mass Media Ethics* 24: 3–21.

Starr, Paul (2009, 19 October). First read: Journalism minus its old public, *Columbia Journalism Review*. Accessed 15 March 2010: http://www.cjr.org/reconstruction/journalism_minus_its_old_publi.php

Stephens, Mitchell (2008) New media, new ideas: Escape from the holy of holies, *Journalism Studies* 9 (4): 595–599.

Tausig, Shuki (2009) Journalism 2010: The survey, The Seventh Eye. Accessed 24 December 2009: http://www.the7eye.org.il/articles/Pages/ 241209_Journalism_2010_Israeli_Media_Consumption_Poll.aspx

Thurman, Neil (2008) Forums for citizen journalists? Adoption of user generated content initiatives by online news media, *New Media and Society* 10 (1): 138–157.

Thurman, Neil, and Alfred Hermida (2010) "Gotcha: How newsroom norms are shaping participatory journalism online." In: Monaghan, Garrett, and Sean Tunney (eds.) *Web journalism: A new form of citizenship*, Eastbourne: Sussex Academic Press: 46–62.

Times Mirror Center for the People and the Press (1993) The vocal minority in American politics. Accessed 20 February 2010: http://people-press.org/reports/pdf/19930716.pdf

Tsoref, Ayala (2006, 9 September) The national sorter of user comments. The Marker Café. Accessed 3 March 2010: http://www.themarker.com/tmc/article.jhtml?log=tag&ElementId=skira20060909_760371

Tuchman, Gaye (2002) "The production of news." In Jensen, Klaus A. (ed.) *Handbook of media and communication research: Qualitative and quantitative methodologies*, London and New York: Routledge: 78–90.

Van Dijck, José, and David Nieborg (2009) Wikinomics and its discontents: A critical analysis of Web 2.0 business manifestos, *New Media and Society* 11 (5): 855–874.

Wahl–Jorgensen, Karin (2002) Understanding the conditions for public discourse: Four rules for selecting letters to the editor, *Journalism Studies* 3 (1): 69–81.

Wahl–Jorgensen, Karin (2001) Letters to the editor as a forum for public deliberation: Modes of publicity and democratic debate, *Critical Studies in Media Communication* 18 (3): 303–320.

Weaver, David H. (1998) *The global journalist: News people around the world*, Cresskill, New Jersey: Hampton Press.

Weiss, Amy Schmitz, and David Domingo (2010) Innovation processes in online newsrooms as actor-networks and communities of practice, *New Media and Society* 12 (7): 1156–1171.

White, David M. (1950) The gatekeeper: A case study in the selection of news, *Journalism Quarterly* 27: 383–96.

Wiles, Roy M. (1965) *Freshest advices: Early provincial newspapers in England*, Columbus, Ohio: Ohio State University Press.

Williams, Andy, Claire Wardle and Karin Wahl-Jorgensen (2009) "Have they got news for us?" Audience revolution or business as usual? Paper presented at the Future of Journalism conference, Cardiff, Wales, September.

World Editors Forum (2008) *Trends in Newsrooms 2008*, Paris: World Association of Newspapers / World Editors Forum.

Zoran, Gabriel (2009) *Beyond mimesis: Text and textual arts in Aristotelian thought*, Tel Aviv: Tel Aviv University Press.

Index

abusive content, as ethical
  issue, 129–30
access/observation stage
  in news production process,
    18–21, 78
  definition of, 203
  workflow trends in, 81–2
"active recipient," in
  participatory
  journalism, 177–91
  battle over fortress
    journalism, 180–2
  conversation facilitators,
    182–3
  description of, 179
  new relationships, new
    roles, 182–3
  rest of story, 179–80
  tools for debate, 179
  working with audience,
    183–6
agenda, news, 76, 171
agenda-setting, 47
  citizens' capability of, 20
  definition of, 203
ancillary reporters, journalists'
  view of users as,
    43–4
animator(s), in creating
  content, 101, 101t
attitude(s)
  of journalists, 102–6

in managing audience
  participation, 80–1
audience, 6. see also user(s)
  changes in, 36
  definition of, 203
  former, 15
  journalist's relationship
    with, 34–55. see also
    journalist(s),
    relationship with users
  participation by, 13–33. see
    also audience
    participation
  in shaping conversation,
    13–33
  working with, 183–6
audience participation
  analyzing of, 16–27
    tools in, 16–18, 17t, 18t
  formats for, 16, 17t
  Internet in, 16
  managing of, 76–95
    attitudes in, 80–1
    best practices in, 89–93
    direct interaction in, 90–1
    facts vs. opinions in,
      78–9
    interpretation stage, 83–5
    materials in, 77–81
    motivations in, 80–1
    newsworthiness of
      images in, 79

placement within website
  in, 79–80
  reporters' involvement in,
    89–93
  strategies in, 77–81
  user contributions-
    related, 85–9, 86t
  users' involvement in,
    91–3
  workflow trends in news
    production stages,
    81–5
audience participation teams,
  182
audience pulse-takers,
  journalists' view of
  users as, 41–2
author role, in creating
  content, 101, 101t

BBC, 4
Belgium, websites and
  newspapers in, 193–4
Black, Conrad, 195
blog(s), 67, 97, 124, 187
  citizen, 22–3, 82
    description of, 17t
  definition of, 204
  journalist, 25–6, 91
    definition of, 206
    description of, 17t

Participatory Journalism: Guarding Open Gates at Online Newspapers, First Edition.
Jane B. Singer, Alfred Hermida, David Domingo, Ari Heinonen, Steve Paulussen, Thorsten Quandt,
Zvi Reich, and Marina Vujnovic.